DARE TO DREAM

Best Wishes

John Ryan

DARE TO DREAM

On Life, Football
and Cosmetic Surgery

Scratching Shed Publishing Ltd

First published by Scratching Shed Publishing Ltd in 2010
Registered in England & Wales No. 6588772.
Registered office:
47 Street Lane, Leeds, West Yorkshire. LS8 1AP

www.scratchingshedpublishing.co.uk

ISBN 978-0956252609

Unless stated otherwise, all photographs are from the personal collection of John Ryan

A catalogue record for this book is available from the British Library.

Typeset in Warnock Pro Semi Bold and Palatino

Printed and bound in the United Kingdom by
L.P.P.S.Ltd, Wellingborough, Northants, NN8 3PJ

For all family, friends and fans of Doncaster Rovers,
who have shared my dream

Acknowledgements

My sincere thanks go to a number of people - alas, too many to mention - who helped me during the production of this book, not least my co-author John Brindley. I am also especially grateful to Kevin Keegan, Sir Bobby Robson, Sir Alex Ferguson, Neil Warnock, Mark Halsey, John Helm, Philip Ryan, Steve Uttley and the Rovers media team, Tony Bluff, Dave Morris, Stuart Highfield, Eric Randerson, Sophie Lassman, Nazar Kazzazi, Gareth Thomas, Dick Watson, Peter Hepworth, Mickey Walker, Harry Bacon, Ian Hornby, Aaron Rea, Dave Parker, The New Football Pools and Peter Catt.

Contents

Foreword (1)
KEVIN KEEGAN
Another of Doncaster's famous sons

MY own dream was destined never to happen. Rovers were always going to be my club as I was born in Armthorpe and lived in the centre of Doncaster in Spring Gardens. I was a regular at Belle Vue from the age of six or seven and from where I stood could also see Doncaster United in their yellow and blue playing on the aerodrome. Great memories.

I watched the incomparable Alick Jeffrey play but I wanted to be a goalkeeper like Willie Nimmo. Unfortunately the goals got bigger and I didn't so I settled on being a striker instead. The nearest I got to fulfilling my dream was a trial at Rovers when I was about 15. But I never got there as I was told the wrong day and soon afterwards signed for Scunthorpe United instead.

Belle Vue was as good as any stadium for a club of Rovers' size and the pitch was of such quality that clubs used to queue up to play pre-season friendlies there. I got to play on the hallowed turf just the once – for Liverpool in an FA Cup replay played at a crazy time on a Tuesday afternoon because of the power cuts in the 1970s.

Dare To Dream

Over the years I saw the old ground deteriorate unbelievably and Rovers went the same way. Luckily, there always seems to be someone willing to rescue football clubs and, thank God, in Doncaster Rovers' case it was John Ryan

What Rovers have achieved since is an amazing story that should never be underestimated. To get where they are is remarkable and a great credit to John. The wonderful thing is that this book isn't finished yet. The Rovers story is still being written.

John's not so unusual in being a fan and a chairman. But what is unusual is how successful he has been. People who come in and say 'I love the club' often fail in the detail but John Ryan has developed the business side of Rovers in a sensible and continuous way. His is one club that is not built on sand.

I was delighted when I was manager at Manchester City that John came to see me and not only brought me a Rovers shirt but the League Three trophy. I showed it to all the players as an example, because it is not easy to win any league.

Since then Rovers have moved into the Keepmoat Stadium which is spot-on and a ground that has the potential to be expanded. It will be the home of Doncaster Rovers for years and years after you and I are long gone. Today Rovers are in the Championship and, although they line up against bigger clubs, the examples of Barnsley, Burnley and Oxford United in recent years show that it is not impossible to get into the Premier League itself. Also they've done it all in real style by playing the game the way I think it should be played with very good management.

I'm proud today that when people ask me which team I support I answer Doncaster Rovers. John Ryan has given my club licence to dream and I say dream on...

Foreword (2)
GARETH THOMAS
Viking Supporters Co-operative Chairman

JOHN RYAN's takeover at Donny Rovers was like something from a Hollywood movie. Our club was dying on its feet and in rode this white knight on his charger to really turn things around. I've supported Rovers for 40-odd years and experienced several false dawns – but John Ryan has been for real. From the start he not only talked the talk, but walked the walk, however uncomfortable that path has been on occasions.

At first, the country patronised us as just a pub team having a laugh. But, oh, how we laughed our way into the Championship and when we consolidated our status so well in 2008/9. Still we get portrayed as 'little old Donny' but, hopefully, John Ryan's story will help capture the imagination of football supporters everywhere. Your club may be floundering in these difficult financial times, but John's message is that where there is life, there is hope. With

John, hope has manifested itself into tangible achievement, and now Doncaster Rovers supporters really can 'Dare to Dream'....

John has achieved everything he planned and forecast when he walked through the door, but I know the dream is still alive and developing. Together we will work to improve the fans' matchday experience at our new home, the Keepmoat Stadium. We need to turn our stadium into a home, a fortress, and create a real atmosphere about the place. We need to build the Rovers 'brand' too. With John, we know it will happen.

It goes without saying we will continue our remarkable upsurge on the pitch itself. Like me, John is a big kid where football is concerned. His infectious enthusiasm invariably brings people on board. I, like so many Rovers fans, can't speak highly enough of John Ryan – I hope that, through this book, you can get to know him better too.

INTRODUCTION
John Ryan

IF I could sum up my life story in just three words, it would be those in the title of this book. I have always been a dreamer and don't intend to change my spots now.

Both as chairman of Doncaster Rovers football club and a pioneer in the cosmetic surgery business, I approach life's challenges in the very same way. The media has often likened me to a schoolboy still living his dream. And, yes, I may be about to turn 60 years old, but that is a very accurate description.

Sorry, ladies, you'll have to forgive me if this book is 80 per cent football but that reflects my personality. I continue to devote countless hours to my life-long love of the football club I discovered more than half a century ago. Read on and I will tell you more about how we have 'lived the dream' over the last decade and proved that David can defeat Goliath, even in this elite-dominated modern age. I promise to tell you the truth about football as I see it, both the good and the ugly - and explain how in an often corrupt and crazy sport, there is still room for good, old-fashioned values.

Similar principles have prevailed in my business life. I have made my name and fortune in cosmetic surgery – not with the knife, as so many still assume, but in running some of the most successful clinics in the country. I have enjoyed every minute of a journey that has seen cosmetic surgery cast off its image as being a controversial luxury for the privileged few to become a life-enhancing option for many. And if, as *Big Brother*'s Imogen Thomas says, I 'have made many women very happy' – that's not such a bad result, is it?

Last, but certainly not least, I have a beautiful domestic life. True love has come into my world in the shapely form of my lovely wife Lynne. She shares my personal paradise Centuryan House in leafy Cheshire together with endless memorabilia from my world of football, the ultimate train set, my own five-a-side football pitch and a tennis court.

But, before you get the false impression that John Ryan is the man whom the evils and problems of this world passed by, allow me to bring you back to harsh reality. In all three areas of my life I have reached rock bottom before bouncing back.

My football club disintegrated into disgrace and a national joke; early businesses bit the dust to raise huge questions marks over my career; and my personal life was blighted by divorce and death. In each case I met the challenge through a combination of hard work and personal vision. The secret, if there is one, is that I've always been able to see beyond my current circumstances and know where I am heading. I hold fast to the view that, if you put your heart and soul into what you are doing and count effort as gain rather than cost, anything is indeed possible. It also helps, particularly if you are a football fan, to have a keen sense of humour.

Welcome to my life story – so far! I hope it will entertain you and should it encourage you to take hold of your own dream, so much the better.

Best wishes
John Ryan

PART ONE:
A TALE OF BOOM AND BUST

1
*
TIL DEATH DO US PART

SIR BOBBY ROBSON, speaking a couple of weeks before his death in July 2009: "I remember very well that day at Belle Vue when John Ryan apparently came to watch his first match. Jimmy Hill scored five goals and we won 6-1, but I'm glad we didn't put John off football!

"I met John many years later when Newcastle United played a pre-season friendly at Doncaster's new Keepmoat Stadium. He was very polite and very proud of the state of the club now – and so he should be."

MICKEY WALKER, Director of Football at Doncaster Rovers: "Make no mistake about it had John Ryan not taken the bull by the horns and taken on board people such as Peter Wetzel, Stuart Highfield and Peter Hepworth, this club would have died before this dream began.

"He had to start from square one as we needed kit, balls, basically everything. They decided they needed a youth policy and that's how I joined. Throughout my time here I've found John to be loyal to his family and his employees. People work for him because he is such an honest man. He has an aura about him and the

success he has had both in business and football has been phenomenal. He has helped to create a friendly family football club, one I am delighted to have worked for in a number of different roles."

MY eyes were transfixed on the coffin, my mind racing through the years. 'King' Alick Jeffrey, Billy Bremner, Alan Warboys, Peter Kitchen, Brendan O'Callaghan, Ian and Glynn Snodin, Stan Anderson, Lawrie McMenemy and countless other heroes flashed through my troubled thoughts. How could things have come to this?

Lost in sober, nostalgic reflection, I was brought back to the present by a policewoman tapping me on my shoulder: "Is there anything you can do about this, John?" she asked earnestly. Not the sort of question you expect at a 'funeral', I'm sure you'd agree. But this was no ordinary day of mourning. For the coffin did not contain a loved one, but the symbolic death of my beloved Doncaster Rovers Football Club. It was Saturday 2 May 1998, the afternoon of Donny's last game in the Football League against Colchester United, yet we all knew we were in very real danger of not just losing our status - but our football club itself.

There weren't too many words shared between the 300 or so solemn folk walking the few hundred yards from the Park Hotel towards Belle Vue that sad last Saturday, accompanied by the regular honking of horns and waves from bystanders acknowledging the grief we were all experiencing.

It was the only time I saw Rovers play that God-awful season. I had been banned from the ground by the club's self-styled 'benefactor' Ken Richardson, the chief subject of our collective fury. Some 40 years after being introduced to the beautiful game when my Dad first took me to Belle Vue

– decades in which I'd backed the club as a sponsor and a director, but always as a fan – I was now totally helpless, merely hearing second hand about the demise of my club. They'd called me 'Mr Champagne Man' as the flamboyant backer from Transform, but just then I was denied even the comparatively small beer of watching my team.

Sitting luxuriously at Manchester United's Old Trafford, watching some of the finest footballers play for one of the greatest teams of the modern generation, I could never be totally at ease knowing that my true love – light years away in a rundown ground and with a side fast becoming the butt of the wider football nation's jokes – was in such a parlous state. I had raised the chant of 'Rovers till I die' many thousands of times, but now I had to ponder the thought that my Rovers could very well die first.

Had things been different, I would have been a key figure at either Manchester United or Manchester City by then, having been approached to buy into United and being backed on another notable occasion to become chairman at City. But there was only one club that really tugged at my heart strings and that was dear old Donny Rovers. So when it came to the very last game I wasn't bothered where the giants were playing, I just had to be at my true football home.

I got into my car on my own for the drive from Cheshire with very mixed feelings. My last direct contact with the club had seen me cast as the villain of the peace. Richardson had bawled me out at a packed public meeting held at the town's Park Hotel. As the last director standing between Richardson and full control of Doncaster Rovers, I was the man seen as holding the club back. I held 28 per cent of the shares and he needed 75. Eventually, with great reluctance, I felt so backed into a lonely corner that I gave the majority what they thought they wanted.

Such things can and do happen in business and much more often in the unpredictable world of football. We'd lived hilariously and often perilously hand-to-mouth for years at Donny Rovers so when someone flashed a bit of cash and promised the earth, my fellow directors snapped his hand off. I honestly think that had Attila the Hun come knocking at our door he'd have received the warmest of welcomes! The historians tell me there was once a gypsy curse put on Belle Vue – I don't know about that but I do know that a businessman from the Isle of Man travelled to England and did a far more destructive job.

To be honest, I'd believed from the moment that I set eyes on the bloke that Richardson was more old devil than Messiah – and not just because of his previous history of being banned for 25 years from the world of horse racing after the Flockton Grey scandal. The story was that the bounder entered the horse as a long shot in a race at Leicester and won by 20 lengths. The stewards scented blood and eventually found that the horse which actually took part was Good Hand and not the hapless Flockton Grey. Richardson also received a suspended prison sentence for his troubles and an extra fine when he launched an unsuccessful appeal. Suspended? If they'd strung him up for life it would have saved Donny Rovers a good deal of trouble.

He then turned his devious sporting mind to football, taking charge of a small Non League club called Bridlington Town. He proved popular at first, pouring in some cash to help the seaside club taste FA Vase glory. But, amid clashes with the council, he then announced the club were quitting their true home and would play their home matches at, of all places, Doncaster Rovers! Didn't make too much economic sense to play football 70 miles away from home, but perfect logic to a green-eyed businessman assessing the future potential of Belle Vue. The ground had always belonged to the council and we held a 99-year lease from September 1965 on the proviso that the land was used for sporting activities.

My eyes spied a shady looking man who rarely looked anyone in the eye, my gut feeling telling me he had no interest at heart other than his own. Boy, how the club was now paying for its misjudgement. Instead of taking Rovers to unprecedented heights, Richardson and his cohorts presided over a chain of events that dragged our name into the mire. The burning down of the main stand may have been the outstanding incident that neutrals recall from this era but there were scores of stories of incompetence doing the rounds, particularly during that dreadful last season in which we won just four Football League games and acquired a pathetic 15 points.

I fought my corner alongside another director Mike Collett, whom I'm delighted to say is still a Rovers stalwart today. I can easily understand why genuine fans thought I was being stubborn but I always acted with the club at heart. I was prepared to sell my shares and even to put more money into Doncaster Rovers but I needed a guarantee that any proceeds would actually go into the club and not ease the chairman's debts. What I wasn't happy about was continually being badgered into giving more money when I feared it would merely prop up Richardson and his cohorts. I made my position as clear as I possibly could when I issued a public statement saying that I had: "grave concerns for the well being of the club when he (Richardson) gets total control. I hope my words will not be prophetic." Eventually I realised that I was in a no-win situation and resigned as a director on 19 October 1993 after four years on the board, to be replaced by no greater a football expert than Richardson's daughter Julie.

Richardson was a crook, a conman, the type of bloke you wouldn't want near any football club - let alone the one I held so close to my heart. By now, the fans knew as well as I did that he was sounding the death-knell for Doncaster Rovers and there didn't seem to be anything anyone could do about it. The man's fraudulent opportunism knew no bounds. He actually put the ground up for sale at one stage, conveniently ignoring the blatantly obvious fact that it wasn't his in the first place. He knew Rovers were failing and he wanted a way out – one in which he would emerge a winner. So he hatched one of the most ludicrous plots in history.

The fire that burnt down part of a stand at Belle Vue in 1995 stunk to high heaven from the moment it was discovered. Richardson's cause in attempting to cover it up was certainly not helped when Alan Kristiansen, the former SAS man he hired to do the bungled job, dropped his mobile at the scene with the message 'the job's been done' already sent to his master's mobile phone. He had even bought the petrol from a service station in town and been caught on CCTV cameras. Rumour had it he got a receipt so he could claim the petrol back on expenses! Richardson got four years at Sheffield Crown Court, but even that was no real consolation and not just because he walked away with £4m when he finally sold the lease. After all, nothing would have compensated for the loss of Doncaster Rovers.

Mind you 'death' would almost have been a release after indignity upon indignity had been heaped upon true Rovers fans over the previous few years. There was the administration order, Richo's threat to pull us out of the Football League and play in the Doncaster Senior League, running rows with the Inland Revenue and the council – and those were the highlights! Heavy and frequent defeats almost paled into insignificance amidst a series of unfortunate, yet highly avoidable events, that kept neutral football fans in gossip for years.

Managers not allowed to pick the team; one-day-a-week 'players' who weren't actually footballers; fans threatened with ID cards in order to quell growing protests; there was all this and more during the reign of the so-called Moss Side Mafia. Ours was the only team coach that would stop at Manchester on its way from Belle Vue to Exeter. We needed to pick up all the 'ringers' that Mark Weaver, whose sole football qualification was that he had been assistant lottery manager at Stockport County, cobbled together to represent us. He even picked his next door neighbour to play in goal.

Sammy Chung, the former Wolves manager, battled manfully for several years to steer the fast sinking ship until he and his assistant George Foster turned up two hours before the official start of the 1996/97 season to be told they were no longer in a job. Chung had already been replaced by former Chelsea striker Kerry Dixon. Then it was the turn of his successor, who turned out to be a terrific guy, to learn that management under Ken Richardson wasn't quite how he'd have imagined it. Dixon famously told a gathering of Donny fans at a public meeting that he was no more than a trainer and advisor to Ken who actually picked the side. The chairman even continued his bizarre role after deciding he would no longer bother coming to Belle Vue, faxing over the teamsheet before delivering his pre-match pep talk by mobile phone.

The papers and media naturally lapped it all up in that dark last season. 'Rovers: the end is nigh' was one of the more optimistic eye-catching headlines and when Channel 4 decided to produce a programme called *Under the Moon*, you can guess where they went for material. They accidentally stumbled upon comedian and former Rovers favourite Charlie Williams during the filming, but the main joke was firmly on us. Rovers were also 'good copy' for stories about potential saviours with even Uri Geller being mentioned at one stage. He could allegedly bend spoons, stop clocks and baffle scientists, but get Doncaster Rovers to win a football match? That would have been a step too far...

Even when we did win, we were bad. A rare home victory over Chester City was clinched when the opposition goalkeeper threw the ball out and it hit one of his defenders and presented us with an open goal to the delight of the crowd of 864. Footage from the season featured on our excellent DVD *Ashes to Glory* and it could just as easily have been used by Jeremy Beadle. We were simply the worst.

On another occasion Weaver threatened to call off our home match against Scunthorpe United after the alleged theft of 14 two-way radios from Belle Vue. If he'd succeeded, Radio 5 Live would have missed out on what commentator Dave Woods famously called "the biggest match taking place in Europe tonight". Needless to say it was the only one and Scunny won 2-1. Another Weaver masterstroke was to dispense with the services of coaches Dave Cowling and Paul Ward, before telling the players they needed merely to report on Saturdays as there was no one to look after them during the week.

By this time Rovers fans knew the score and fought furiously for the sake of their club. The magnificent efforts of the Save the Rovers group and other concerned supporters were an inspiration to football folk everywhere. They lobbied MPs, held public meetings, instructed David Mellor's Football Task Force and put forward the more truthful version of events at Belle Vue to the local and national media. Without people such as Ray Gilbert, one of the organisers of the mock funeral, there might not have been a Doncaster Rovers to revive. The 'Fans United' match against Brighton that season, when both sets of supporters came together in protest at what was happening at our respective clubs, sent out a very clear message. This was the right type of fan power – the people of Doncaster letting it be known that Rovers would always be their club. If only we had never allowed Richardson to get his feet under our table.

But this was no time for 'I told you so'. The state of Doncaster Rovers was so obviously sick that I dragged my heavy heart to take a last look at Belle Vue without a thought about the moral high ground. One look at the dear old place and it was obvious why the Conference would need a lot of reassuring before they offered Rovers a place in their league. Dilapidated and semi-derelict, it was past the need for a make-over, it required major heart surgery.

I took my place on the popular side to witness the final 'wake'. With Rovers well and truly already relegated, the 90 minutes that followed had meaning only for our promotion-chasing visitors from Essex, managed ironically by Steve Wignall, a former Donny player and later to become our manager.

I preferred to think of happier times from the hundreds of games I'd witnessed at Belle Vue. I had my own special spot in front of the main stand, near the halfway line. There I used to rendezvous with some salt-of-the-earth characters, who shared my sporting passion.

Good old 'Jimmy Hill'. I never did know his real name, but he was re-christened that after the then *Match of the Day* presenter because he never stopped his own unsolicited running commentary on the game. On one glorious occasion, he got so excited about Rovers scoring a goal that his false teeth were sent flying over my shoulder – I swear they continued to chatter until finally landing on the ground. Then there was Kevin, another friendly guy, who nevertheless used to launch into the players whenever they made a mistake. His volley at man mountain Alan Warboys whom he implored to 'get his finger out' was so loud that the striker turned round in disgust and reduced my mate's legs to jelly with a withering look. That was surpassed when, after laying into a certain Jack Lewis throughout one afternoon, Kevin inadvertently bumped into the player in the social club and fawned all over him to my undisguised delight. Daft, funny moments recalled years later are almost as precious as the most spectacular of goals. I'll always recall Albert Broadbent, known to the fans as Yogi, bearing his bottom to the crowd when we gave him a bit too much cheek.

I was as vociferous as any fan. But my target, as many of you will not be surprised to know, was invariably the man with the whistle rather than the players. I could never hope to score a goal for Doncaster Rovers, but if by contesting every decision I could help bend an official's ear into giving us a throw-in, free kick or, the ultimate prize, a penalty, that would be a successful afternoon.

If you are a genuine football fan, I'm sure you can appreciate the emotional turmoil we at Doncaster Rovers felt that later Saturday. But for the grace of the unpredictable football gods go you and your team, particularly in these turbulent economic days. The odd professional football club has perished over the years, although more often than not a white knight has charged in at the very last minute to rescue them. But white knights are thinner on the ground than ever in 2010 and I honestly believe and fear that we are on the very edge of seeing a major name or two bite the dust. The huge debts that clubs have accrued are fast becoming as important as points.

Football may not be more important than life or death as the incomparable Bill Shankly was quoted as saying, but I'd happily go this far - when a community loses its football club, it loses part of its very soul. People need reminding that our game runs deeper than the riches of the

Premiership, the Champions League or even the World Cup. When there's suffering at the game's grass roots, we all suffer – whether we realise it or not.

Put it this way: there are places many of us would probably never have heard of save for their football team. The depressing effect losing Rovers would have had on the town of Doncaster should never be underestimated. A possible conversation a few years hence flashed through my mind. "Doncaster? Isn't that a rundown industrial town up north somewhere?" "Yeah, it's got a really good racecourse. But didn't it have a football club once?"

There will always be mega-rich folk attracted by the prospect of reflected glory, but it defies logic why anyone should devote themselves to rescuing an organisation that had plumbed such depths as Doncaster Rovers. But then football is more about love than logic.

The club itself actually dates back to 1879 – a little bit before my time – when an 18-year-old fitter at the town's Great Northern Line works got a team to play against the Yorkshire Institute for the Deaf and Dumb. Afterwards, the lads got together to make things more formal and the name Doncaster Rovers came into being for the very first time against Rawmarsh a month later. We were elected to the Football League in 1902/3 and then re-elected after a spell in the wilderness.

I fell head over heels in love with Rovers from the age of seven, when my Dad took me to Belle Vue to watch Fulham demolish our local heroes 6-1 in the old Division Two. The real Jimmy Hill – not my chattering friend - blasted in five goals, but if he'd scored 15 it would have made no difference. Rovers were my club through thin and thinner. Not for me a brief, passionate affair – the sort that begins all guns blazing, but fades once the going gets tough. This was the full gut-churning, heart-stopping thing that will continue as long as I draw breath. Only a fellow football fanatic knows how your very being can be enraptured by a thrilling victory – or, more commonly, your spirit crushed by the bitter disappointment of defeat. It's crazy, child-like and completely inexplicable to the outsider, but that's football.

Supporting Doncaster Rovers was an emotional rollercoaster with far more lows than highs, even before Richardson hitched his wagon in our town. Within 12 months of that first game, we lost our status in the equivalent of today's Championship and, worse still, a further season later we were in Division Four. From then on we were the proverbial yo-yo club between the two bottom leagues.

I used to bag a few goals at a very modest level in my time as a tearaway centre forward. But Sunday football was basically my limit, so when Saturday came the only way I'd make it to my hallowed Belle Vue was as a spectator. Luckily for me – and countless others – supporting a football side feels every inch like taking part. There are never, ever just eleven men kicking a ball for Doncaster Rovers when they cross that white line and run out onto the field. That's what the so-called beautiful game has always been about. Indeed, at heart, it remains a game for ordinary folk to vent their emotions as a wonderful distraction from the more mundane things in life. If God had intended the game to be for prawn sandwich-eating billionaires he would have put Gordon Ramsay instead of Sir Alf in charge of the England team.

They say that when close to physical death, your life actually flashes before you and I could relate to that too. Great Football League Cup victories over giants such as Manchester City and Aston Villa, promotions gained, relegations lost and the awesome presence of the great Alick Jeffrey, undoubtedly the greatest Rovers player of all time, all came flooding back into my mind. What would King Alick be thinking as the club he once almost single-handedly put on the soccer map slumped onto the soccer scrap heap?

So, on 2 May 1998, a modest Colchester United side walked away with one goal, three comfortable points – and my broken heart and dreams. That was no reflection on the largely youthful side whom we clapped from the pitch. They were merely the sacrificial lambs, incidental to the wider picture.

We didn't go out of the Football League fighting and screaming – more kicked mercilessly into touch, nursing our own self-inflicted wounds. That post-war lowest points record and a goals against column for which we could offer no defence were just the bare statistics of ten months of football hell. All that was left from Richardson's wreckage was a team that would scarcely have spread fear in the Northern Counties East League – with the facilities and infrastructure to match.

I looked around at grown men and women who also had tears in their eyes – people who needed and deserved so much more. Yet, strangely, even right there among the ashes existed a reason for optimism. For, if folk cared so passionately as to join this macabre procession or even honk their horns in approval, there must still have been plenty around with Rovers in their hearts.

Not one, but two, and then three folk asked me the same question: was there anything I could do about all this? After all, many of them knew I was Doncaster-mad and had previously been on the board. I'd be a spin doctor if I told you that I provided an instant answer; that I knew at that moment I could breathe new life into the corpse that was Doncaster Rovers. Yet scarcely three months later I was installed as the new chairman and beginning a journey that few people in football can have experienced.

Today, as I survey the magnificent Keepmoat Stadium and reflect on a team that won so many plaudits in our first season in the Championship, it's almost difficult to remember how close we came to losing our football club. Yet we do so at our peril.

So how did the young boy from a modest council estate become the man to save Doncaster Rovers? Part one of my story looks back at the years and events that led me to one of the most important decisions of my life.

2

*

STARTING FROM SCRATCH

SILVER spoon? Search me, if you like, but there wasn't one. In fact, there was nothing remotely amazing about my start in life. After being born in the maternity ward of Hexthorpe Annexe in Doncaster in 1950 to parents of very modest means, I lived in a council house in Cantley until I was nine, when we moved to a semi-detached house in Intake. Dad Oswald was the son of a miner, who had died during war time, and mum Ada, a salt-of-the-earth woman whose work was our modest home. Her father William Horace Wren was also a miner and a good footballer, too, whose brother played for both Derby County and Nottingham Forest.

Like so many remarkable stories, mine probably shouldn't have happened at all. During the war Dad went out with his squadron to Cape Town, ironically where I have one of my homes today. They were camped out on the racecourse for about four months and Dad's role was working as a mechanic on the aircraft, with which he had a life-long fascination. Apparently he was itching for active service but when the names of the 90 per cent of men bound for Singapore were read out, his wasn't among them.

Instead he was part of the ten per cent sent to the much safer territory of India. My point is this – when Dad did go out to visit the country he had missed, it was to view their memorials. The great majority of men sent there sadly died serving their country. He could so easily have been one of them and John Michael would never have been the first of his three children. That's fate, I suppose...

Life was tough for the family although we knew no different. I was soon joined by sister Janet and brother Philip. Dad, who had plied his trade as a mechanic in a garage in Doncaster before the war, got a good job as chief inspector with International Harvesters, whilst Mum toiled away at home, keeping the family ticking along. Dad was a big powerful man, more than six feet tall and impressively built. Gregarious and sociable, he was rarely short of anything to say, so you can see where I got some of my personality. Dad also had his moment of fame when he became only the second person in Doncaster to pass the driving test, a feat remarked upon in the local press.

My first taste of school life was at Hawthorne School in Cantley and I didn't like it much. I was there until I was nine and it won't surprise you to know the only thing I was really interested in was football. It made me laugh when I made contact with my old school a few years ago to donate a full Doncaster Rovers kit in memory of my time there. The headmaster Mr Skinner thanked me and then revealed they don't play football there anymore. "Goodness me," I said. "If that had been so in my day, I would never have gone to school at all!"

My form teacher was a Miss Tollerfield and the only other thing I can remember that was remarkable about the place was a pupil called Margaret Bond. She was absolutely gorgeous; the first of many beautiful ladies I was to set my eyes upon. I did make some friends, despite my limited interest in the classroom. Fellow pupil Geoff Jenkinson became a life-long friend and another was a lad called Mark Hudson. Strangely enough, the latter bumped into me at the airport in about 1985 – he recognised me straightaway, but I must admit I needed a few prompts before I could make a positive identification.

Dad had an interest in watching Doncaster Rovers and so I eventually got my chance to accompany him to Belle Vue. Rovers were in the equivalent of today's Championship, dizzy heights in the context of the club's overall history. It's strange to think back now and reflect that two of the Fulham lads who made my 'debut' so miserable that day went on to make such an enormous impact on the game – and are both men for whom I have the ultimate personal regard.

Jimmy Hill became one of the sport's great movers and shakers with his role in helping to abolish the 'maximum wage' - back then just £20 a week - and also a very highly regarded media pundit and presenter of the timeless *Match of The Day,* as already described. Hill may not have done Donny any favours that afternoon as he tore our defence to shreds, but he was just the sort of friend we needed when things got so tough for us many years later. Jimmy is one of those football men who has never forsaken the game's roots and didn't want to think of a club with such a great name and reputation as Doncaster Rovers going through perilous times.

The other famous name in the Cottagers' ranks was none other than the now sadly-departed Sir Bobby Robson. A tremendous player in his own right, Sir Bobby later became one of the greatest managers the game has ever produced. He led Ipswich Town to FA Cup and European glory and was unlucky not to add a Football League title or two to his collection of silverware at what was a comparatively modest Suffolk club. One of so few to become a success at virtually every club he managed, Sir Bobby was a big hit in both Holland and Portugal and, of course, led England to the very brink of the World Cup final in 1990, the game made famous for Gazza's tears and the first of our traumatic penalty flops against Germany. Sir Bobby was my boardroom guest at the beginning of the 2008/9 season when we also had the joy of welcoming another of Doncaster's most famous sons, Kevin Keegan, to the Keepmoat as Newcastle United played us in a friendly. It was good to see and hear Sir Bobby in good form, despite his recurring illness, and for him to compliment us, both on our new facilities – so markedly different from the Belle Vue he had graced that day – and the style of our football. We lost a true gentleman and giant of the game and of life when Sir Bobby was finally defeated in his long battle against cancer in July 2009. It was typical of him that he kindly gave me the benefit of his thoughts at the beginning of this chapter when he was almost too ill to talk. Rest in peace Sir Bobby, we will never forget you.

Returning to Fulham, however, I'm glad to report that seeing my team crushed in such an emphatic fashion didn't put me off the game for good. Perhaps a fair few people, referees included, wish that it had! Afterwards Dad took me every now and again to Belle Vue, although I can't remember any other matches nearly so well as that memorable introduction.

School life carried on in much the same way when I moved on to Intake Juniors. Again I made the odd lasting buddy – in this case Howard James – but hardly much of an impression with my studies. Every youngster has his day, however, and mine was one that took a few folk by surprise. I'd missed my original date with the eleven-plus exam because of an untimely attack of mumps. But on one golden day I took it in the education offices in the morning – later learning that I had passed – and capped the occasion by netting a hat-trick in a five-a-side school tournament during the afternoon. My team 4A 'B' weren't supposed to defeat 4A 'A' as the ranking suggests – but we did and, as you all know now, it wasn't the only time when one of my teams upset the form book.

Young Ryan, the player, was always a centre forward. Scoring goals was my forte, although I never pretended to have anything more than very average talent. How I would have loved to have been more like Rovers' Alick Jeffrey. If ever a lad deserved the word 'legend' to be associated with his name, it was Alick. A goal-hungry forward, whose thinking and execution seemed in a different league to everyone else on the pitch, he could so easily have been one of the greatest English players. It was my privilege to have watched the master at work at Belle Vue after he broke his leg playing for England Under 23s against France in 1956 and effectively left his future behind him. More, much more, about the great man later....

I wasn't cut out to be a Ryan of the Rovers and, if my form teacher Mrs Kirkland was to be believed, was all set for a quick return to the local secondary modern. She never did know how I passed that exam. Mind you, she had good reason to disbelieve. Life at Danum Grammar School, a haven for all boys, started pretty badly. I came a miserable 29th out of a class of 31 at the end of my first year. That was despite coming top in history, a subject I always enjoyed, and starting my interest in chemistry, which I was later to study at university.

The subject that really let me down was English, as the staff weren't slow in reminding me. My spelling was terrible and my command of the language pretty limited. So much so, in fact, that one particular master grabbed me by the lapels and told me very pointedly: "You, young man, are going to be a total waste of time unless you learn how to spell!" That was another potential psychological blow for a lad sent reeling by my parents splitting up when I was 12 – a much rarer occurrence in those days, of course.

But my story has always been the same: I've started at the bottom of the league and reminded myself that, from there, the only way is up. There's a good deal of stubbornness in my nature that resents the thought of being beaten or unfairly labelled. Time and again I've made it my mission to show someone what I'm really made of when they have done me down, although on this occasion I wouldn't necessarily recommend the method.

I tell this story with a fair bit of hesitation. After all what I actually did was theft and that is a criminal act, not something I can condone. But this is my story warts and all and, as what actually happened is relevant to another stage in my journey, I'll reveal the whole truth. I went into a big store called Taylor and Colbridge in Doncaster and my eyes feasted upon a book. Why I didn't go into the library and legally take out the helpful journal I really have no idea. It just didn't enter my mind at the time, I suppose. The book, although I've forgotten its title, was about English words and their meanings. There I was in the store, knowing I didn't have enough pennies in my possession to actually buy the book yet realising that I needed and wanted it nevertheless.

So I shoplifted that book – sorry Taylor and Colbridge, but I hope it gave you some compensation that it genuinely changed my life. The book became my educational Bible. Every night at bedtime, for as long as I can remember, I trained myself to digest 12 words – their spellings and meanings. And my language ability, as with the rest of my education, began to turn for the better. People who know me today will appreciate that my vocabulary is quite large and

I'm rarely at a loss in using it, particularly as I handle quite a lot of the media attention at the club. But I don't think that would have been possible, save for that one book. It was with great sadness that I heard many years later that the store had closed, as it will always have a place in my heart.

I managed to finish fifth in class 2Z, winning promotion to the far loftier sounding 3A. By now, I was much more in the swing of education and my 'O' levels brought more success – and a big boost to my confidence. I passed all ten subjects with good grades and my overall result was the second best in the entire school. Naturally, I achieved a top grade in history. It was more than enough to encourage me to do my 'A' levels in which I managed to tame Maths, Physics and Chemistry, with the seemingly irrelevant General Studies thrown in for good measure.

Young Ryan was developing as a physical being and half a footballer too. I suddenly shot up to the heights of 5'11" inches, although I think I've probably come an inch or two closer back to earth since! This helped me to turn the tables on my sports teachers. For, after not being selected for the school team during my early days at Grammar School, I managed to score six goals in a 9-3 victory over a local side, and then go one better with seven as we won another match by an unlikely 11-0. Sadly that was as good as it got for me playing-wise. I played local league soccer after school, but that was my limit. Yet like most football officials, I suspect, I've always stayed in love with the playing side of the game and still take a mean penalty on my own six-a-side pitch in the gardens of my home in Cheshire. And my soccer skills, or lack of them, have even won me a place in the *Guinness Book of Records*. More of those three minutes of fame a bit later…

Naturally, one of the subjects you want me to talk about is sex – me too! I was by today's hectic standards a bit of a late developer. Going to an all-male Grammar School helped to keep me on the sidelines for a while as did another factor you may not readily associate with the John Ryan of today – I was actually very shy.

I'm sure a lot of you men out there will readily relate to this story. During my later school days, I used to go along with some of my male mates to a place called the Top Rank in Silver Street, Doncaster. They hosted regular dances, a chance to perhaps catch the eye of that thus far foreign species – the female sex. I'd arm myself with a few Black Velvets, the poor man's version consisting of cider and Guinness, and get into the usual routine of ogling the girls dancing around their handbags. Let's face it, we've all been there, haven't we? However much we may feel attracted to anyone, it is just impossible to do anything about it. The fear of outright rejection was just too great, so I used to stand there like a rabbit in the headlights having as good a time as I could with my friends.

Eventually, after a fair spell as a bird watcher, I developed a cunning plan. I would reduce the chance of rejection by identifying the ugliest looking young woman on the dance floor and asking her for a dance! Anyway, this particular Friday night I summoned up the courage – and the Black Velvets – to do just that. I spied this girl who was just about the opposite of what I was looking for - overweight, not pretty, not the best dancer and a bit short of offers (I'm sorry if this sounds horrible, but I'm telling you the story as it was). My heart was thumping as I made my way across the dance floor to this unfortunate babe from hell, rehearsing my short speech. Eventually I caught her attention and somehow spluttered out the words: "Would you like to dance with me?" Can you guess her reply? "F--- off!" she said.

My friends didn't know where to put themselves, it was

the highlight of their night by a mile. I would gladly have thrown myself into the nearest waste bin – I was flabbergasted, gutted, heart-broken, you know the rest. If the worst-looking bird in the building thought I was such a clown what chance would I have with anyone else? John Ryan was destined to be a monk.

Well, after Plan A went down the drain, I quickly considered and rejected Plan B. Becoming gay might solve my immediate problem but, looking at all those attractive girls out there, I didn't think that was a viable option. So, like all good football managers when their tactics go completely awry, I decided on something totally different. This time I would go for broke by looking out for the most attractive girl on the dance floor and ask her. Sounded high risk and I still wasn't blessed with the greatest of confidence, but there was method in my madness. I worked out that attractive girls were more likely to say 'yes' because they were accustomed to male attention and at ease dancing with strangers. And, you've guessed it, I cracked it!

The first young woman I fell in love was a gorgeous brunette called Debbie Brunt. I was 17 and she was 15 when our eyes first met across a crowded room at the Top Rank and we ended up going out for about 18 months or so during my schooldays. Naturally we thought it would last forever but first loves rarely work out that way and we fizzled out before I went on the next very important leg of my sexual education at university.

I had offers from Salford and Aston, but my mind was set on Nottingham. The course suited me just fine and the well-known saying that this was the city of gorgeous girls who outnumbered the boys by about three to one had absolutely nothing to do with it. Well, that's my story and I intend to stick with it. Suffice to say that university is the ideal place for young men and women to learn about sex and I had a fantastic time. It was like being let loose in a sweetie shop and was all good innocent fun. I know the stakes are much higher these days with the increased spread of sexual diseases and other moral issues, but my version of the swinging sixties was closer to heaven on earth. I went to university not just to study chemistry, but live it as well!

Before I get myself into too much trouble, I better change the subject back to football. I ended up in a flat in Charnwood Grove, West Bridgford, sharing with a couple of my mates Pete Palmer and Micky Finn. One of the obvious advantages of the location was that it was within walking distance of both Trent Bridge cricket ground and, of course, the City Ground, home of Nottingham Forest. These were pre-Brian Clough days but extremely good ones in the club's history as they boasted terrific players such as Terry Hennessey, Henry Newton and Ian Storey-Moore in what was a genuinely good Forest side who finished second to champions Manchester United in 1966/7 and reached the semi-final of the FA Cup. I thoroughly enjoyed watching Forest, even then renowned for playing entertaining football, and this is one reason why they remain one of the clubs that I look out for to this day.

So two of my main needs - sex and football - were satisfied. What about the third part of life's dream; money?

My family circumstances at the time when I went to study in Nottingham meant I was entitled to a full grant, but it didn't stretch too far. My initial payment was supposed to last throughout my first ten-week term, but I ran out of cash in just the third week. Where could I turn? I was at rock bottom again and, unlike some of my contemporaries, I knew that going back to my parents and asking for a few bob wasn't an option. My future was very much in my own hands. I'm not sure quite how it happened but some very useful information came my way at just the right time. I'd never done anything with sales before, but I was given the task of selling encyclopedias door-to-door on the streets of Nottingham for a company called Chambers. Whether I'd swallowed a manual on sales techniques or it was just the gift of the gab, I'm still not sure, but it went far better than I could have ever imagined. I've always seemed to have the ability to persuade people to do what I want. As you can imagine, that's a definite help in the highly competitive world of business.

My mischievous tale of how I'd developed my own life with the aid of a book seemed to go down very well with the folk of Nottingham and within a month the company was offering me a full-time job as their area sales manager. Naturally I was flattered by the offer, but my heart was set at the time on being a forensic scientist and that still seemed more attractive than the world of sales and books. So I contented myself with the consolation prize of a spanking Sunbeam Alpine sports car for the grand sum of £299.

As on many occasions afterwards, my friends thought I must have come from a rich family or have a benefactor. But, hand on heart, it wasn't and never has been the case. Success and riches have come through my own efforts – 90 per cent determination and, let's say, ten per cent inspiration. John Ryan, the would-be businessman, was rarely short of ideas, even if not all of them would see the light of day.

While I was still in Nottingham, we went through the trauma of the three-day week and power cuts as the Prime Minister of the early 1970s, Ted Heath, faced a huge revolt from the labour force. The result wasn't very good for us poor students. Studying is hard and bleak enough at the best of times, without having to do it in the dark. To make it still worse, Nottingham began to run seriously short of candles. Enter Ryan and flatmate with an idea that could have made us into better-off bright sparks.

I took it upon myself to ring Brussels and put in a mass order for candles. I could see them helping me with my exams and, more importantly, my own cash tills registering. An estimated £400 would certainly have been very welcome in my coffers. The idea went as far as me driving down to Folkestone to collect the goods. But this was one occasion when my beloved car let me down. Not to put too fine a point on it, the big end went and left me by the side of the road cursing my luck. It was a good job it was still light at the time.

During the latter part of my student days I met up with the second young woman for whom I fell head over heels, a delightful young lady called Gay Wilson. Not only was she a striking blonde, she was also the daughter of Frank Wilson, who had been one of the most successful chairmen of Doncaster Rovers. Small world, isn't it? We embarked on a very passionate two-year relationship during which I was privileged to get to know both Frank and his lovely wife Celia. Bless her, countless were the times when we'd go back to Gay's home after a night out and Celia would cook me a delicious steak. They really made me feel at home.

Mind you, I didn't always do my utmost to endear myself to Frank. One day he very kindly invited me to have a look at his Bentley. "Come and have a sit in it, if you like," he said proudly. Half of me longed to take him up on his kind invitation, but then the visionary part of young Ryan took over. "No, thanks," I replied. "I don't want to sit in it until I get a Bentley of my own." Talk about the arrogance of youth, but there was more. "And another thing, Mr Wilson, I am going to be the owner of Doncaster Rovers and will be the most successful chairman in the club's history." Later when I was at Transform and sponsored some Rovers matches, I made similar claims to a local journalist called Peter Catt of the *Doncaster Free Press*.

I'm not quite sure what Frank thought of my super confidence at the time. But it was a huge personal joy when I spoke on the telephone to Frank, not so long before his death at the grand old age of 95, and he reminded me of exactly what I'd predicted and congratulated me heartily and generously for our achievements at the club he cherished so much. Gay and I didn't last the course, but so many precious things came from that time. Celia is still a lovely lady, now aged 92, and it was a poignant moment for me when I spoke with Gay for the first time in 34 years at her father's funeral.

I may have wished that my happy student days would last forever but all too soon it was time for John Ryan to get down to business. I got my inspiration for my next move from my love of pondering the criminal mind. It has always been an abiding fascination for me. If there's ever competition at home for live sport on the TV today, it's the Crime Channel. As with a lot of folk, I suppose, the process of uncovering evidence and discovering exactly what happened is a source of constant fascination. Perhaps it was also a strange form of destiny as the founder of DNA, which has done so much to influence criminal investigations, was one Alick Jeffrey – not the Rovers legend, I hasten to add, but a professor at Leicester University.

It was with great enthusiasm therefore that I set out to work as a forensic scientist at Aldermaston, the famous nuclear site. The work itself didn't disappoint, but somehow things didn't add up for the ambitious young Ryan. Just as with the encyclopedias at university, the natural entrepreneur rose to the surface. To supplement my small income this time, I turned to selling central heating systems around the doors. Again I hit the spot almost immediately. It's alright having a job you enjoy but when you consider I was making £20 a week as a forensic scientist and £200 selling central heating in my spare time, you would probably come to a similar conclusion.

After just 18 months I gave up the day job, so to speak, and set up in business on my own – this time selling cavity wall insulation. I got premises in Boar Lane in Leeds and Modern Plan Insulation was born. I was at the helm of my own business at the comparatively tender age of 24. The next couple of years were successful enough for me to net a Jaguar and a Datsun 240Z and expand to a workforce of 24 people. It was the right product at the right time and everything in the garden looked set fair. Enter then that great enemy of the English entrepreneur – the Government! They smothered us all in red tape by insisting that we needed to get council approval to fill small cavities. It meant delays in our work that neither we nor many of my competitors could cope with. In such circumstances you can moan and groan and scratch out a living, or move on. I chose the latter.

3

*

OPERATION TRANSFORMATION

HAVING found that forensic science wasn't for me after all and a few salutary lessons about business, I discovered cosmetic surgery. Or, more accurately, it discovered me.

I didn't wake up one morning and decide I wanted to change the shape of the nation. My route to my future career off the football field was a bit more circuitous than that. Yet, when I look upon it, there was a curious sense of destiny about it all. Back in the 1970s, Dad lost his job and needed to bring in some cash. So he took a role as a travelling salesman for a small company called Transform, who were wanna-be big wigs, you might say. I, meanwhile, was working for Sheer Lighting after my initial dips into the business world had come to a standstill. It wasn't exactly a case of seeing the light, although the company car was a nice perk. And, conveniently, it gave me the time and vehicle to accompany my father on some of his sales calls.

This was a new environment that suited me fine as I've always had the gift of the gab and could sell electric fires to Eskimos. So when Dad couldn't make one particular call, I volunteered to take his place. Cue the born salesman I'd first discovered as a student. Just take a second to imagine the scenario. There I was, a young man blessed with a full head of hair, taking the bold - and bald - step of talking to men who generally had been on the planet a fair bit longer about the benefits of hair transplants. I'd never given a second's thought to the issue before, yet it suddenly seemed to be the most natural thing in the world.

Good salespeople, in my view, are usually born not made. You can attend scores of training courses and still not be very adept at it. Rather like the art of man-management, you can either do it, or you can't. I'm just fortunate that I've always had the knack. Of course, you need to get to know something about the product that you are selling, but the rest is all to do with personal qualities.

The key, I think, is to listen rather than preach to a potential client. But when you have heard what they have said, you must act on it. Looking back, I have a lot to thank those folically-challenged males for. They got me thinking about a very important principle I have taken through my business life. All these men wanted to do was to improve their physical appearance in order to feel more confident about themselves and how others viewed them. If I could play a small part in helping folk to enjoy their lives more that would be fantastic. And, of course, I could see that making me a lot of money.

I was soon heading for bigger things. Transform offered me a post as a salesman, then as a clinic manager in Manchester. I was hooked – and not just by hair transplants. Today I say that if you work in this line of business for a couple of years, you will be in it for life. So it proved with me. I bought ten per cent of the business in the early 1980s for £10,000 and, after becoming managing director in 1984, took a further 50 per cent, this time for £150,000, two years later. By the time I sold Transform back in 2002 in a multi-million pound deal, the very line of business that used to be a bit of a laughing stock had made me my fortune.

What you've got to appreciate here is that back in the not-so-swinging seventies few folk could have envisaged I was sitting on a potential pot of gold. Far from it. That's why the media have quite rightly referred to me very frequently as a pioneer of cosmetic surgery. Fortunately, it's not just hair styles that have changed since the 1970s, society has moved on a great deal too. And the public perception of cosmetic surgery has changed with it.

Seems like a distant memory now, but in the early days I was subjected to a fair degree of ridicule, even anger. Try to imagine the scene because it happened on countless occasions. There I'd be at a lovely dinner party. The wine and food would be flowing, just enough to loosen the tongues and enable the females of the species to say what they really thought. "I can't believe that women subject their bodies to that..." "I would never allow a cosmetic surgeon to get his knife into me, not in a hundred years..." "It's vain and plain dangerous, any woman who'd do that must be round the twist...". The abuse went on and on.

Cosmetic surgery was regarded as a luxury, at best. At worst, it was a crude violation of nature. But you can be sure that when a subject attracts such strength of emotion, there must be plenty of interest in it. So guess what? Quite a few of those women tiptoed up to me a few months later to ask me what my cosmetic surgeons could do for them! I jest not. Human nature is a very strange thing sometimes and cosmetic surgery proved to be a subject that women felt they should distance themselves from publicly even if it fascinated them in private.

I regard the American actress and role model supreme Jane Fonda as a great example of what I'm trying to say here. When young and at her physical peak, she was a beautiful woman who spoke out against cosmetic surgery. But in her 50s and in need of a little help, she was at the front of the queue. Hypocrisy? Not really. People change over the years and their opinions can change with them.

When you are venturing into the comparative unknown it is always good to draw upon very special people for inspiration. The late and great Dr Harold Shapiro, the world-renowned nutritionist and dietician, certainly fell into that category for me. We met during the 1970s at a time when I was looking at ways of taking Transform forward and became a very good friend. Dr Shapiro helped me a great deal with my business and, interestingly enough, had links with both major fields of my life as he was at one time the nutritionist at mighty Manchester United.

Being a remarkable man with rich and broad experience, he was one of the finest exponents of positive thinking and I believe that I owe some of the positive mental attitude that has benefited me so much to him. Some may scoff but in the early 1990s he came to watch a Rovers match at Belle Vue and gave some time to Eddie Gormley, one of our midfielders who had been struggling and hadn't scored a goal for a fair while. The magic didn't take long to work as Eddie went out and scored in the very first minute. Harold, sadly, is no longer with us, yet I still draw upon his influence. Taking on board something he taught me, whenever I'm in urgent need of a parking space, I'll shoot out a quick plea to Harold to help me and it's amazing how quickly a convenient space will open up in front of me.

Early experiences taught me a great deal. I knew almost from the beginning that the potential for cosmetic surgery in the UK was huge. From being the almost exclusive reserve of the rich, I could see ahead to the time when it would become one of the most sought after and profitable businesses. I wouldn't be telling you the full truth if I didn't admit that one of my main motivations for developing this business was to make money. I make no secret of the fact that I wanted to be rich and successful and can see no problem with that.

But where I do draw the line is the accusation, put forward more sparingly these days it has to be said, that I have been at the forefront of an industry that exploits human frailties. If you had been on the journey I have experienced, I don't think you would give credence to that point of view. I've always been someone who wants to make a contribution to other people's lives. As my good friend Neil Warnock so rightly says, I didn't go into football to make a fast buck, but my profit is in the personal satisfaction it has given me and the smiles I have helped to put on people's faces. This has also been the case, to a certain extent, with me and cosmetic surgery. I couldn't have put my heart and soul into it unless I actually believed in it.

So now you begin to see where I am coming from, I trust. Going around the wards in our clinics and speaking to our patients, particularly after their surgery, was a very useful and enlightening experience. No one human being can tell another how they should feel. We should all speak for ourselves. The positive message I received was that the women were genuinely appreciative and excited about their new image.

It's difficult to pick out too many individual examples but some have stood the test of time in my mind. One of the most moving was an operation that we wouldn't normally have performed at all. We had a rule that the minimum age for surgery was 18 – a figure I still consider realistic – but this story involved a young boy who was just FOUR years old.

I recall very vividly the sadness in his father's voice as he told me about his son who was refusing to go to school. It was nothing to do with the teachers or his dislike of education, but the things that did stick out in the poor boy's mind were his ears! As I witnessed when the lad came on a subsequent visit, his ears were at right angles, making him an obvious, but ill-deserved, subject of abuse. The probable repercussions for that young boy's future, all caused by a physical problem over which he had no control whatsoever, were potentially enormous. We are all more acutely aware these days of how much a young person's formative years can affect him or her for life. As I have indicated, this young boy's problem was actually beyond our normal remit. He was too young and, in any case, we didn't perform ear operations. But I'm a great believer in finding solutions rather than problems and thinking outside of the box. And I was helped in my mission by the fact that the surgeon I recommended the youngster to was of similar ilk. He told the lad and his father there was no practical reason why he couldn't perform the operation. Indeed it only required a local anaesthetic.

The boy came in very bravely for the procedure and I saw him as he left the clinic heavily bandaged up. I remember thinking that this could very well be the day that changed his life. Two or three weeks later the father again phoned me and there was a completely different tone in his voice. Gone was sadness and despair, replaced by optimism and joy. "I can hardly believe it," he told me. "It's as if I've been given my son back." A shy and frightened boy had been changed into a confident, happy and contented young soul determined and able to live life to the full. There aren't many professions in which you can inspire such profound and positive change.

I rode the wave of changing public opinion and continually drove the business forward. I have never settled for second best, or the status quo. In business, as in life, you either go forward or you sink fast. This young businessman wasn't for sinking. The number of treatments increased, advertising mushroomed and two clinics became many more. But the development that really saw cosmetic surgery take off came in the 1980s and was one very good idea from the other side of the Atlantic. They say the United States usually takes the lead and we follow a few years down the road and so it was with breast surgery.

It always made perfect sense to me. Women are acutely aware of their body image, which is so important to their self-esteem. And the most sensitive area of all is a woman's breasts. If you can do something to improve a woman's confidence, without causing any harm to her general health, then why not? But we needed the X-factor, a role model for ordinary women to look up to. We needed a messenger and were so grateful for one - Melinda Messenger.

It's amazing what bigger breasts will do and they certainly played a major role in the almost overnight rise to fame of the one-time customer services manager from Swindon. Armed with two impressively improved assets, courtesy of one of our clinics, Melinda became known as the 'Girl of the Thrillennium' and one of *The Sun*'s most celebrated topless models. Melinda's success over the past decade has shown that she is far more than a woman with gorgeous breasts. But they set her on her way to an impressive career as a TV presenter before her popularity boomed even further in 2008 when she became one of the darlings of ITV's *Dancing on Ice*. Of all the glamourous girls that have passed through our clinics, none has been so frequently linked with me as Melinda. At one stage we were bracketed in the same sentence so often that you'd have thought something was going on – and I played along to the full. After a famous Carling Cup victory over Aston Villa in 2005 I said that winning was 'even better than seeing Melinda Messenger naked'. The truth was my surgeons saw a lot more of Melinda than I ever did, but our success stories were intertwined. Melinda was a great example of a woman making the best of herself – and she helped to inspire many of our patients to do the very same.

Talking about models, we did perform one operation on Katie Price, or Jordan as she is even better known. But you won't find me linking myself with Katie too much, not at any price. There is a sense in which cosmetic surgery can be overdone and abused and she has long since crossed the line. Her operation with us was her second on those now famously huge breasts and it wasn't too long before she made enquiries about a possible third. We always, however, made a point of counselling our would-be patients in their own best interests and told Katie that we didn't feel comfortable with what she was doing. So I became one man who stood up to and turned down the demanding Jordan. It's sad really as I still find it hard to understand why such a naturally beautiful young woman needed to go so far. On the other hand, it's difficult to argue that her breasts have played a massive role in her rise to top celebrity status.

There's no doubt that the rise of our celebrity culture has suited cosmetic surgery just fine. Women, in particular, look up to the powerful and the beautiful, but I don't believe that means they are exploited as a result. It's important to reflect that for every Melinda Messenger or Katie Price, there are hundreds and hundreds of less well-known women who have experienced similar change in their lives.

I can still see before me now a very ordinary looking Yorkshire couple who came in to see me about the wife's proposed breast augmentation. The man was a particularly dour character and I quickly realised that he had a fair few misgivings about his wife having such surgery. That was significant as she was clearly under his thumb. Yet now he had come to the conclusion that it was the lesser evil to do something about his partner's flat chest.

The woman herself was in her thirties and the only word I could use to describe her was dowdy. She was obviously suffering from a severe lack of confidence and her slightly rundown appearance reflected that inner torment. Yet, as we spoke further, I could see there was a spark, a hint of something far different and brighter about this woman. I don't think she knew herself just how much an operation could help her, but she wanted to give it a try.

When I saw her in my office a few weeks later, I could barely believe it. In fact I had to look more than once to confirm that it was the same woman at all. Apart from the obviously enhanced figure, she had dyed her hair a striking blonde, dressed herself in a smart suit and, let's be totally honest, was now incredibly attractive.

What happened afterwards caused me mixed emotions. My next contact was with an angry husband telling me the story of how his more confident wife had subsequently run off with a younger model. Understandably, he was in no mood to appreciate the surgery and demanded that, as he had paid for the operation himself, we should refund him the full amount. When I told him that wasn't really possible as the woman herself had been fully satisfied with the procedure, he came up with another idea that left me not knowing whether to laugh or cry. He insisted that he wanted his wife's new boobs re-possessing! I don't think I've ever heard anything like it either before or since. Without getting any joy from marriage break-ups, I got the impression that the bloke probably got what he deserved. The fact that the woman discovered herself was a positive rather than a negative in my book.

Cosmetic surgery can and does meet many of our clients' expectations and, as the tributes later in this book reveal, enhances the lives of countless people. Never have I been so crass as to suggest that boob surgery, or any other surgical procedure for that matter, will actually change your life, but it can certainly help the way you look at it.

On the other hand, I have always been wary of promising miracles. We were always going to get a small percentage of women who would wave a photograph of Marilyn Monroe, or whoever was the pin-up of their time, in front of us and say they wanted to look like that. In such circumstances I did have to counsel some women against such surgery as their expectations far exceeded what we were able to do. To be successful over a lengthy period of time, you need more than a glamourous image and good PR – you need substance and that's what I have always striven for. I've always ensured that we enlisted the very best surgeons. Indeed there are plenty of professionals, Jan Stanek of *10 Years Younger* fame among them, whom I helped to get a start in cosmetic surgery.

Although the business generally prospered over the years, there were, of course, some very sticky moments. In the mid-1990s my subsequent success story could so easily have come to a very unfortunate end. For various reasons Transform was going through a period of struggle but I felt that, given our previous success and good reputation, we would indeed get backing from the bank when we asked for an increased overdraft to ease the worst of our troubles. But I was hugely disappointed and disillusioned as the bank, so glad of our business during the good times, threatened to shut its door firmly in our faces. Their emphatic 'no' could so easily have meant me having to close down Transform and that would have had a huge knock-on effect in my life. Certainly I would not have had the money with which to rescue Donny Rovers a few years down the road. But there was to be a saving grace. I had put £1m away into a pension fund and was able to get access to half of it, £500,000, to plug the potentially terminal gap in our finances. The good times then returned and the rest is history. But this was a pretty close call and an experience I put away in my personal locker marked 'do not repeat'.

MY life has always included a place for play as well as work and one of the joys of being successful in business was that it did indeed give me the perfect platform to indulge my main passion – Doncaster Rovers, of course. Being at the helm of a fashionable company meant I could offer my support not just as a spectator, but as a regular sponsor. I got my reputation as being Mr Champagne man for adding a bit more bubbly and sparkle to the club's man of the match awards.

I took things a major step forward in 1989 when I joined the board of Doncaster Rovers as a director. As ever, the club was in a state of uproar. We were in Division Four at the time, Joe Kinnear had departed Belle Vue after a row with the board and the Inland Revenue had slapped in a winding up order. It was also a time when football was attempting to come to terms with the horrors of the Hillsborough disaster in which 96 Liverpool supporters lost their lives after going to watch the FA Cup semi-final between their Merseyside heroes and Nottingham Forest. One outcome for Rovers from the safety-conscious Taylor Report was that our own capacity at Belle Vue was reduced to a mere 7,294.

The traumas were nearly too much for Peter Wetzel who threatened to withdraw his backing, only to return to the Belle Vue boardroom in the coup that saw my entrance. Both of us were delighted when Billy Bremner, who had twice led Rovers to promotion back to the Third Division in his first spell in the Belle Vue hot seat, returned to replace Kinnear as manager.

It was then I gave that highly significant interview with

Peter Catt in which I revealed it had always been my ambition to make a lot of money in order to help my football club towards the then First Division. I know that my comment raised his eyebrows and probably those of many readers of the *Doncaster Free Press*, but I was speaking from the heart.

It was a great honour for me to join the board and I thoroughly enjoyed the experience. But I tell you what I learnt from being a director - there's one thing harder than being in charge of a football club and that is not being in charge! I had 28 per cent of the shares, enough to make me a significant player but not to have full control.

Naturally, I went into the club with loads of enthusiasm and optimism and thought that a highly respectable Third Division side including the likes of Ian and Glynn Snodin, John Buckley and Colin Douglas had the potential to take us into that era's equivalent of the Championship at the very least. But we were always battling against the financial odds despite all the cash that I and fellow director Peter Wetzel, who held 40 per cent of the shares, put into the club.

There were good folk associated with Rovers at the time, but it's fair to say that we were never the most professional of organisations. Many times a hefty bill from the Inland Revenue was greeted almost with a shrug of the shoulders and a laugh. Next question was not the whereabouts of the cheque book but which player would be out of the door to give us a fighting chance of paying. That explains why a promising young striker called Brian Deane was allowed to go to neighbours Sheffield United for the scandalously low price of £30,000. Deano was a powerhouse of a striker who became one of the Blades' goal scoring legends, most notably in partnership with the equally fearsome Tony Agana, before being sold to Leeds United for a cool £2.9m He won three England caps and went on to play for Middlesbrough and

Benfica. Being financially stretched obviously makes you vulnerable to the richer clubs cherry-picking your players at favourable prices. Another bargain from the Donny basement was Mark Rankin who left for Wolverhampton Wanderers, again for the sake of the taxman.

A very important bonus for me was that I got to know Peter Wetzel. A businessman with Donny Rovers running through his veins who later became my partner when we took over the club, Peter had been a great servant to Rovers from the early 1980s when he sold his business, SR Gent, for a substantial sum. However living the dream on gates of around 3,000 proved too great a task in the end and led to Peter selling out to the awful Ken Richardson. But his time had yet to come.

The crux of the problem was that we were financially weak, yet had the very attractive carrot of that 99-year lease at Belle Vue to interest prospective buyers. It was always my view that the lease was the first thing on Richardson's mind. I did try at the time to launch a takeover with Mike Collett but the chairman Jim Burke, in his wisdom, decided that Richardson was the better option. What a mistake that was.

Armed with Peter's 40 per cent, Richardson went round the other minor shareholders to gain a majority share with the pressure increasing on me to sell up. As I have already said, I was actually cast as the villain of the piece during this fraught spell, as unsuspecting supporters accused me of being the stumbling block. I walked away a sad, but wiser man. I never wanted to leave my football club behind, yet with opinion swinging so strongly against me, I really had no choice. So I continued to watch our unequal struggles from the terraces until Richardson hit me with his crazy ban.

Come 1998 I was a far different human being from the one who had set out tentatively in life and in business. I was more confident and aware, both of the hardships and pitfalls as well as the rewards. I'd learnt a great deal in my personal life, too, particularly as I'd encountered some extreme emotional heartache.

My confidence with women was high after Gay and my university liaisons. And it wasn't long before I met the woman who was to become my first wife and mother of my two daughters Claire and Gemma, a beautiful brunette called Denise Flanagan.

I always looked out for attractive young women as they were more at ease with themselves and therefore easier to talk to. I also was attracted by the idea of women who wanted to better themselves. Denise certainly fell into the first category, although she was never the most ambitious person. We met at the Airport Club in Doncaster where I showed that I'd learnt my lessons about the perils of being shy and missing out on the 'catch'. I noticed that quite a lot of young men were ogling her but all were keeping their distance, so I came straight to the point. I walked across the dance floor and asked her straightaway if she wanted to dance. She said an immediate 'yes' and remarked that mine had been the first such invitation she'd received all night!

We married at Slough Register Office in August 1978 and lived together in a two-bedroom bungalow at Tickhill, near Doncaster. This was the first house that I'd ever bought and cost me £8,000. Sadly, for both of us, it proved to be a difficult marriage. Despite having two beautiful daughters, we gradually drifted further and further apart. We were together for 15 years and I must admit it was my decision to move on and seek a divorce which happened in 1993. No parting of the ways is easy, even from the point of view of the party who leaves and this provided me with one of the most challenging periods of my life.

Those weren't quite the heady days of multi-million pound settlements but the break-up cost me £1m. However all that paled into insignificance when Denise died suddenly in October 1997 as a result of a tragic accident at home. You can talk all you like about how hard a particular event may have been in football or in business, but few things compare with the harrowing task of helping my two daughters to come to terms with the impossibly awful fact that their mother was dead. That's not to mention my own personal sorrow.

It is fair to say that few, if any, events have affected me so profoundly as the death of Denise. It made me think long and hard about this mortal existence of ours and what it all means. However, without disregarding the pain this caused all of us, I believe that some good has come from it. I put Denise's untimely death down as a marker in the sand and decided there and then that nothing could ever be as bleak and as dark as that in the future. It also put the relative trivia of life into a more accurate perspective. How could I, for example, be worried about small issues such as speaking in front of hundreds of people when I'd gone through the experience of losing my former wife and the mother of my children?

All our experiences, whether good or bad, play a part in making us the type of person we are and without them I would never have been able to answer that all-important question: Is there anything you can do about this, John?

I could now see how far I'd come along my personal journey and, moreover, where I still wanted to go. Most folk never get the opportunity to indulge themselves and do exactly what they want to do. But by this time I was in a very privileged position despite my recent loss. My business life was extremely successful and I had folk I could happily hand over the reins to in order to take a back seat. As far as fully declaring my hand and giving my football club a real go was concerned, it really was a case of now or never.

PART TWO:
MY FOOTBALL MISSION

4
*
FIVE STEPS TO HEAVEN

PETER WETZEL, former co-owner and vice chairman of Doncaster Rovers: "I admit that when I first left Rovers as a director I was absolutely fed up with it. I'd been out of the game for many years when John Ryan phoned and asked whether I'd like to come back. Our years in the Conference were very tough but a real learning curve for us. Every step forward was a gamble, buying the club in the first place, the training ground and players, but you have to speculate to accumulate – and we did."

ROVERS director Stuart Highfield: "I remember John telling me in the 1980s that one day he'd own a Bentley, be a millionaire and chairman of a football club. Since then his premonitions have often come true, including when he predicted four months before the game that Rovers would beat Leeds United in the play-off final. It's no coincidence that we have almost the same board of directors we had since John and I started - and a lot of the backroom staff have remained as well. In those early days we were in uproar but we never fell foul of the authorities for our administration with the likes of secretary Joan Oldale staying and doing a great job We don't chop and change for the sake of it and Rovers remains a family club today.

SIR ALEX FERGUSON, Manchester United manager: "May I take the opportunity to congratulate you and your club on a marvellous achievement in gaining promotion to the Championship league. It has been an amazing journey for you over the last few years and, although there may have been one or two hiccups along the way, your drive and determination has proved a big advantage to your club. I now hope you establish yourself in the Championship and, from there, keep rising. It is not impossible with the ambition shown by your team. I have written personally to Sean O'Driscoll to congratulate him and his players. I am sure he realises that having the backing of a good chairman is equally important when it comes to progressing to the next level of football and I wish you every success. I will be watching your results."

IF the 'funeral' brought home as never before how much I needed Doncaster Rovers, our continuing plight in the summer of 1998 convinced me beyond doubt that my football club also needed me.

The exact circumstances leading to my becoming chairman are a bit of a blur now but the opening gambit was made by Ray Thomas, a friend and colleague, who let it be known that I was once again interested in becoming more involved. My first meeting as we explored the way forward was with a gentleman called Kevin Phelan, from Westferry. He had already started to assemble some of the jigsaw but felt that the key piece needed to be someone with an interest in football and in business who either lived in the Doncaster area or had the club and the area in his blood. All takeovers take time and it was July 1998 before Westferry officially ended Mr Richardson's reign and I was installed as non-executive chairman on the understanding that I would buy the footballing side of the club as quickly as possible.

Fast forward a little and I held my famous, or infamous,

press conference at Belle Vue where I made FOUR very specific promises – to restore Rovers to the Football League, provide us with a new stadium, win a national competition and elevate us to the level of football we enjoyed when I first started watching – the modern-day Championship. I don't believe for one moment that the small group of journalists and club officials present took me totally seriously. After all such words are uttered over and over again about 'sleeping giants' who generally remain dormant. But, yes, I meant and believed every word.

However, it is one thing to have a dream, quite another to try to put it into practice. I knew well enough from my previous links with the club that it was never going to be a case of waving a magic wand – or even a magic chequebook – and instantly putting to rights what had been going wrong for so long. The five Conference years, in particular, tested my love of Donny Rovers and football to breaking point. I think all fans suffer far more than they celebrate – but that only goes to make success, when hard and long earned, all the more enjoyable.

It's an interesting thought that I can almost divide today's Doncaster Rovers fans into two – those old enough to remember the days when we slipped to the bottom of the pile and the rest who have known only the last few years of virtually non-stop success. I'd like to dedicate the next section of my story to both groups and football supporters everywhere who have a passion for their particular club. Learning from the past is an underestimated art.

5

*

STEP ONE: OUR GOLDEN GOAL

Doncaster Rovers 3 Dagenham and Redbridge 2
Saturday 10 May 2003, Britannia Stadium, Stoke,
Conference play-off final.

'SIR' FRANCIS TIERNEY, scorer of Doncaster's most important ever goal and now a lorry driver: "I remember that goal as if it happened yesterday – the build-up down the left, a low cross from Paul Barnes and the ball coming to me. I was surprised that when I hit it my legs were like jelly – when it went in, it was unbelievable. I spent the most enjoyable years of my football life at Doncaster and it gives me great pleasure to see where they are now."

JOHN HELM, TV broadcaster, journalist and proud fan of Bradford Park Avenue: "Such has been the phenomenal success achieved during John's tenure at Doncaster Rovers, the club should be held up as a blueprint to the rest of the Football League. I'm happy to say I've been there to share in several of John's triumphs – the most notable being that day at Stoke in 2003 when league status was restored. I like the fact that he is living a boyhood dream with the club he has always supported, and yet whenever we meet never fails to ask about the well-being of my club."

DAVE MORRIS, Doncaster Rovers chief executive: "There's no way I would have joined the club but for John Ryan and his sheer enthusiasm. He can walk into a room and by the time he leaves you're almost jumping for joy! At first we didn't even have any accounts – a legacy of the Richardson era – and I was brought in to try and sort them out. There were only three of us working off-the-field, the others being Albert Paget, our safety officer, and Joan Oldale, a survivor of the old regime who stayed on and did a great job for us. It took years to build up trust in us again but we have developed into a club people are once again very happy to do business with. The biggest day in the whole history of this club was at Stoke. For a few seconds after the golden goal went in it was as if none of us knew what to do. Then it hit us – we were back in the Football League!"

TIME almost went into slow motion when the goal of all goals was scored. I have relived the moment thousands of times since because it was one of the most significant in the entire history of Doncaster Rovers.

There were barely a couple of seconds between our skipper Paul Barnes crossing the ball and Francis Tierney striking it low into the Dagenham and Redbridge net for the golden goal that won Rovers our place back in the Football League. But I'll tell you how long it seemed in my anxious mind - FIVE YEARS! For that was the time it took to haul ourselves back from the 'death' and ashes of relegation.

Yet that only made the actual moment when we clinched promotion and our subsequent successes back in the Football League all the sweeter. Rome wasn't built in a day, nor Belle Vue re-built in a few months, but then the most important battle I faced when I came through the door wasn't just winning back our league status but ensuring the very survival of the club.

I still tell friends, with a twinkle in my eye of course, that Peter Wetzel and I bought Doncaster Rovers for £50,000 on 1 May 1999 plus £50,000 more when the new stadium was produced – and we were had big time! Honestly, the mess I inherited wasn't worth 50 pence, but this was a job for love, not money. Most folk in my position might have expected a present on his 49th birthday; I bought myself a dying football club!

I don't think many Rovers fans would have been surprised had the club folded completely after the debacle of that awful last season in the Football League. And I can truthfully say that I discovered a club in a far worse state than even I suspected. But then if you are going to reverse a decline, you might as well start from the very bottom. And, believe me, few clubs can ever have sunk as low as Doncaster Rovers.

Important decisions were made by the consortium seeking to buy Rovers in the months prior to my re-emergence on the scene – one being the appointment of former Rochdale player and sports consultant Ian McMahon as chief executive, to give the club some much-needed organisation and drive. I think Ian found Belle Vue a bit of a culture shock but unearthed enough material during his short stay with us to write an amusing book. It was a time when a sense of humour was an absolute necessity. Also able to testify to the Rovers revival story from day one was Paul May who worked closely with Ian from the start and was announced as overall boss before I took over. Paul is a great example of what the last decade has been all about as he is still a director today.

Then there was our secretary Joan Oldale, a rare survivor from the wreckage of the Richardson days, who stayed loyal to us and ensured that somehow we kept ourselves above water as far as the paperwork in particular was concerned. Thank goodness, too, for Eric Randerson, who despite getting no encouragement at all on the community side from our previous owners, kept the faith and is now part and parcel of a thriving club and one of Rovers' many friendly faces.

One of the first priorities was to ensure the Conference was happy to take us – and that was anything but a formality. To play in any league, you need to be able to satisfy their conditions and Belle Vue fell a fair way short. August dawned before our admission was confirmed on the grounds of my assurances that we were seeking a new venue. Otherwise we would have kicked off in the Northern Premier League. Not that we had a team anyway! Just two weeks before we were due to return to training there were only four professionals on the books – not all of them footballers – and no manager. It looked for a while as if we'd have to ring round all of Mark Weaver's mates just to try and raise a side. Rumour had it that a young lad called Mason Van Basten – yes, a relative of the great Dutch star – was interested in playing for us. That's until we put him in the side for a friendly at Worksop and he failed to turn up!

I was bank rolling the club months before officially becoming chairman. Basically we identified a need – be it a player to sign, or some work that needed to be done and I paid for it. It was the only way forward. We needed something special to capture the imagination of the general public – a move to dispel some of the gloom and give Rovers supporters genuine belief there were better times around the corner. And I'm not referring to the appearance of page three model Amanda Robbins to model our kit! It came instead with the capture of a slightly older model and one the fans could genuinely look up to – our new manager Ian Snodin.

Ian was a Doncaster Rovers legend who never forgot his roots even after becoming an England Under 21 international and swapping Belle Vue for the more celebrated surroundings of Everton and Leeds United. Speaking in the *Daily Mail* shortly after he took the job, Ian's passion shone through: "I watched the club stumble out of the Football League. I was playing for Scarborough at the time, but lived in Doncaster. I paid my £6 along with everybody else to stand and watch. Fans would recognise me and ask when I was coming back to do something about the mess the club was in. I'd just laugh, but deep down I really wanted to come back and put things right." It was a fantastic move for Rovers when out went Mark Weaver, Richardson's right-hand man, and in his place came a big name and a man with the club's well-being at heart.

There could be no one better to assist him than his brother Glynn, a fellow Donny legend and former Leeds United star. It took a little longer to lure the second Snodin back to Belle Vue, but by now I was firmly on the case, offering to fund Snodin II's wages if we could persuade him to join Ian at the helm. I negotiated Glynn's release from Scarborough to put the dream management team in place. Needless to say Scarborough's initial demand for more than £30,000 compensation needed a fair bit of revising. Never underestimate the role the Snodin brothers played in Donny's revival – I certainly don't. I know they would have loved to have seen the full mission accomplished yet, without them, it would never have got off the ground.

People often think that a football chairman lives off the fat of the land, but nothing was further from the truth, particularly at that embryonic stage of our redevelopment. Put it this way, the playing budget would have been spent many times over but for me putting my hand in my pocket to give us a fighting chance. I don't think the fans have much of a clue about how costly it is to run a side at Conference level and I invested heavily for some time with little sign of much on-field progress. By the time we finally achieved our promotion I estimated my input at £4m including a club record £100,000 waste of money on striker Justin Jackson.

Initially, I had a hot list of players whom I would have loved to have brought to the club – former England international Chris Waddle, ex-Aston Villa starlet Dalian Atkinson and Tommy Wright were just three of them, with the latter being the one who actually put pen to paper. But getting a kit and training facilities was a good enough start. Our friends from Sheffield United provided us with some shirts and shorts and we managed to find some land at Cantley Park, which we have since transformed over the years into an excellent training base.

Don't be fooled by the phrase Non League. The Conference, or Blue Square Premier as it is now known, is deadly serious stuff. This is where grass roots football and the big time collide. Grounds may be a little more rundown and defenders kick forwards an extra six inches in the air, but in its own way this is football at its very finest. I met some great folk during our five years in Non League soccer and just because we've moved on to bigger and better things now doesn't mean I will ever forget them. Non League football is everything the Football League is except a million times harder. It saddens me hugely whenever I hear about yet another of the clubs who make grass roots football so special struggling or even going out of existence altogether.

Today the Blue Square Premier is the fifth division in all but name, literally packed with clubs who have graced the Football League in the recent past and those still dreaming of getting there for the very first time. You only have to look at Morecambe, Accrington Stanley, Dagenham and now Burton Albion in the last few seasons to appreciate that the divide between this division and League Two is wafer thin.

Yet re-wind just a few years and automatic promotion and relegation in and out of the Football League was still new enough for Conference clubs to regard Donny Rovers as big-time charlies. Perhaps they weren't too far from the truth, although there was nothing remotely big time about our team that ran out for our very first Non League match at Dover.

You can imagine my mixture of excitement and apprehension on Saturday, 15 August 1998 when more than 300 travelling Rovers fans gathered to witness the start of the next chapter in our history. Our 'big match' preparation, however, wasn't quite ideal. In true Non League-style we picked up some of the team from a service station and when we emerged from the tunnel it was unaccountably in shirts with East Riding Sacks – the company owned by the damned Mr Richardson - on them. In the circumstances, a 1-0 defeat was almost a moral victory.

Monday morning brought a couple more tumultuous announcements as Westferry declared they had taken over from Dinard – therefore officially banishing the Richardson regime to history - and the signing of a certain Neville Southall in goal. Yes, the Neville Southall, of Everton and Wales fame! Again, I agreed to fund the deal after Ian had used his powers of persuasion. The following day I was unveiled as the new chairman and the Welsh mountain our new guardian at a do at the Grand St Leger Hotel, the event being cut short as we had the small matter of our first home match against Southport later that evening

If we needed a reminder that Doncaster folk were behind us it came that very night as an amazing 3,663, our largest opening crowd for many a year, came to cheer us on. Not that we gave them a great deal to shout about against the previous season's FA Trophy finalists and another former Football League side. The game was lost 1-0 to a goal from Justin O'Reilly in the 25th minute, meaning we were without a point or goal from our opening two fixtures. But that was scarcely the issue, as *Doncaster Star* reporter Steve Hossack observed in his match report: "Rovers have now lost both opening games – hardly surprising in view of the circumstances. But they have competed well in both and they will only get better once they have had time to gel and player manager Ian Snodin has had the opportunity to fine-tune his charges." Ian Snodin, 36 at the time, was in the team and Southall had a good game, being blameless with the winning goal.

Big names, however, didn't add up to big results. Neville conceded some sloppy goals and former Leeds and Republic of Ireland international John Sheridan, a strolling, confident player at his height, was also well past his best. Both soon had their match-by-match contracts cancelled. Steve Nicol, the former Liverpool star, was a far different proposition, becoming hugely popular with Rovers fans before moving on the following March to America. You never quite know what you're getting when a big name goes into Non League football, but Nicol was a diamond and we'd have loved to have kept him for longer.

Perhaps the most significant signing was Dave Penney, the former Derby County player. I liked Dave from the beginning as he was a gritty player who put his heart and soul into the club, although I had no idea then that he would become such an important figure in Rovers' revival. Our first and biggest problem was persuading Dave to come – he freely admitted that when he first saw his colleagues he didn't know whether he wanted to play with us. He recognised instantly this was never going to be a quick fix. How right he was.

Keeping our heads above water in the Conference was the limit of our ambition that season. We were actually rock bottom around Christmas, whilst I was carrying out the usual task of due diligence to establish fully the club's financial state before officially taking over. Worries over our league position were too immediate, however, to wait for such niceties so, having spoken with Ian, I promised to continue funding any new recruits if they could help us avoid going down. And, another thing, I dangled the carrot of an end-of-season trip to Magaluf for the Rovers family just as long, of course, that we avoided relegation.

It therefore came as a mighty relief when within the space of a few days my due diligence was completed and Ian Duerden's hat-trick earned us a 3-1 victory in January at Rushden and Diamonds, three vital points in our survival bid from the home of one of the Conference's high flyers. We could even afford the luxury of a rare Steve Nicol own-goal.

With Richardson's trial rumbling on in the background – disrupting us both through negative publicity and the need for some members of Rovers staff to give evidence – I tried my best to assure everyone that, once the takeover was complete, I was looking for stability. That meant keeping the services of Ian McMahon and Peter May as well as loyal office staff.

We inched closer and closer to mathematical survival – and to Magaluf – with a 2-2 home draw against Northwich Victoria and were then officially safe after suffering a 1-0 defeat at Farnborough, as other results went our way. In the end we finished 16th with 48 points. Sixteen more than Leek Town and Farnborough who occupied the bottom two spots.

There was a major bonus on the horizon that showed once again the potential of this club if only we could get our act together. The Endsleigh Challenge Trophy, basically a Conference league cup, might not have meant too much to most people, but to folk who hadn't touched silverware for decades and had nearly gone out of existence it was worth the Premiership and Champions League rolled into one.

The timing of the final couldn't have been better as it also coincided with the takeover being officially confirmed. We'd already taken a one-goal lead from the first leg at

Cherrywood Road against Farnborough with Dave Penney, appropriately, getting the score. So Peter Wetzel and I had the lovely task of going out onto the pitch prior to the all-important second leg to tell Rovers fans the news – we had new owners. I'm not normally a fan of traffic jams but couldn't help but feel a tinge of pride when the kick off was delayed 15 minutes due to crowd congestion. An astonishing capacity crowd of 7,160 turned out and Belle Vue was rocking. It would have been harsh if Farnborough spoiled such a wonderful party and they never came close. Player of the year Colin Sutherland doubled our aggregate lead after just five minutes and hitman Duerden netted a couple more as we triumphed 3-0 on the night and a convincing 4-0 overall. Yorkshire TV cameras were there to record the carnival and the looks of sheer joy on the faces of Ian and Glynn Snodin when they held up that cup said it all – the 'dead' club really was back in business.

We'd kept Rovers alive, staved off the very real prospect of a second successive relegation and won a trophy – if you or I were writing this story our second season, 1999-2000, would have seen the club building on that platform and concentrating on the other end of the Conference table.

Certainly we entered the next season in sound enough shape. Ian moved quickly to get his summer signings in place and we looked to have improved the side. The most significant addition in terms of their future contribution to Rovers on the field was undoubtedly goalkeeper Andy Warrington, who arrived on a free from York City and gave sterling service both throughout our Conference years and all the way through to League One. And there was a huge addition off-the-field, too, as we managed to bring in Mickey Walker to head our youth section. A local man with a strong affinity with Rovers, Mickey had held similar posts at both Leeds United and Forest and again turned out to be one of the heroes in our revival in this job and later as assistant manager to Dave Penney and now as Director of Football. I'm a firm believer in the importance of football clubs nurturing and developing young players but, unsurprisingly, this was another area of the club that had bitten the dust under Ken Richardson

There's nothing like the arrival of a star striker to set the pulses racing and it was not every day that a club such as Rovers could attract a forward with a Premier League winners' medal. Mike Newell arrived at Belle Vue with the impressive CV of having been Alan Shearer's partner up front during Blackburn Rovers' fairy-tale rise to the very top in 1992/93.

For most of the campaign it looked pretty good for us. We may not have been serious promotion challengers at any stage but by the end of January we were handily placed in seventh spot. Season two also had its fair share of surprises – not least seeing our name appear in the first round of the Sheffield Senior Cup. We started against Northern Counties East League Brodsworth Welfare with the father and son team of Glynn and Lee Snodin in our ranks. This was the first time in our history that two generations had appeared on the same teamsheet – and both scored in our 5-0 win. Wombwell Main provided a sterner test at Belle Vue going down by just 1-0 and our run was halted at the quarter-final stage when we lost 2-0 to Frickley Athletic, of the Northern Premier League. The referee, by the way, was a young man from Rotherham by the name of Howard Webb. I remember telling him afterwards that he would never make it!

There were fun and frolics in the other national cup competitions, too. The fourth qualifying-round of the FA Cup brought us a club from the hotbed of football, the north east. But our opponents were Crook Town rather than Newcastle United and we were four up inside 16 minutes after Newell began the rout. Glenn Kirkwood, a striker we'd signed from Eastwood Town the previous season, helped himself to four. Our exit in the next round was also at Belle Vue in front of BBC's *Match of the Day* cameras and, ironically, at the hands of Halifax Town, who had replaced us in the Football League.

We had our designs on the FA Trophy, particularly after the extraordinary events in our third-round tie against Halesowen Town. A 1-1 draw at Belle Vue took us to Halesowen for a replay that proved anything but straightforward. The team left Doncaster at 1.45pm but was so badly held up in traffic they didn't arrive at the ground until 7.30pm. Kick-off was eventually put back until 8.30pm. In the circumstances the very last thing we needed after such a late arrival was extra-time, but that's just how it turned out. By the time defender Dean Walling nodded the winner the clock was ticking towards 10.45pm. The stage was set fair for us to continue our good run at Dover Athletic in the next round and it was on occasions like this that we expected Newell with all his nous and experience to come to the party. Dover went 1-0 up against the run of play and, sure enough, the moment arrived for Newell to step forward. Duerden's cross eluded the home goalkeeper after 71 minutes and the Premier League winner just had to nod the ball into the empty net to equalise. But the ball bobbled up and he managed to lift his shot against the bar from just two yards – one of the worst misses I've ever seen. It may not quite have been so blatant as Rocky Baptiste's open-goal blunder against Harrow Borough in 2009 that attracted so many internet hits but, believe me, it was a cracker of its kind. The result was that we disappeared from the Trophy and Newell himself left a few days later as he was transferred to Blackpool. A home-sick Sutherland also went north, this time to Clydebank.

Simon Marples, a youngster we had signed from

Stocksbidge Park Steels, won representative honours with the England C team and even attracted a very large bid from Sunderland, which we turned down. By now, however, our only other hint of light was coming in the League Cup as we closed in on a second successive triumph with a 3-1 aggregate success over Telford United in the semi-final. We then went on to retain the trophy in a 2-0 one-off final victory over Kingstonian. Penney was among the scorers.

But the most important competition was always going to be the league and our slump to 17th spot in late April, just seven points away from the dreaded relegation zone, prompted me to take a very tough decision. I fully realised that there was a lot of sympathy and support for the Snodin brothers, both of whom I regarded very highly. But you have to look at these things as dispassionately as possible and I was concerned that we could be exiting the Conference in the wrong direction. So it was the job of myself and Peter Wetzel in the closing weeks of the 1999/2000 season to step in and relieve both Ian and Glynn of their duties – an unenviable task indeed. The fear of going down another division was too awful to contemplate. Looking back on it now I would venture to say that Ian perhaps wasn't cut out to be a manager – top-class players rarely are, it seems - but Glynn was a different kettle of fish altogether. I'm not at all surprised that he still has a niche in the game as assistant manager at both Leeds United and Northern Ireland.

Temporary reins were handed to our two most experienced players, Penney and Mark Atkins, who duly averted any threat of relegation with three wins and a draw from our last five league games. Perhaps I should have gone with my gut instinct then as I'd already spotted Penney's leadership potential, but instead we opted for Steve Wignall, another former player with a tremendous proven track record for building up clubs that had fallen on hard times –

fans of Aldershot and Colchester United would happily have given references. He worked in partnership at first with Alan Lewer. We made Penney player-coach with responsibility for the reserves and he responded in promising style by guiding them to the First Division of the Avon Insurance League at the very first attempt.

We made some progress in 2000/1 winning five successive home games early on and moving up to seventh spot by Bonfire Night. The fans would have liked more touchline fireworks from the more understated Wignall, but were impressed with his passion when he spoke at a public meeting at the Earl of Doncaster in front of 400 fans and a suitably pleased chairman.

There was still the odd crazy moment, of course, with our youth team manager Mickey Walker having to pick defender Ciaran Kenna in goal for an important FA Youth Cup tie on the grounds that he'd played Gaelic football and therefore knew how to use his hands. We beat Chester City 2-1. Then, in November, Belle Vue was broken into one Wednesday night and all our boots were stolen. Instead of calling up Sandy Shaw or Zola Budd, we stretched the budget to some new footwear for the next game against Rushden and Diamonds. Then we had the distinction of playing Sheffield Football Club, officially the world's oldest, in a Sheffield Cup tie at the Don Valley, going behind early on before shaking off the cobwebs to win 4-1.

All was overshadowed by the huge sadness of losing Alick Jeffrey, our club president, with 750 people turning out for a very moving memorial service at Belle Vue (see later chapter: King Alick Jeffrey). Proof, I suppose, that life and football goes on was that we won 14-0 the following night, albeit against modest Yorkshire Main, in the Sheffield Cup. Ian Duerden hit them for six. The strangest of all Rovers cup runs continued with wins over Ecclesfield Red Rose 7-0 and a Worksop Town team, including a certain Chris Waddle, 2-1 in the semi-final. That took us to Hillsborough for the final against Emley where we needed a tongue wagging from Steve Wignall to turn a half-time deficit into a 2-1 success that ensured yet more silverware was put into the Belle Vue trophy cabinet.

We were fifth going into March, although promotion was out of the question as there was only one promotion place and no play-offs. You better believe a certain John Ryan was doing his level best to iron out that anomaly. In the end we finished ninth.

Things didn't go Steve Wignall's way in 2001/2 – and that was even before the season started. Negotiations with the Conference about an extra promotion spot got very sticky as the Football League, although voting in favour, were unhappy about the financial ramifications. The result was the ridiculous suggestion of having the play-offs but still only one promotion spot – thankfully the FA put the lid on that rubbish. In addition the season started with Steve's wife seriously ill – a very sad and unforeseen course of events that obviously made his difficult task all the harder. Despite all this, we started well enough and I agreed to boost us still further by lashing out that £100,000 on Justin Jackson, from Rushden and Diamonds, a lad we'd put in a £30,000 bid for when at Morecambe a couple of seasons before. Poor Justin missed a couple of good chances on his debut against Woking and took it from there.

November brought my infamous 'I quit' speech which I also deal with in part four of this book. Suffice to say that having already put about £1.5m into the club personally, I was distraught that the council could no longer guarantee us a new stadium, putting our plans to get back into the Football League in severe jeopardy. I decided to continue as a director, however, taking a £10,000 fine, £8,000 of which was suspended, on the chin from the FA for my emotion-charged comments.

We were actually sixth at Christmas, but financially challenged without my cash and that played a part in the unfortunate dismissal of Steve Wignall on 10 January. To be honest, the lad had no luck at all, with his wife's illness taking up an understandable amount of his emotional and physical energies. Again it was seen by some to be a questionable decision when we sacked Wignall, a man who had also served us well as a player, but subsequent events proved us right. By this time Penney was Wignall's number two as the Lewer partnership had struggled to take off and it was an obvious decision to make him caretaker manager and promote our youth coach Mickey Walker to be his assistant after he'd done a fantastic job with our youngsters. We lost 1-0 in Penney's first match in charge at Scarborough, but then won the next six on the bounce, making the duo's permanent appointment a formality.

As we prepared to kick off the 2002/3 season, our fifth in the Conference, I chatted to Dave and told him to do his best to get us into the play-offs. The Football League and Conference had by now come to an agreement over two-up two-down, giving our chances of gaining promotion a pre-season lift. There was a wave of optimism about Belle Vue once again.

Certainly the campaign couldn't have started with a more positive omen. Opening day was Dave's birthday and we battled our way to a 2-1 victory over Barnet at Belle Vue. But it was far from a party. A rare error by our capable goalkeeper Andy Warrington presented Ben Strevens with the opening goal for Barnet after just a couple of minutes. Jackson, doing his utmost to make some kind of amends for an injury-ravaged previous season, came on at the start of the second half and we started to pour forward and make chances. Finally, Jackson and Simon Marples helped set up a chance for teenager Paul Green to thump home a 69th-minute equaliser. Still, it looked like a point was all we'd get until, in the 84th minute, we had that rub of the green that you long for in any closely-fought match. Defender Dave Morley's header looked goalbound but took a flick off a Bees defender, hit the bar and went in off the goalkeeper's legs.

By 7 September we actually topped the Conference for the first time and here we didn't need any luck. A thumping 5-1 home victory over Dagenham and Redbridge had the supporters singing delightedly 'we are top of the league, we are top of the league'. A sixth victory in seven outings meant Penney was now being fully extended to keep his emotions under control as the town started to believe in us once again. Winger Andy Watson got the all-important opening goal, youngster Robert Gill added a second and a goalbound shot from Jamie Paterson took a deflection to leave us leading 3-0 by half-time. It crossed my mind after Paterson had made it 4-0 from the spot that we had somehow managed to throw away just such a huge lead at Telford but, on this occasion, the force was with us. Danny Shipp did pull one back for Garry Hill's shell-shocked side, who were among the promotion favourites themselves, but we deservedly had the last word with Paul Barnes netting our fifth.

It wasn't always going to be that convincing, of course, but performances like the one at Yeovil six weeks later when we ground out a 1-1 draw showed we meant business. Huish Park hosted the biggest Conference gate of the season and Yeovil came into the game on the back of 13 unbeaten games. Yet we were never overawed against a team well clear at the top. Midfielder Danny Hudson gave us a dream start by netting with his first touch of the ball as early as the second minute, as he started a loan spell from neighbours Rotherham United. And what a spectacular strike it was as he picked the ball up 40 yards out, made his way to the edge of the area and drilled a low shot to the right of goalkeeper Jon Sheffield. Yeovil, however, were far from beaten and replied with a great goal of their own after 15 minutes when Gavin Williams left Andy Warrington with no chance at all from fully 30 yards. Thereafter we had to defend doggedly, but pushed forward with enterprise whenever we could in what was, by now, typical Rovers fashion.

Belle Vue was becoming a bit of a fortress, particularly defensively. The 2-0 victory over Hereford United on 2 November meant we had conceded just two goals in ten home games – an impressive record indeed. Outstanding at the back that day was another lad instrumental in our rise through the leagues, Tim Ryan. No relation to yours truly, but possessing similar grit and determination, Ryan picked up the player of the month award before kick-off and celebrated at the end by being named man of the match. There were signs also of an emerging midfield partnership between Mark Albrighton and Gareth Owen and it was Albrighton who got us on the scoresheet after a shot from Jackson had taken a deflection. Not everyone agreed with referee Parkin's decision to award us a penalty in the 23rd minute when United defender Andy Tretton was ruled to have brought down Jackson in the area. But, ever the true professional, Barnes kept his thoughts to himself and duly dispatched the spot kick into the net to take his tally to eight.

Around this time my sale of the Transform Medical Group was completed and, although I had other business interests, my heart was with Rovers and I promised more cash in the bid to get back into the Football League. In December we reached the heights of joint-second with Chester City, three points behind leaders Yeovil, but plumbed the depths again in the LDV Trophy, thrashed 8- 0 by a classy Crewe side – shades of Leyton Orient and Forest!

We celebrated the festive season with a 5-2 Boxing Day feast at Scarborough to leave us second on our own but, after eight games unbeaten, were brought down to earth with a bump by Telford who whipped us 3-1 at Belle Vue. It should have been four but somehow the referee failed to notice that a fierce shot had hit the stanchion at the back of the goal and rebounded back into play. We nearly scored at the other end whilst Telford players celebrated.

We kept up the pace with a couple of four-goal displays at Southport and Gravesend and Northfleet but any hopes of catching leaders Yeovil virtually disappeared when Dave Morley and Jason Blunt were sent off at Chester City where we lost 1-0. The last two months were therefore all about the play-offs and that was no certainty with Dagenham, Chester and Morecambe all going equally well.

Attendances were disappointing and the 2,800 for the Margate victory prompted me to question our support. The answer came with 4,155 turning up to see us lose at home to Scarborough – but that was one too many, according to Dave Penney. He was apparently annoyed that former Barnsley boss Steve Parkin was being used as Radio Sheffield's match summariser as the ex-Tyke had presided over four successive defeats. Good job my record in the commentary seat was a bit better.

Fortunately we steadied the ship with a fairly lucky 2-1 win over Forest Green Rovers and, with results going our way, our play-off berth was assured come the visit of champions Yeovil. Good job, too, as manager of the month Penney saw Rovers get thumped 4-0 – I wonder if Mr Parkin was watching?

The remaining games didn't matter that much as, due to an agreement with the racecourse relating to the use of the car park on match days, we were duty bound to play the second leg of our play-off semi away from home. This went down okay as our opponents would have chosen to play that way around anyway.

This gave me a chance to shock the world with my world record-breaking appearance on the pitch at Hereford United. I'll never forget the tumultuous reception I received from our fans whilst racing down the touchline to warm up and no-one else will let me forget that I never as much as touched the ball during my brief substitute's appearance.

Yet nothing could take away my pride at fulfilling my dream of playing for the Rovers. As a schoolboy many folk dream of playing one day for their favourite team. The lucky ones usually make that dream come true because of their ability. I was slightly different because I owned the joint. Not that Dave Penney really thought I was going to go through with it. I'd innocently told him that I'd like to make an appearance for Rovers, providing there was nothing at stake result-wise. But when I spoke with him a week ahead of the Hereford match and said I was going to make my debut, I'm sure he hoped I'd sleep on it and think better of it. The press were all in on my plans to become the world's oldest professional footballer at 52 years and 11 months and I was deadly serious. After all, I had signed the necessary forms earlier in the season to register myself as a Rovers player and even stepped up my pre-match training schedule in Majorca.

The occasion caught the imagination of the football media who provided me and Rovers with plenty of hype. But it so nearly went wrong on the day itself. My fiancée Lynne was at the wheel and, to be quite honest, we got a bit lost on the way to Hereford. Indeed, as BBC Radio Five Live was announcing the historic occasion at 3pm, I wasn't trotting out onto the field but was still some way from the ground. So this was one occasion when the chairman had to humbly apologise to the manager before I took my place on the bench. The one thing I wasn't going to do was to back out – not with such a throng of media watching.

Calling me a super sub might be stretching a point, but the sight of me warming up on the touchline did make some sort of difference. We were trailing 2-1 when I began stretching my limbs, but 4-2 to the good by the time I trotted onto the field of play. Perhaps the ignominy of fearing that they could be the one to make way for a 52-year-old galvanised our lads into action. It was none other than Paul Barnes, our skipper and the winner of the Conference's Golden Boot for most goals that season, who eventually gave way to the old maestro, handing me the captain's armband as he did so.

Oldster or not, I got the traditional welcome from Hereford's centre-half who said: "If you touch that f---ing ball, I'll break your f---ing leg." In reply, I showed him my legs and said: "They're twice the size of yours, you could end your career right here." In the event neither of us had to worry too much about out future health as those bloody professionals whom I admired so much weren't able to provide me with a single pass. I'd envisaged becoming King Alick II, weaving through the tiring Hereford defence and curling a 30-yard shot into the top corner before sharing a high FIVE with my astonished colleagues. But, hey, you can't have everything. As the final whistle went – and I tried to get my breath back – I accidentally tripped up the referee! Caught up in the amiable atmosphere, Mr Broad jokingly threatened to send me off. Now that would have created a few interesting headlines The papers reported afterwards that I'd paid £4m for my few minutes of fame and in a way I did. But it was worth every penny and not just because it earned me a place in the *Guinness Book of Records*. I'd made a certain Neil McBain, the New Brighton manager, who selected himself at the age of 52 years and four months in 1947, look like a youngster.

In the end we finished third on 78 points, just behind Morecambe, with Chester and Dagenham taking the other coveted play-off spots. So all was set for me to celebrate my 53rd birthday by watching us blow away Chester City at Belle Vue in front of the live Sky cameras in the first leg of the semi-final. Only it didn't work out that way. Former Rover Kevin McIntyre gave City a first-half lead and we huffed and puffed all the way to the 93rd minute, before Tristan Whitman gave us some hope for the second leg with a terrific shot from 20 yards.

The odds were marginally on Chester for the return game on the Bank Holiday Monday and all the more so when Steve Foster's goalline clearance fell for Hatsell to give the home side a 2-1 aggregate lead in the first half. There were several periods during that game when our promotion hopes were kept alive by a shred or, more accurately, the inspired goalkeeping of Andy Warrington. But that goal poacher supreme Paul Barnes got us back level on 57 minutes after his initial effort had hit the bar and even extra-time couldn't separate us.

Penalties are both the best and worst thing in football, depending on whether your team wins. This shootout started badly with Paterson seeing his shot saved, only for super Warrington to even things up by stopping Chester's first kick. Blundell, Blunt, Morley and Ryan then netted for us and it was down to that man Andy Warrington again to send this chairman into dreamland by saving Chester's last spot kick and booking our place at Stoke's Britannia Stadium on Saturday, 10 May for what I still maintain was the biggest game of my life.

What could be better than seeing 10,000 Rovers fans decked out in our colours on a beautiful day? The problem was that there was still one formidable opponent in our path. Garry Hill's Dagenham, who had gone so close to promotion in previous seasons, also that believed this was destined to be their day. After all, they'd been within a minute of going out in their semi against Morecambe before winning on penalties. A play-off final has to be the worst game of all to lose. It's the culmination of a league and a cup campaign all rolled into one. Fail and we'd be back to the Conference drawing board for a sixth successive season. I chatted merrily away to fans with my wife-to-be Lynne but by the time the game kicked off I was much more nervous than usual. People told me afterwards that when the Sky cameras focused on me that afternoon my face told a thousand different stories. It was that kind of cliffhanging game - everything a neutral could have longed for, but sheer emotional pandemonium for those really involved.

We wanted to make a good start and get our noses in front. Only some brilliant saves from Dagenham goalkeeper Roberts kept the scoresheet blank until Greenie got on the end of a cross from Tim Ryan and his header thudded into the net after 39 minutes. Two minutes later Steve Foster had another header cleared off the line. We went into the interval happy, but wary.

The second goal is so often the clincher and as Dave Morley's header soared into the net ten minutes after the break my celebrations were hysterical. But Tierney put a free header wide soon afterwards and I couldn't help wondering whether that miss could yet prove significant. When the opposition pulls the score back to 2-1 momentum can change instantly. That old fox Brian Stein got Daggers back into this one after 63 minutes and suddenly from being in control, we were very much on the ropes. Our normally calm defence was at sixes and sevens and after Mustafa cut in and drove past Warrington, Hill's side scented blood. I was just relieved we hung on to take the tie went into extra-time.

I hoped and prayed that Dave could lift the lads for one last push. Just five of the allotted 30 minutes of extra-time had elapsed when Sir Francis Tierney scored the last golden goal in British football before the rule was rescinded.

It was difficult to put into words how I felt – joy, relief, exhaustion and more. This time there was nothing Garry Hill and his valiant Dagenham side could do about it. The fans shouldn't have run on the pitch, but who could blame them? I, for one, was totally overcome, so I wouldn't preach to others. Ask any Donny fan what was THE most important victory in the last decade or so and almost all will point back to Stoke's Britannia Ground and the moment that Tierney put that ball into the back of the net. He will always be known to us as Sir Francis for getting the goal that put us back where we belonged in the Football League.

I treated the players and staff to a four-day celebration in Spain. The celebrations did justice to the occasion, although you'll have to forgive me for sparing the details! Part one and the most important part of my promise to Rovers was complete – but, boy, I'll never underestimate how hard it is for former Football League clubs to turn things around. Rather you than me lads.

6
*
STEP TWO: CELEBRATING A TITLE

Boston United 0 Doncaster Rovers 0
Monday 3 May 2004

ROBERT CRAVEN www.thelittlegazette.com: "If Doncaster Rovers are not involved in a relegation fight, then it will be a major surprise to a number of people."

CHRIS MALLINSON, owner of Doncaster Cables: "When Dave Penney and Mickey Walker brought the League Three trophy to show all our employees, it was a great morale booster. Rovers are a football club which realises that the fortunes of the club and the whole town are linked. Like everywhere else Doncaster is feeling the pinch economically, but John Ryan and his Rovers have put a smile back on many faces."

STRIKER Leo Fortune-West: "Rovers may have only scraped up through the play-offs, but even before we ran out at Leyton Orient for the first game that season I knew something was on. All promotion teams I have been involved in have got on very well and had a sense of togetherness. That was just what I discovered after signing for Rovers."

SETH BENNETT, sports presenter at Radio Sheffield: "John Ryan was alongside me in the commentary box on a great day at Boston United. Winning the league was a fine achievement and John was mobbed by the fans afterwards; he had a squeaky voice and was close to tears. I began commentating on Rovers the previous season, when they and John had their greatest day of all at Stoke – without getting out of the Conference, the success that followed could never have happened. Back then, John was a commentary box regular, perhaps because our facilities were often better than those for the directors! I have a good relationship with several chairmen but John is a man apart. Wherever he is in the world, he will pick up the phone, be very friendly and we'll talk together about football. Yes, Rovers can go further still. They are a very professionally-run club. One thing is for sure: while John Ryan is alive, Doncaster Rovers will never go back to those darker days."

WHAT a way to celebrate my 54th birthday. There I was in the commentary box at Boston United's York Street with 2,096 Rovers fans watching the lads clinch the League Three title, ensuring I had a gleaming trophy to match my smile at my forthcoming wedding!

I only wish I could bottle such moments when life suddenly seems almost too good to be true. Already promoted after our 2-0 victory over Cambridge United at Belle Vue on Easter Monday, this was an afternoon in which we could almost guarantee a Boston party – with plenty of champagne, rather than tea.

Yet I'd have been equally glad had time stood still way back on Saturday 9 August. I was so happy and proud about merely being back in the Football League that I asked our media manager Steve Uttley to take a picture of me at exactly 3pm as we kicked off at Leyton Orient. It still has pride of place in my office at home.

I had recently been officially re-appointed as chairman

with Trevor Milton becoming president, Stuart Highfield vice-chairman and Andrew Smithson and Paul May joining the board. Yet the most important 'meeting' I attended that pre-season, the one that set us on our way to confounding the bookmakers, actually came in a toilet at the Conference awards dinner a few months previously. That's where I inadvertently came across Michael McIndoe, the inspiration behind Yeovil's title-winning campaign. Unaccustomed as I am to chit-chat in such circumstances, I congratulated Michael on how well he'd played – particularly against us – and said that he'd certainly be welcome in our team. The incident was then largely forgotten but clearly set off a chain reaction! For a few months later I received a phone call from Michael's agent saying he was having problems with Yeovil and asking whether we would be interested in signing him. I nearly jumped off my seat – the one in the office, not the toilet. You bet we would! Here was a player I knew could set League Three alight. This country hasn't been hugely blessed with talented left-sided players in recent years but McIndoe certainly fitted that category. He could beat his man, produce excellent crosses and possessed an eye for goal. Allied to that he had no shortage of faith in his own ability. Not bad for a £50,000 snip.

The bookmakers, looking at the way we'd scraped up via the play-offs, duly installed Rovers as favourites for instant relegation. That suited us just fine. There's seldom a problem motivating players when they've been written off even before a ball has been kicked. And this Rovers side was already a far stronger proposition than the one triumphant at Stoke. Dave Penney, who had already pulled off something of a transfer masterstroke by bringing in Gregg Blundell to bolster our forward line, also delighted Mrs Ryan-to-be by signing a giant of a man called Leo Fortune-West, from Cardiff City. Put bluntly my wife always thought

Leo was hot and that was not necessarily a comment on his football prowess. He may have been popular with the fairer sex, but I think it was fair to say that Leo's physical power and presence made him a total nightmare to play against.

Prior to kick off at Brisbane Road I received a word of 'encouragement' from Orient owner Barry Hearn. He kindly reminded me that our last visit there had seen us lose 8-0 and suggested we could be in for another beating. I told him that he was in for a real surprise – and there was good reason for my bravado. I knew we had a damned good team. That day would have lived long in my memory, whatever the result. It was quite simply one of the hottest days – if not the hottest – I've ever encountered in football. The official temperature was an astonishing 38C - more akin to Brisbane, Australia, than the East End. As it happened, the football matched the build-up. Blundell settled our nerves by opening our scoring for the season on the very stroke of half-time before that man Fortune-West put us well in command with two more in the first 20 minutes afterwards. Orient got a goal back before the end, but a 3-1 victory left Hearn and company well and truly snooker loopy by the final whistle. Our fans were delighted, too, as 6,000 turned out to see us come back from a couple of goals down to shipwreck Grimsby Town 3-2 in a thrilling League Cup tie and another 5,500 were there when dear old Charlie Williams re-opened the Town End, before we saw off Southend United 2-0 back in the league.

It was a great tonic of a start, but didn't last for long as we then went six matches without a win and slipped to a disappointing 18th in the table. Sky Sports have invariably been well entertained by us but chose the wrong time to call at Belle Vue for live coverage of the derby with Hull City, a scoreless draw that was decidedly a blankety-blank. Yeovil then got their usual three points from us with a 1-0 victory in which Fortune-West got himself an early bath. Andy Johnson, who has since gone on to a glittering Premiership career and represented his country, halted a spirited Rovers display in the League Cup with two penalties for Crystal Palace, but it was now for the good news as we sandwiched this with successive wins over Oxford United and at Bury to move up to a heady sixth in the early table.

Meanwhile the earth was definitely moving for Rovers fans – and this was nothing to do with Fortune-West. Sponsors showed their faith in the new-look Rovers as Earth Mortgages turned Belle Vue officially into the Earth Stadium and the main stand into the Earth Finance stand. We celebrated by showing everyone just what we could do when Bristol Rovers came to Donny and found themselves on the receiving end of a 5-1 hammering. McIndoe not only scored a number one and a number two, but also completed his hat-trick. And to think it all stemmed from him spending that fateful penny.

Rovers fans made up almost half of Macclesfield Town's biggest crowd to date, 2,831, and enjoyed the trip as McIndoe was spot on again to seal a 3-1 away day. Then we had our biggest crowd for 15 years to see Mansfield Town well beaten 4-2, despite taking an early lead. Things couldn't really have got much better as we extended our winning run to a magnificent seven when Paul Green's lone goal beat Torquay United just three days after we received some of the best news in our history.

After all the seemingly endless political football, the green light was finally given to the new Community Stadium by Doncaster Council's Cabinet Ratification Committee. The project that had so nearly caused me to jump ship would finally come to fruition with the proposed opening being the start of the 2005/6 campaign. Suddenly the full significance of this particular Rovers return was beginning to take shape.

In the circumstances, clearing the decks in the remaining cup competitions – disappointing though the respective exits from the LDV Trophy and the FA Cup were at Blackpool and Scarborough – may also have worked in our favour. We were just beginning to scent something good, so concentrating on the league was no bad thing, I suppose.

York City did manage to put an end to our winning run with a disputed penalty but we finished November in a very healthy second place, just a point behind leaders Oxford United after wins at home to Boston United and at Carlisle. The extension of Chris Brown's loan from Sunderland brought about the end of the road at Rovers for another of our star turns, Paul Barnes. The goal machine who had powered our Conference promotion challenge will always be remembered fondly by us all but, by now, was struggling to get into the side and opted for a move to Tamworth.

I wanted to see Rovers top the table at Christmas to put the icing on the cake and successive 3-1 victories over Cheltenham Town and Swansea City ensured our festive joy was full. We drew an even bigger crowd of 8,961 for the Boxing Day visit of Scunthorpe United whose forwards showed signs of plenty of Christmas spirit as they missed a host of chances and went down to a goal from the dependable Gregg Blundell.

But that crowd was nothing compared with the amazing 23,006 who turned out two days later for our first-ever trip to the KC Stadium. It was, not surprisingly, the highest crowd of that entire League Three season for a clash between two clubs beginning their recovery from the hardest of times. Fortune-West gave us an early lead before Jason Price, of all people, went and scored a hat-trick for Hull to give them a 3-1 victory. Would you Adam and Eve it? JJ proved he was a lethal finisher – against Donny Rovers. It was the first and, so far, only treble of the highly popular striker's career.

That victory kept the Tigers on our tails, although the immediate beneficiaries were Oxford United who went into 2004 topping the table with Rovers two points adrift in second spot. We then fell foul of another striker who went on to bigger things, Huddersfield Town's Jonathan Stead, who scored twice in another 3-1 reverse to bring in the New Year in disappointingly sober style.

There was important news on the horizon with the club announcing that we would be going ahead with our youth policy for the coming season, although we still needed a lot more financial backing to make it a success. Two defeats in succession meant the critics had something to bite on but a visit from Mr Hearn's Leyton Orient was just the break we needed. Fortune-West virtually pocketed the points with a hat-trick inside the first 18 minutes – now I was loving the big man too – and two more goals in the second half completed a 5-0 victory. There was a certain symmetry about this when you think about it. We'd shipped eight goals to Orient in our relegation season and now smashed eight of our own past the Londoners, albeit in two games, on our return. So whom do you think you were kidding, Mr Hearn?

The big time was definitely here as the visit of Lincoln City's Imps was made all-ticket. Yet the majority of the 8,774 fans were disappointed as the visitors left for home with a 2-0 victory. The scoresheet included a Ryan own-goal – although I swear it was nothing to do with me! We were grateful then for three points on a horrible Friday night against Northampton Town at Belle Vue. Greenie got the only goal to leave us drenched, yet singing in the rain.

Scunny, this time, had their shooting boots on as they led us 2-0 and were in complete command. But a shocking challenge by Jamie Price that cut us down to ten men somehow sparked an unlikely comeback. McIndoe pulled one back from a penalty and Fortune-West stole a point in

Above: The earliest recorded sighting of yours truly with my mum Ada.

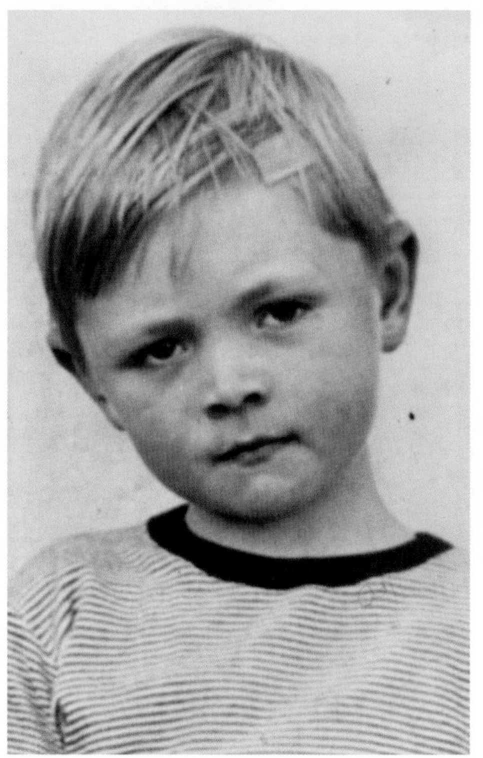

Left: A young lad from a Doncaster council estate with a dream.

Above: I was a late developer at Danum Grammar School. You can spot me third from the left on the back row.

Above: Football was always my goal and I scored my share at schoolboy level. In this team photo I am second from right on front row.

Above: Owning a Bentley was part of my dream. Here I am with Peter Wetzel.
Below: An assortment of MYA's satisfied customers.

Left: Mr Champagne Man. Here I am with Rovers boss Kerry Dixon and man of the match Jon Schofield.

Pictured: 'King' Alick Jeffrey takes on Rob Newman during his comeback spell with Rovers. Needless to say he netted a hat-trick against Peterborough.

Above left: My first wife Denise – her early death devastated me.
Above right: My beautiful daughters, Gemma and Claire.

Above: Another family shot - me with my mum Ada and brother Philip, who is honorary club photographer at Rovers.

Above: Dr Harold Shapiro, one of my inspirations, with Chrissie Davies and Cheryl Inglesias at a cosmetic surgery event.

Left: My bosom buddy – I will forever be linked with model client Melinda Messenger.
Photo: David Fisher/Rex Features

Above: S(no)w play today at Belle View, for so long my spiritual home.
Photo: Philip Ryan

Below: Fond farewell – we said goodbye to Belle Vue with a 1-0 victory over Nottingham Forest.

Above: John Ryan - officially the world's oldest striker.

Right: It cost me £1million a minute and I never touched the ball against Hereford.

Above: All good fans should look the part!

added time. There are occasions when a draw seems like the very best of wins – this was one of them.

We made hard work of beating struggling Macclesfield 1-0 but if there was a game that convinced me we really could win the title it was the next one – at Field Mill against fourth-placed Mansfield Town. Once again the Stags scored the opening goal and this time they threatened to make the most of their important advantage. Cometh the hour, enter Gregg Blundell. Two opportunist strikes in seven golden minutes midway through the second half not only turned this particular match on its head, but confirmed that we were back in business – and on top again, two points clear of Hull City.

It was very good timing that our next game was on the Friday night so our main rivals had to wait until the following afternoon to try to strike back. And we couldn't have picked much more obliging visitors than fast fading Kidderminster Harriers. Our toughest obstacle on this particular night was the cold and frost, ignored by an amazing 7,000 who braved the freezing temperatures to back us. We were two goals clear at half-time by which time the weather had turned to snow and sleet. Scott Stamps ensured he was just about the only warm person in South Yorkshire by getting himself an early bath and Ricky Ravenhill soon added a third goal. By now, so much snow was falling I was nervously looking at my watch and hoping that the game wouldn't be abandoned. But instead there was time for Blundell to add his second goal and full-back Dave Mulligan, a recent acquisition, to score one of his long-range specials. I defy anyone to feel the cold when you've just won 5-0 and our hearts were warmed still further the following day when Hull lost to Lincoln. Suddenly after a head-to-head fight for most of the season we had the luxury of a five-point lead with matches fast running out.

Even the relative disappointment of a couple of 1-1

draws against Swansea City and Cheltenham Town were overcome by a trip to our bogey side Yeovil Town on a Tuesday night. For once the long journey was well worthwhile as Ricky Ravenhill bagged a 72nd-minute goal to give us three more points towards almost inevitable promotion. The Yeovil fans weren't too impressed with the return of their one-time conquering hero Michael McIndoe as they held posters with the word Judas on it and launched a regular volley of foul-mouthed abuse in his direction. I'm all for freedom of speech but that sort of thing is way over the top and does football fans no credit whatsoever. I'd like to compare that with the reception our fans gave Paul Green on both occasions when we met Derby County last season – they were disappointed, as I was, to see the lad go, but gave him a good reception based on what he did whilst he was with Donny Rovers.

Three more successive draws followed as we threatened to limp over the line. Substitute Adebayo Akinfenwa, who'd just been signed from Rushden and Diamonds, saved us a point with an equaliser five minutes from time against Darlington at Belle Vue. Akinfenwa, a born-again Christian, was an interesting character who came back to haunt us on a few occasions after his short spell at the club.

Chris Black, a right-sided midfielder, also proved a memorable acquisition. Let's put it this way, Akinfenwa almost qualified for a testimonial compared with this young man's stay at Donny. He showed up well on his debut in a 0-0 draw at Oxford United, who were in the temporary charge of Doncaster-born Graham Rix at the time. Perhaps Black thought he was in a Brian Rix farce because he went home after the game and was never seen at Belle Vue again. Then Mark Albrighton scored the latest of late equalisers as the seconds ticked away in a rearranged game at Rochdale The run of just one win in six did little to dent our promotion chances but gave Hull the chance to close the gap at the top to just a single point - with a useful match in hand. Fortunately, we soon got our goalscoring act back on the road as two from Blundell and one from Akinfenwa accounted for Bury 3-1, and Ravenhill and Akinfenwa netted at Bristol Rovers to ensure a 2-1 win. Both teams finished a player short with the not-so-saintly Akinfenwa the Rovers player dismissed. That increased the lead over the Tigers to a useful six points and meant that we could confirm stage one of our mission – automatic promotion – with victory against Cambridge United in front of our own fans at Belle Vue on Easter Monday.

That turned out to be a genuine day of celebration for everyone at Doncaster Rovers football club. A sell out crowd of 9,644 turned out to cheer us on our way and finished the afternoon in wild celebrations as we overcame a nervous start to end up convincing 2-0 winners. Our assault gained some momentum shortly after half-time when Ravenhill rapped a fierce volley against the bar before Akinfenwa wrote himself into Rovers folklore – albeit briefly – by scrambling home a cross from Greg Blundell. As the minutes elapsed, the fans began to realise that this was going to be our day. Any remaining tension was lost amid unrestrained joy five minutes from time when Greenie put the seal on our win and promotion with a diving header - shades of his strike 12 months previously in the play-off final.

With the pressure now largely off, we could concentrate on the title, although a determined Torquay United side, themselves well in the hunt for an automatic slot, didn't help us when edging past ten-man Rovers with a first-half goal from Kevin Hill, who had earlier been involved in the tackle that resulted in Dave Mulligan seeing red.

There were no such worries in the next home game, however, as two goals inside the first eight minutes settled any nerves against struggling York City. The eventual 3-1 margin was enough to relegate the visitors to the Conference from where they have struggled to return. Nobody likes to see a famous old club in strife so I suppose there were mixed emotions for me. Like ourselves at the time of our demise, York have gone through some stressful times financially and now find themselves just one of around a dozen Blue Square Premier clubs striving to get back to where they surely belong.

I couldn't have timed our big day better if I'd organised it myself. We kicked off at Boston United six points clear of Hull, so needed to win to completely take the issue out of City's hands, but knew that a point, or even none, would suffice if our rivals lost any further ground. In a lovely gesture, Boston's players applauded Rovers onto the pitch before they produced a professional enough display to keep me on the edge of my seat. I was co-commentating on the match on Radio Sheffield and was delighted when it was confirmed that our 0-0 draw was indeed good enough for us to take the title.

Looking back on the day now, again it is sad to reflect that our hosts have since gone on to experience much of the pain that we endured at Donny, not only returning to Non League football but living on the very precipice over the last couple of seasons. The crowds they attracted to York Street for the modest fare of UniBond Premier League football in 2008/9 tells an important story - there is still a demand for a football team as a big part of the Lincolnshire town. I hope they will be able to turn the corner once again.

The beauty of clinching the title one game early was that 9.720 were able to watch us entertain Carlisle United, who had already been consigned to joining York in the Conference, without any reason to hold back their celebrations. It was presentation time before kick-off with

Dave Penney getting the Manager of the Month award for April, Michael McIndoe being awarded Third Division player of the year and even the referee getting in on the act as a memento was presented to David Pugh to mark his final game.

The Cumbrians provided noble resistance as their fans chanted defiantly that they would be back. Even when we were awarded a second-half penalty, Greg Blundell saw his effort saved by United goalkeeper Matt Glennon before the same striker headed the only goal three minutes later. Twelve months later Carlisle fans were indeed celebrating instant promotion back into the Football League before equalling our feat of back-to-back promotions to move into League One, where they became close rivals in the race to the Championship. Amazing, isn't it, how quickly this game can turn!

The champagne certainly flowed a few weeks later when Mr and Mrs Ryan took their wedding vows – and, yes, the League Three trophy took pride of place in the celebrations.

7

*

STEP THREE: HOME FOR KEEPS!

Doncaster Rovers 3 Huddersfield Town 0
The first match at the Keepmoat Stadium
Monday 1 January 2007

PREMIERSHIP referee Mark Halsey, who officiated at the historic game: "It was a pleasure for me to be selected for this important occasion. I've always got on well with John Ryan from the day I refereed Rovers in their Conference days at Southend in an FA Cup tie. John will talk to you as an adult and give you praise if he feels you warrant it. Unusually, I had to send off three players in the Huddersfield match, but I got the usual honest reaction from John afterwards. It was also a cracking game."

Sir Bobby Robson: "I was totally impressed with everything I saw when I watched Newcastle play a friendly at the Keepmoat. Such friendship and warmth emanating from everyone. It took me back to my Ipswich days. The stadium was a beaut'."

MENTION Doncaster Rovers to the general football public these days and many folk will instantly think of the Keepmoat Stadium – our magnificent new home on the Lakeside development. How quickly things change! For years and years the idea of a new stadium seemed no more than a pipedream, something that crazy bloke John Ryan used to bang on about but never seriously likely to happen. But the real story behind the eventual £32m project goes back well beyond my association with Donny Rovers and has more twists and turns than a murky plot in *EastEnders*. Of all the promises I made when I took over as chairman, this was the most important and the one that so nearly defeated me. It also involved so many conflicting emotions. I loved Belle Vue, plain and simple. It was my football home for nearly half a century and will always have a major place in my heart and in my memories. Of all people, I am in a position to empathise with those fans who mourn its passing and shake their heads sadly when they pass the now derelict old ground and wonder what will eventually become of it. Saying farewell to wonderful rickety old Belle Vue and then hello to our modern dream of a stadium at the Keepmoat was like attending a funeral and a wedding on the same day. More than a few tears, both of sadness and of joy, were spilled as I shared a thousand memories with some of the greats of Rovers' past during the social events leading up to our final match at Belle Vue against Nottingham Forest just before Christmas 2006. Yet the over-riding feeling, I believe, was that we were standing on the very threshold of an exciting new future barely a couple of miles down the road.

I may have a reasonably sized chequebook, but I don't possess a magic wand – and that was the reason we had to move on from Belle Vue. The talking actually started as long ago as the swinging sixties when chairman Frank Wilson made an unsuccessful bid to buy the lease from the local council. Then there was the experience of my vice-chairman Peter Wetzel who went down the cul-de-sac of attempting to persuade the council to develop the ground. How I would have loved to have watched stars such as Ian and Glynn Snodin, Brendan O'Callaghan, Peter Kitchen and Colin Douglas performing on a stage more appropriate for their rich talents. If that had happened perhaps the late and great Billy Bremner would have launched the Donny Rovers revival long before I took over at the helm. We will never know because the project never got off the ground and, as greedy Ken Richardson discovered, just about the only thing about Belle Vue that was worth its salt in its final years was the lease itself.

From the press huddled rather too closely together for anyone's comfort on antique benches, to fans risking life and limb to navigate the terracing in search of a meat pie, Belle Vue was both bloody awful and bloody marvellous at the very same time. Away supporters, particularly that very dedicated fraternity that loves to attend as many Football League grounds as possible, used to speak of it in highly irreverent terms. Many used to describe it as the worst ground they had ever ever visited, yet I guess they too left with a sense of what Rovers fans loved about it. The atmosphere was always very intimate and quite often electric. There really was nothing like the feeling of being in a good old-fashioned Football League ground with its wooden seats, concrete terracing and sense of history.

At least we all had a fantastic send-off as the dear old ground was at its creaking and rocking best in that highly emotional last year or so, when it arguably hosted three of the most memorable games in our history.

I doubt very much whether the Carling Cup featured at the top of many fans' agenda that year, yet the magic began when we discovered the identity of our third-round opponents – mighty Manchester City at Belle Vue. Okay, it was the pre-foreign takeover City but Stuart Pearce's side was still a huge draw for us. Big enough to tempt Sky TV to show the game live, a cause for any League One chairman to rub his hands together with financial glee. They knew and we knew that this had the makings of a classic David and Goliath confrontation, for 'Psycho' is one of those guys who doesn't dance to the modern tune of cheapening cup ties with lower-strength teams. He wanted to win the competition with every fibre in his ultra-competitive body. No question about it.

City may not have been pulling up any Premier League trees at the time, but their line-up still had plenty of big names to conjure with. David James, the alternately brilliant and dodgy England goalkeeper; no-nonsense hardman Richard Dunne in the centre of defence; and the twinkle toes and raw international talent of Darius Vassell up front were just for starters. Joey 'bad boy' Barton was absent from the midfield – Belle Vue would certainly have given him a hot reception – but a young lad called Stephen Ireland, who went on to become a firm Eastlands favourite, made his debut. All this would surely be too much, so the nation presumed, for a Rovers team still containing a good number of players from our Conference days and having made a sluggish start in League One.

My emotions were churning as I excitedly took my seat with my fellow directors. I looked across at my friends from Manchester City – I could so easily have been sitting among them as I've already explained. And yet this was the kind of night to make me realise why I could never have forsaken my first love. There was something stirring in the Belle Vue broth that night, a major cup upset perhaps?

The game that followed was predictably frantic and scrappy rather than classical and easy on the eye. Clear-cut chances were in far sparser supply in the first 45 minutes than good-natured Yorkshire banter, as our fans let City's slickers know for sure they were in the bull ring. Eventually the drama started to unfold. James, almost predictably unpredictable, spilled a shot from James 'Copps' Coppinger, allowing us a brief glimpse of glory. But as time ticked by and the prospect of emotion and energy-sapping extra-time began to go through my find, City turned the screw in the final moments. Vassell produced a moment of class amid the general hustle and bustle, Lee Croft centred the ball and Sun Jihai suddenly had the goal at his mercy. Somehow he lifted his shot and it hit the bar rather than the gaping net – I could hardly believe my good fortune.

It wasn't to last too much longer. In the first period of extra-time, Dunne bulldozed into our penalty box where he was met by an unfriendly challenge from Phil McGuire. My body language may not have suggested it at the time, but I wasn't too surprised when referee Graham Salisbury pointed starkly to the penalty spot. Up strode Vassell, Andy Warrington did his best but the ball nestled into the net and City looked to be on the way through.

It's at such moments when chairmen dream of the ball hitting the backside of one of the Rovers players or some other piece of outrageous fortune to somehow suck the ball into the opposition's goal. Instead it was break a leg for luck! Naturally I wouldn't have wished what happened to Andy Warrington that night, not in a million years. A true Rovers hero from our Conference day and a giant of a gent to boot, the collision he had with City's Nedum Onuoha played a huge role in his future. He was sidelined for many months and was never quite able to re-establish himself as our number one before moving on. Yet the referee's decision – reversed after he had the reviewed the video evidence – to send off Onuoha inadvertently brought us back into the tie and prompted the unscheduled entrance of our man mountain of a substitute goalkeeper, Jan Budtz.

But, first, we needed a break at the other end of the pitch

and again Mr Salisbury was in generous mood. There appeared little danger as we smuggled the ball into the City box and the handball awarded against Sylvain Distin was hugely disputable, yet I was grateful that the ref's finger of fate again went against the defending team. I could feel my heart pounding, so I don't know how Michael McIndoe felt as he stepped up to take that spot kick. All I know is that he made it look as easy as shelling peas and we were level once more.

That left us with a shoot-out and enter giant goalkeeper Budtz as an instant hero. The guardian routinely saved penalties in training and here, on his debut and a big, big occasion, he repeated the feat twice as we triumphed 3-0. You can imagine the euphoria as the media got to work and I gave my animated views. It was always going to be a fairly late night back home in Cheshire, where the most cruel twist of fate awaited Lynne and I.

The background was the ill-health of my father. After losing a fair deal of contact with him following the split from my mum, I'd been delighted when he came to work with me whilst I was at Transform. Then, about ten years before he passed away, it had been my pleasure to give him £5,000 to allow him and his partner to have a really good holiday. They chose to go to Jersey where, by some magical co-incidence considering Dad's love of aircraft, the famous Red Arrows display team were staying in the same hotel. By the day of the City tie, however, Dad had become very ill. Only the Sunday before he'd gone out to Woodhall Spa for lunch and suffered a stroke. So instead of thinking about events at Belle Vue, Dad was in hospital in Boston, Lincolnshire.

What happened next will live with me for the rest of my life and was as real as the cup tie itself. It was 1.40am by the bedroom clock when I suddenly woke up and nudged Lynne. "My dad's just died," I told the love of my life as she struggled to come to her senses. "How do you know?" she asked, trying to gauge the seriousness of what I was saying. "I just know love," I answered. "He was here just a moment ago at the bottom of the bed. I smelt his tobacco smoke." Later we went back to sleep only to be awoken again in the morning by a call from Boston Hospital. "We've got some sad news for you, Mr Ryan," whispered the gentle voice. "Your father passed away this morning." Fighting back the tears, there was one more thing I needed to know – the time when he died. "Yes," the caller said. "It was about 1.30am." "Strange," said Lynne. "Did you know our bedroom clock is ten minutes fast?"

Another interesting event happened a few days later when my personal assistant Sue Matthews and I went to register the death. Firstly, we had to drop off in Hull to collect Dad's birth certificate, then we made our way on the long road in the middle of nowhere towards Boston. Suddenly we spotted the Red Arrows doing a full aerial display. There were no other vehicles in sight and it seemed as if this was happening just for us. People can interpret such events as they want, but they certainly provided me with some comfort at a very difficult time. What a shame Dad hasn't been there to witness some more of our triumphs at Doncaster Rovers in the last couple of years. He was, after all, the person who introduced me to my beloved football club back in the 1950s.

Drawing Aston Villa in the next round was just about perfect. Another Premiership club, another chance to shine on Sky TV, it couldn't have turned out much better. But there was a disagreement between chairman and manager over exactly what we were expecting. Jan Budtz had been our number one since his City heroics and I wanted to publicise the match in the programme as the clash of the Vikings with Budtz lined up in one corner and fellow Great Dane Thomas

Sorensen, Villa's goalkeeper, in the other. But Dave Penney both surprised and greatly disappointed me by telling me that Budtz was going to be replaced by Dino Seremet between our sticks. I got the impression, to be honest, that he had taken the hump.

The tie almost brought back some interesting memories for yours truly. There was that incredible marathon FA Cup battle about half a century previously when Alick Jeffrey was emerging on the scene and we finally disposed of Villa at the fifth attempt, with all the games being crammed into 18 tense and hectic days. There are no dangers of such deadlocks these days with even FA Cup replays being limited to just the one, although such games will live on in folklore.

At that time both I and Villa's long-serving chairman Doug Ellis were much nearer the beginning of our respective journeys, but the two of us have met on several occasions on yachts in the Mediterranean. Naturally I was greatly looking forward to welcoming deadly Doug to the slightly less salubrious surroundings of Belle Vue on a raw Tuesday night, especially as I reckoned he might be in for a surprise.

He was certainly taken aback by our excellent performance in the opening 45 minutes during which we established a very valuable lead through another Michael McIndoe spot-kick. Doug had already taken delight in telling me prior to kick-off that a repeat of the Manchester City upset was out of the question. His manager, David O'Leary, had picked a very strong side. Trying his best to digest what he had seen, he now added: "You can't possibly play as well as that for another 45 minutes!" Oh yes, we can!

In fact, the second half turned out to be even more spectacular than the first as we put on another absolute treat for the cameras. Instead of getting back into the tie, as Ellis and probably most of the nation anticipated, Villa fell further behind to a well-taken goal from Paul Heffernan. When Sean Thornton smashed home a long-range third via the underside of the bar, we were well and truly in dream land – Doncaster Rovers THREE, Aston Villa nil! What a fantastic scoreline. Yet, as the media agreed afterwards, the result was one thing, the way we did it was something else. That night has to go down as one of our greatest ever performances and victories. I was in full flow afterwards telling the nation we had produced champagne football and comparing our success with the very best view of Melinda Messenger.

Media attention was well and truly on us as the quarter-final draw handed us yet another plum Belle Vue draw: mighty Arsenal in a tie played four freezing nights before Christmas. In sharp contrast to City and Villa, we knew Arsene Wenger would field a young side – as he traditionally does in this competition – but take a look at some of these names: Manuel Almunia, Emmanuel Eboué, Pascal Cygan, Alexander Hleb, Robin van Persie and Nicklas Bendtner were all in that team of super-skilled young Gunners. That's not to mention their two goalscorers Quincy Owusu-Abeiyie and Gilberto Silva.

Anyone who witnessed the tie, either in the packed Belle Vue crowd or on TV, will surely agree it was a magnificent game of football in which we matched the Premiership side stride for stride and skill for skill. We got the ideal start when McIndoe slipped through for an angled shot past Almunia as early as the fourth minute and Almunia was the busier of the goalkeepers throughout a frantic first half. There were chances – and good ones too – for us to go further ahead shortly after the break before Owusu-Abeiyie unleashed a long-range shot that took a cruel deflection past Jan Budtz off Sean Thornton

Still we came on strong and when Philippe Senderos hesitated fatally, Paul Green restored our advantage in extra-time. And that is how the scoreline stayed until the 122nd minute! How the referee found an additional two minutes at the end of the second period of extra-time I'll never know, but it certainly suited Arsenal. One last heart-breaking assault was time enough for Gilberto Silva to slip the ball into the back of our net.

Penalties were yet to come but, in that moment, our cup dream ended. You could see the energy drain from our brave bodies and the look on Wenger's face afterwards spoke volumes. The legendary Arsenal boss was extremely complimentary when we spoke together afterwards, saying that several of the Donny players on view could play in the Premiership and conceding that his young side had been lucky to win through. I always make a point when I see the referee from that night, Phil Dowd, to ask him whether he has got himself a new watch.

So instead of lining up to face Wigan in the semi-finals, I gave our players the gift of a four-day trip to Cyprus, which proved an ill-fated decision. For this was the holiday that resulted in us parting company with both Steve Foster and Tim Ryan, two players who had certainly played their parts in our revival, due to breaches of club discipline.

Back to our big move. Put simply, the stadium was the bricks and mortar on which my dream at Donny Rovers was built. It's so easy to have a vision of what you'd like to see happen, as I did, when I said I wanted to take us from the Conference to the Championship. Replacing players with new ones was within our grasp, but turning dear old Belle Vue into a venue fit for some of the country's top sides was always going to be a miracle too far. Those of us who had Rovers in our hearts – and the facts at our fingertips – knew from day one that if we were going to build a great football club we needed a new arena in which to accommodate it.

Joining me on the journey were a great team of Rovers

officials – and fans – who painstakingly pleaded our case until they were red and white in the face with the local council, and simply refused to give up until that great New Year's Day in 2007 when we entertained our Yorkshire rivals Huddersfield Town in our very first match at the Keepmoat. Certainly the new stadium took a little longer than we originally expected, but without the collective will and effort of so many well-meaning folk, it wouldn't have happened at all. Thank you to everyone who supported our cause.

Officially, it all started with the formation of a Stadium Steering Group, including Andy Liney, who had just been elected as our fans' director, fellow director Peter Hepworth, plus the council's head of development. Our president Trevor Milton was another prime mover for us. As always in such projects, the initial outlook was very promising and upbeat, but progress soon stalled as politics took their toll and the fans became more and more disgruntled.

The local authority and I had appeared to be singing from the same hymn sheet. They welcomed my involvement and we made a verbal agreement that had mutual benefits for the authority, the community and the football club. They were relieved to be rid of Ken Richardson and, as the owners of the land at Belle Vue, had good reason to share my vision for a new stadium. For once we moved on, they could get on with developing the old site. Basically the deal was that if I put in the money to sort out the football side of the club, they would provide a new community stadium. I was more than happy.

The problem was only one side kept the bargain. I stumped up the cash but things went very quiet at the Mansion House. Eventually I arranged a meeting and was told that the community stadium was off the council's agenda. That was when the proverbial you-know-what hit the fan. Next, I fired a warning shot across the bows of the council. I stepped down officially as chairman and installed Trevor Milton in my place. But, in truth, it was more a gesture, a symbolic move, a means towards an end than a statement of resignation on my part. For during the 18 months. I was officially 'away' I was still, in effect, running the football club.

I also gave an ill-fated interview to Colin Mafham, a reporter for the *Non League Paper*. I very much doubt whether I ever did say the words: "there could be blood on the streets". Certainly I wasn't intending to provoke a riot. It was a piece of sensationalist reporting, yet I don't dispute another much-publicised quote in the same article. It read: "I wouldn't like to be a councillor in Doncaster now. Doncaster has not seen the likes of what is going to happen. There are 62 councillors in Doncaster and we know where they all live."

What I was unashamedly doing was sending out a message to the council not to mess about with the football club and therefore the community. They had made us a promise and needed to be held accountable. But when I went to York 'Assizes', or more accurately, the railway station, to account for my strong words, it was my turn to get a shock. Instead of just being one of a number of cases, as I'd imagined, they'd put on a special session just for me with three on the panel to consider a charge of bringing the game into disrepute. Two were local FA officials from Cheshire and Manchester but the chairman, Peter Heard, chairman of Colchester United, was the most sympathetic of the trio. As he said some time afterwards, I got a £10,000 fine but that was a small price indeed to pay for a football stadium. Very true.

My words certainly did the trick. I genuinely think the council were worried about 3,000 Doncaster Rovers supporters marching down to the Mansion House and turfing them out of their comfort zone. Incidents like this remind me that I am in quite a powerful position as chairman of a football club to mobilise people – although I could never condone violence or threatening behaviour. Instead a good number of peaceful Rovers fans attended a council meeting bedecked in our club colours to hear the decision overturned and the local authority reinstate its commitment towards a community stadium. It was fantastic news – not just for us, but for the whole of Doncaster.

To achieve our goal we had to play a lot of politics ourselves and indeed our supporters' co-operative elected our very own representative, Richard Haley, as a proposed candidate for the role of Doncaster's directly-elected Mayor. The idea was for Richard to stand on the sole policy of supporting the new stadium and this was another legitimate wake-up call for the authority, particularly as the successful candidate Martin Winter pledged to deliver a stadium for Doncaster in his personal manifesto. Mr Winter made his pledge at a Rovers event at The Dome and there was a fair amount of controversy flying around afterwards. But I think that merely strengthened his resolve as he stuck to his guns. The red tape that afflicts local councils is almost unimaginable and trying to assess exactly where we were after presenting our plans to various committees, as well as the full council, was rather like trying to do a safety check in a minefield. But amid all the numerous one steps forward and three steps backwards I became more and more grateful to the people of Doncaster, who had pledged their support for the new form of Mayoralty. Without the office of a leader, we might still be going round in ever decreasing circles to this day.

Folk held differing views on the overall performance of Martin Winter, the first person to be elected to the new office, but he certainly got behind the town's football club in this vitally important issue and was the one person who got things done. In contrast, I'd long since worked out that a significant number of Doncaster councillors did not support their local club, but were far more interested in Leeds United and Sheffield Wednesday. In the 1990s it was very publicly shown that a lot of our elected representatives had their snouts in the trough and were principally interested in their own personal gain, yet Martin Winter proved to be someone with the best interests of Doncaster at heart.

The problem with drawing up plans for a football stadium is that you are constantly on shifting sand – quite apart from the eccentricities of the council. To be honest, it would help if you had a reliable crystal ball. It was vital that we not only negotiated a deal but the right deal for the future of the club.

The first firm offer on the table was for a simple 10,000-seater stadium near the end of Potteric Carr Road, just past the sorting office. That would have been an improvement on Belle Vue, even though we'd somehow managed to extend the old ground's capacity to just over 10,000 without having any prospect of achieving what we really wanted – long-term security and room for future expansion. So why should a football club with gates struggling to scrape into four figures need a stadium with a capacity of 15,000, or even 20,000? The reason was that we were planning ahead for Championship football with our heads as well as our hearts.

We managed to get the stadium on the agenda of the Lakeside Redevelopment Committee, therefore opening up the possibility of a prime location in a town which, with the opening of Robin Hood Airport, was growing and expanding with its football club.

The priority then was to lobby for the increased capacity and work on the business plan to ensure the stadium could be self-financing. The very last thing we wanted after the disgrace of the Richardson era was to land the authority and its people with a financial millstone around its neck. The community deserved something far better than that. Throughout the long process we were grateful for the support of fans who attended council meetings in Rovers shirts when proposals were put to the full council. The people of Doncaster were instrumental in the stadium project becoming reality because they were invariably there to assure councillors that there was mass support for the venture.

I know that a lot of Rovers fans would have liked to have seen standing at the new stadium – indeed 98 per cent voted in favour of it in one poll – but this was never going to be possible as we would not have qualified for an important £2m grant from the Football Foundation. Being totally honest and, as someone who used to enjoy standing on the kop at Belle Vue, I think we have lost out on the atmosphere created by fans huddled together on the terraces. There would be no real risk in having standing behind the goals at today's grounds. Yet considering the way things have moved on following the Taylor Report into the 1989 Hillsborough disaster it is difficult to see those days ever returning.

It was around the time of Euro 2004, just after Rovers had clinched the Third Division title, that we got the great news that the Mayor had come up with a scheme that did match our vision. Martin Winter put forward a stadium with an initial capacity of 15,000 that could be expanded to 20,000 – alongside a sports complex comprising external grass and artificial pitches, seven and five-a-side pitches, plus an athletics track. In short, a major community asset and a dream beginning to come true.

Things were never going to run that smoothly, of course, and political changes as a result of a council election meant that the lobbying campaign had to start all over again. But, with Andy Liney making an impassioned plea, councillors gave the Mayor's visionary proposals the green light and soon there were the first visible signs that something was happening – hoardings going up at the entrance to the proposed new sports complex.

With the politicians on our side, our next obstacle was the great crested newts! English Nature identified that there was an area of wetland suitable for breeding - as they are a protected species. So arrangements had to be made to fence the area, organise their detection and capture, and prepare a location to which they could be moved. In the event there weren't any randy newts to be seen, but all such things take time and money and need legitimately to be done.

Renewed delays left many fans saying they'd only believe the new stadium when they were sitting in it. Totally understandable stuff but the wheels were still turning, however slowly. Finance became an issue as none of the shortlisted contractors was able to complete the project within the £32m budget agreed by the council – the nearest being £4m over. One major stumbling block was the fast-increasing price of steel during the lifespan of the project. This meant cuts to the design with the floating roof being one of the casualties, along with the City of Manchester Stadium-style external staircase and access pods. True, some of the iconic features were lost but, most importantly, none of the actual facilities were touched. The below-stand space remained just as large and we were still looking at a first-class arena with what has now become 15,300 seats, all with excellent views and leg-room under a continuous, pillarless, cantilevered roof.

We did, however, lose several more months as the miscalculations meant literally going back to the drawing board. It wasn't until August 2005 that, with new plans in place, the council was able to identify a preferred contractor in Mowlem, now taken over by Carillion. And so on 19 September 2005, Andy Liney officially put our name to the various contracts and leases for the new stadium and at the stroke of a pen catapulted us towards a brand new era. Construction began in late December, almost a year after the start date on the advertising hoardings.

Roll forward just a few short months on the pitch and we were saying farewell to Michael McIndoe, who was initially packed off to Derby County on loan before signing permanently for Barnsley. He has since played for Wolves, Bristol City and Coventry City, carving out a good career at Championship level. The lad was destined in the end to fall a little way short of his own great expectations, as he always envisaged playing for Scotland and in the Premiership, and he wasn't always everyone's cup of tea during his days at Rovers. To his huge credit he got his life well back on track after acknowledging his alcohol problems whilst at Luton Town earlier in his career. But his intensity and focus – quite characteristic of those who do fight such addiction – didn't endear him to all. I, however, will admit that McIndoe's departure disappointed me. I had agreed a new deal with him, but Dave Penney wasn't 100 per cent committed to keeping Michael so it was a losing battle. I suppose the zenith of his career was that goal against Arsenal and his excellent displays in general against the Premiership sides in that Carling Cup run, yet I wonder whether we both could have gone a little further had he stayed into our Keepmoat days.

By now, I was in the enviable position of having not one but TWO football homes – Belle Vue was the place where I still watched my football, but when I wanted to dream about the future I would wander down to the Lakeside and take a first-hand look at how our new stadium was progressing. I walked down the road, now named Alick Jeffrey Way, donned my hard hat and surveyed the newly-laid terracing. The new boxes were mere shells and I wandered 'offside' more than once, as the angry-looking site foreman was only too quick to remind me. But my mind was alive with the vision of a magnificent completed Keepmoat Stadium, packed with excited Rovers fans.

Various dates were mooted before it became clear that we would be changing homes some time within the 2006/7 season. Most switches take place during pre-season but it became clear that Christmas was the most likely time - what a present for our loyal fans. I also appreciated the huge efforts of our loyal staff as we lived in two different sites for a good few months.

What we wanted – and expected – was to put everyone in the mood to party by kicking the season off in great style on the pitch. All seemed so rosy in pre-season when we'd signed Kevin Horlock on a two-year deal after he'd spent time on loan with us, splashed out £130,000 on James O'Connor from Bournemouth, snapped up Adam Lockwood after his release from Yeovil and added Gareth Roberts and Bruce Dyer to the fray.

There would been changes behind the scenes, too, with the Penney-Walker partnership broken up with Mickey accepting a new role as Director of Football and Mickey Lewis taking his place alongside the manager on the touchline.

But, for whatever reason, our flying start just didn't happen. Five points from the opening five games was a major disappointment and, allied to injuries to Horlock and Dyer, led to a few furrowed eyebrows. What a lot of folk weren't expecting, however, was that it would lead to the departure of our manager.

Now, if you've learnt anything about me by now, you'd appreciate what a difficult decision this was. The five games in themselves would have counted for nothing had I been convinced that Dave was still the best man to take us forward. And, let's face it, he was hugely in credit as a manager after his previous achievements. As Rovers fans know, it was a topic of heated discussion for many months afterwards and I can fully understand that. I had nothing and still have nothing against Dave Penney; he has been a welcome visitor to the Keepmoat since his departure and will always remain so. His part in the remarkable revival of Donny Rovers was one that should never be under-estimated, certainly not by me. As both a player and a manager, he can look back on his time here with huge pride.

There are times, however, when as a chairman you have to live or die by your gut feeling and I queried whether he was the right man to take us that extra step into the Championship. He still had the abiding respect of the players and would no doubt have continued to do a good job. But I needed that X-factor, that hard-to-define something else, to kick us on still further. We spoke things through and departed on very good terms. Naturally he was disappointed but Dave appreciated where I was coming from. My subsequent surprise was that he went down a division to manage Darlington where again he gave excellent service before taking on League One Oldham Athletic. I gave Dave a heart-felt positive reference and I wish him every success in the future. Football being the ironic game that it is, Dave Penney's last game was a 1-1 draw at home to Bournemouth, for whom a certain James Hayter levelled the scores with a late penalty.

If Dave's departure sent shock waves through the club, we were indebted yet again to that human dynamo Mickey Walker for his loyalty and expertise. Although he'd naturally become very good friends with Dave Penney, Mickey stepped into the breach as caretaker-manager and lifted the spirits of the lads so effectively that we gained an excellent 2-1 win in our next match, a televised affair at Port Vale. The lads even bounced back from going a goal down and seeing a Lewis Guy spot-kick saved before Paul Heffernan won the day with two late goals.

Shortly afterwards Rovers and the people of Doncaster in general were dealt another sad blow by news of the death of our former player and life-long fan Charlie Williams at the age of 76. A very good defender in his own right who played 171 first team games for Rovers, Charlie was also a most engaging and warm human being, known to millions by his popular catchphrase: "hello, me owd flower!"

Perhaps the most remarkable testimony to Charlie as a person was that in the years before anti-racism became such an issue in English football, his colour was never an issue with the many people who loved him. He was one of the first black footballers in this country after the War and also broke similar ground in his subsequent career as a comedian. In my view and that of countless others, Charlie broke down far more barriers than he ever created, despite criticism he received in later years from the politically correct brigade. He made a fantastic double act with Alick Jeffrey both on and off the pitch and was voted our number one cult hero of all-time by viewers of BBC TV's *Football Focus* in 2004. I had the joy of meeting Charlie on many occasions and am poorer for his loss.

It was in the midst of all this emotion that I set about creating a bit of a smokescreen for my next move. Yes, it was true that Kevin Keegan had reportedly said he would like to be the manager of his home-town club. Yes, it was true he embodies the X-factor and would have grabbed the total imagination of the players and the public. And, yes, he was out of the game at the time. But, no, it was never realistically going to happen. I knew for sure that KK was immersed in his business interests and I knew who I wanted for the job - and he couldn't have been more different to the former England captain if we'd tried.

You know, if Rovers hadn't come knocking, Sean O'Driscoll would almost certainly still be on the south coast, fighting almost impossible odds at Bournemouth, a club he loved dearly and served so magnificently. The guy had all the qualities I was personally looking for - and that didn't mean a CV full of trophies and a huge public profile. Nor was I looking for a man who could give the press a good story every day of the week. I wanted someone who could do his talking with the team; someone with the tactical know-how and intelligence to get us into the Championship, play entertaining and watchable football and hold in tension both the limitations and the fantastic potential of Doncaster Rovers Football Club.

Sean's a quiet, highly intelligent man; an introvert in some ways who doesn't enjoy dealing with the media very much. Yet pound-for-pound he is as good a manager as there is in the game. Anyone, up to a point, can manage Manchester United, Liverpool or Chelsea, with the greatest of respect to some very good folk who actually do so - but to keep a club such as Bournemouth afloat and play great football with such limited resources was the X-factor I was looking for.

When I went to see him, Sean was surprised but delighted. In all honesty, I don't think he expected anyone to come knocking on his door, let alone someone who actually wanted him. That, along with the famous John Ryan sales pitch, turned Sean O'Driscoll towards a bright new future at Donny Rovers. I couldn't promise him heaven on earth, but I could guarantee him more resources to do exactly what he was already doing albeit on a slightly higher stage. It took Sean O'Driscoll a couple of days or so to see the light and many loyal Rovers fans a good deal longer to appreciate their new manager, but I knew from the start he was the right fit for us.

Every time we played Bournemouth - and not just in that infamous 5-0 drubbing - we'd received a football lesson and that was saying something for a team of our pure qualities. They passed the ball brilliantly, weaved pretty patterns and almost always belied their comparatively lowly status. That spoke to me of a top-class coach with very high principles.

Another important part of our jigsaw was Mickey Walker who resumed his role as director of football. No doubt he was disappointed not to take over as our number one as he was on the short-list of three interviewed for the post. But Mickey, being Mickey, handled it in a first-class manner. I said at the time - and I'll reiterate it now - there was no way I was going to countenance a managerial team without Mickey Walker being a part of it. That guy proved he is Donny Rovers through and through from the moment he joined us to rejuvenate our youth section, which was literally at square one. He did a great job with Dave Penney and is currently proving beyond any doubt that there can be a role for a director of football at a club where people are pulling in the same direction. Mickey's testimonial season in 2009/10 was a fitting tribute to a man who played a major role in our success story.

We appointed Richard O'Kelly as Sean's number two to continue the partnership they had developed with the Cherries. Very much the more extrovert of the duo and in many ways the joker in the pack, O'Kelly has also proved an excellent acquisition to Doncaster as assistant manager.

A minute's silence was observed for Charlie before the Gillingham game - Mickey's second and last in charge - and Sean moved into the hot seat on 11 September 2006, on the back of a disappointing 2-1 defeat. On the very same day the council announced that the road around the new Keepmoat Stadium would be titled Alick Jeffrey Way. I'd love a road to be named after me one day but, as I'd have to die first, I'm quite happy to wait, thanks very much.

It's fair to say that the press conference in which we formally welcomed Sean wasn't the most tumultuous tub-thumping affair - no Barack Obama-style celebrations here, but then hype and conviction aren't necessarily the same thing. Sean answered all questions politely but was probably more glad of a cup of tea afterwards and getting his thoughts in order for his first two challenges - both local derbies.

It didn't take him long to sign Brian Stock, on loan from Preston North End. As we'd found out to our cost a few times, Stockie was one of O'Driscoll's key men at Bournemouth before moving on to higher things in the Championship. Sean couldn't have made a more influential move had he brought in a £10m player for Stock, now the Donny skipper, has been magnificent for us. A sublime passer and striker of the ball, he is an obvious and vital cog in the O'Driscoll engine room and has always been one of the players our opponents fear most.

Stockie took his bow at Huddersfield Town on the Tuesday night, a game in which two strong defences prevented a goal. Then it was on to Millmoor where we got rather less than a friendly welcome at Rotherham United. Considering the help we'd gladly given Rotherham the previous season it was a huge surprise to arrive at the ground to find that our fans had been totally slagged off in the match programme. In the column usually reserved for pre-match pleasantries, Rovers fans were, totally unfairly, singled out for a real slating. It turned out afterwards that the article, submitted by a London-based Rotherham fan, had slipped in unedited and normal relations between the two clubs were quickly restored after a particularly good game finished in another 0-0 draw. It was also particularly gratifying that a number of Millers fans took the time and trouble to contact Rovers to apologise and thank us once again for our support in their time of need.

Sean's first victory looked an almost certainty as we promised another Carling Cup upset against Championship side Derby County at Belle Vue. This was one of Jonathan Forte's hot nights. He scored twice and Stockie once to blast us into a seemingly unassailable 3-0 lead. Yet we were then given a rude awakening as Rams boss Billy Davies ranted and raved from the touchline and Derby responded with three goals in the final 18 minutes. Derby then had a player sent off as we dominated extra-time before we re-established our prowess from the penalty spot by converting eight out of eight spot-kicks for another dramatic shoot-out victory.

League success continued to elude us in the manager's first month as we drew against Blackpool and Bradford City in totally contrasting fashions. The first game was scoreless and the City clash a 3-3 thriller. That man Dean Windass again proved a huge nuisance, netting after just 40 seconds and then luring Graeme Lee into a challenge that resulted in us going down to ten men and the Valley Parade side getting an equaliser from the free-kick. It doesn't take long for fans to get on a manager's back and that first became apparent after Rovers followed up a dreadful display at Scunny with a disappointing 1-1 Friday night draw with Oldham at Belle Vue.

Usually a new incumbent goes through a honeymoon spell with even a struggling side turning things around with a few wins, but this never happened for Sean. We couldn't wait for September to end as we were in a desperate 19th spot. The first green shoots appeared in the next game at Cheltenham where we triumphed 2-0, but it was still rollercoaster stuff as a piece of outrageous fortune allowed Forte to down Chesterfield, before the lads lost the plot, or rather the spot, as they crashed out of the Carling Cup on penalties at Wycombe. No chance then of a repeat of the previous season's heroics.

There was considerable unrest from the Belle Vue faithful as Leyton Orient stifled us at Belle Vue to get exactly what they were looking for – a bore draw. For the first time in goodness knows how long, a Rovers team was booed off our own pitch at both half and full-time. I would have ensured temporary top billing in a Mr Doncaster popularity contest had I declared my Sean O'Driscoll venture null and void and given him the boot. It was never going to happen. That's just the sort of knee-jerk reaction blighting modern day football everywhere. Granted it was taking time to adapt to the new style of football, with an even greater emphasis on passing and moving, but the only thing that is instant in this life is coffee.

At least we managed to relieve the frustration with a 1-0 victory at Brentford in the FA Cup. Lewis Guy was the man on target although Mark McCammon had a reasonable claim to a goal bonus as well. His 76th-minute shot went into the net and through a hole in the rigging! Had the scoreline been 0-0 I might not have looked back upon this bizarre incident with quite the same amount of humour. It's amazing what you can forgive when you've just won a football match.

We were becoming harder to beat as we drew at Millwall and snatched a 1-0 win over Brighton. That trend was even more likely to continue after Sean pulled off a masterstroke by signing goalkeeper Neil Sullivan on loan from Leeds United. There were a fair few more obstacles to overcome before Sully eventually became a full-time Rover but he was worth the wait. We'd been very unfortunate with goalkeepers – Andy Warrington's injury woes becoming just the first in a long line of seemingly cursed guardians – before we relieved Ken Bates of one of his main assets. These days it appears that goalkeepers, along with heavyweight boxers, are the two groups of people that genuinely get better and better with age. Sully has been an inspirational and reassuring figure between the sticks for us.

Off the pitch, a number of events were held to mark the impending end of an era at Belle Vue, the most memorable perhaps being the Farewell Banquet attended by more than 600 guests at The Dome in Doncaster. Among the former players on that amazing occasion were Ernie Moss, Alan Warboys, Laurie Sheffield, John Buckley, Stan Anderson, Brendan O'Callaghan, Peter Kitchen, Brian Makepeace and Daral Pugh. It was a great opportunity to remember the past with fondness and raise a toast to the future.

There could have been no more fitting opponents to finally bring down the curtain on Belle Vue on the final Saturday before Christmas than Nottingham Forest. As I've revealed elsewhere, I've always had a soft spot for Forest since my university days in Nottingham. At the time, they were the big fish in League One and top of the table.

There was a scare in the lead-up to the big farewell as the previous Saturday's match against Yeovil Town at Belle Vue was called off due to a waterlogged pitch, but the weather relented and the lush turf was in as good a condition as ever as fire eaters and fireworks greeted the two teams. The special atmosphere was enhanced still further by the inspirational opera singing of Martin Toal.

A crowd of 8,923, including a good contingent from Nottingham, settled down to what was an appropriately rousing 90 minutes. Forest goalkeeper Paul Smith did most to prevent Rovers from going ahead in the first half before being beaten by one of the strangest goals the dear old stadium ever witnessed. On-loan Theo Streete blasted the ball in from tight to the right touchline and Smith belied his earlier heroics by fumbling it into the net. It looked a dreadful mistake although, as I watched the incident on the DVD afterwards, Streete's effort spun like a Shane Warne leg break. Theo's number 33 shirt is another priceless memento on my office wall at home.

Actually, that wasn't the very last game. Rovers heroes gathered on 28 December for a charity match in which we played our final, final respects to the stadium. A certain John Ryan appeared for 12 minutes alongside such legends as former Rovers loanee Tony Woodcock, Ian Snodin, Colin Douglas, John Buckley, Vince Brockie and Scott Maxfield as well as Hull City chairman Paul Duffen in a charity match in aid of Brian Makepeace, a Rovers skipper in the 1950s. We tackled teams of supporters in games lasting 25 minutes. Our loyal supporters paid £50 each to play on the sacred turf and helped us raise £6,000 for Brian. The very last act at Belle Vue was the taking of penalties – poor Brian, who never scored for Rovers, still couldn't break his duck!

So, after a hectic Christmas, we finally arrived at the day we'd waited so many years for – New Year's Day 2007 and our first ever match at the Keepmoat. If the Forest game was a good one to end on, we could have asked little more from the fixture computer than a Yorkshire derby against Huddersfield Town.

This was one day when the X-factor was guaranteed, even before the kick-off. For the pre-match entertainment included the operatic sensation Katherine Sayles and Alexandra Burke, who was introduced to the Keepmoat as a soul singer from the hit ITV show *The X Factor* and "a girl with a massive future". Alexandra, of course, went on to re-enter and win that show in 2008, topping the charts at Christmas into the bargain. The crowd was a near-capacity

14,470 and all we needed now was a rousing Rovers performance. We were not to be disappointed.

There is always a fair amount of tension, not to say mystique, about the first goal in a new stadium and naturally we were desperate that it was scored by a Rovers player. Well, big Mark McCammon was the man who wrote his name into modern Rovers folklore with a thumping volley as early as the ninth minute. It was a moment he'll always remember with pride and I recall virtually every day of the week. You guessed it, his shirt from that auspicious occasion is also on my wall.

There weren't too many chances over the rest of the first half but it didn't take long for Rovers fans to raise the roof in the second. Paul Heffernan increased our advantage to 2-0 barely two minutes after the restart and the Keepmoat was ablaze with celebratory Mexican waves. The party was in full swing five minutes later when Jonathan Forte shot past Matt Glennon to virtually wrap up the points.

That was the end of the scoring but certainly not the drama, as the goals were then matched by three red cards produced by Premiership referee Mark Halsey. The first was for a dreadful challenge by Adnan Ahmed whose team-mate Pawel Abbott was also dismissed in the bust-up that followed. Rovers' Gareth Roberts was sent packing for a more disputable challenge nine minutes from time. That, however, could scarcely take the edge off a great carnival day. Years of dreaming, not to mention huge amounts of hard work, came to fruition as the fans walked away from their first helping of football at our lovely new stadium

Few things in this weird and wonderful game of ours have given me so much pride as helping to provide the people of Doncaster with a stadium that is both a fine place to watch football and also safeguards the future of our club. It may have taken a little longer than Frank Wilson or I first envisaged, but I believe it is proving well worth the long wait.

Getting over the threshold and then turning the Keepmoat Stadium into our home have understandably proved to be two very separate tasks. There have been plenty of ups and downs in the stadium's first few years. As many Rovers fans will recall, the arm's length company running the complex made a net loss of £1m in its first six months and we agreed to up our rent significantly after reports that they could even call in the administrator. Later, we experienced severe problems with the playing surface as a result of the difficult balance of staging football matches and other big public events at the Keepmoat.

Rovers fans understandably called for more signs to be erected confirming to them and our visitors that this was indeed the home of Doncaster Rovers, and that has been done.

Having said all that, the positives have always outweighed the negatives. Our supporters have taken to the new stadium very well and, across the football nation as a whole, people now naturally associate Rovers with the Keepmoat Stadium.

Gone forever are the days when we would seek to hide our ground from potential signings, and take them to Cantley Park instead as we didn't want to put them off. The Keepmoat speaks of a successful club with a great future.

8
*
STEP FOUR: OUR TROPHY FLOWETH OVER!

Doncaster Rovers 3 Bristol Rovers 2
Johnstone's Paint Trophy final, Millennium Stadium, Cardiff
Sunday 1 April 2007

DAVE MORRIS, chief executive of Doncaster Rovers: "I recall a media man describing this as a tin-pot trophy during the first round at Huddersfield and I told him he wouldn't be saying that when we were at Cardiff . It was like an old-fashioned day out with two trains carrying 12 carriage-loads of Rovers fans to the final. John was on the pitch and I texted him to say that this was a day well worth £10m – and he waved back. Staff were treated to two nights in a hotel and it was a brilliant weekend for all of us. Winning the JPT was a huge boost for the entire club and lifted our confidence that we could get promoted the following season."

ONLY as an April Fool's joke would I have predicted that our national cup success – the next part of my pledge – would come in a much-maligned competition given a makeover and named the Johnstone's Paint Trophy.

Yet absolutely nothing could take the gloss off my joy, because this particular 1 April had everything I had dreamt of – 20,000 excited Rovers fans packing a huge stadium for an unforgettable day out, and a gleaming trophy to take home to South Yorkshire at the end of it.

Most clubs, it seems, used to loathe rather than love this competition. The old Freight Rover and LDV Vans offered the less than inviting prospect for lower League clubs of being given a good going over by a Non League side in front of a near-empty ground. The only way to make a few bob was to somehow manage to battle all the way to Wembley itself. If you thought Premiership clubs invented the rotation selection system, you should have seen the sides selected for this cup.

Yet, although the competition hadn't exactly been a roaring success for Rovers – the 8-0 defeat in our Conference days at Crewe Alexandra being the obvious lowlight – I did harbour a confession. For some reason, I actually liked the event and that was well before it was given a much-needed lick of paint and extra credibility by the sponsorship of Johnstone's.

Call it pragmatism, call it fanaticism, frankly you can call it what you like -the fact is that during these elite-dominated days there may still be a glorious opportunity for so-called smaller clubs to play at our national stadium via the league play-offs, but winning a national cup is between improbable and impossible. However much the Premiership clubs use and abuse the FA Cup and the Carling Cup, they always seem to be the only guests at the end-of-term parties as the gap between the 'haves' and the 'have-nots' widens by the season.

We, of course, had our magnificent run to the Carling Cup quarter-finals in 2005/6 – but that equalled our best ever cup run in our proud history.

You can begin to understand then that one reason I've always had a soft spot for this competition is that it almost guarantees an unfashionable winner. Blue Square Premier sides may be rather unfairly sidelined these days but the new rules requiring the League sides to pick strong line-ups means the Johnstone's Paint is gaining a grudging respect.

It was said that Cloughie used to give his teams a dressing down if they dared to lose a pre-season friendly, or even a testimonial. Well perhaps I would have got on with the great man famously if I'd ever been his chairman. For I always take great joy out of Rovers winning football matches, even if it adds to our fixture list and the worry lines on Sean's face.

There's an oft-quoted saying in life that 'you have to be in it to win it'. I'd like to Ryanise that a little to explain my view on competitions such as the Johnstone's Paint: 'You can't win it, unless your heart's in it!' Don't think about sparse grounds and aching limbs, lift up your head and you might see what I saw that April Fool's Day – my club having a fantastic adventure we will never, ever forget.

Young and old alike waved their flags, sung their anthems and let an old softie like me know that all the hard toil of winning seemingly meaningless matches at the back of beyond on a freezing Wednesday night was worth its weight in silver.

We haven't always sent out our strongest team in this cup – we took a second team to a near full-strength Barnsley a few years ago and whipped them 5-2 (I just had to get that one in!) – but what we will never do is go into a game content to lose. It's unfair on the fans, it's unfair on all who work for the club and, anyway, I hate losing. Catch it if you can because winning is one of the few bugs that's worth having – I want us to win, win, win because winning breeds success.

The other point that strikes me about the Johnstone's Paint Trophy is that it takes me back to my first success in the hot seat at Donny – the Endsleigh Cup in our Non League days under Ian and Glynn Snodin. Both victories were heavily symbolic. Back then success over Farnborough in front of a packed Belle Vue told the football world that, contrary to public rumour, the death of Doncaster Rovers had been greatly exaggerated.

Now, time had moved on. And in 2007 we had a different point to prove. More than a few fans doubted my judgment when I appointed Sean O'Driscoll and Richard O'Kelly to manage the club – in fact that's putting it mildly. With a place in the play-offs by then looking very unlikely, we were looking to add extra spice to our season and send out a message that the new era at Rovers was up and running.

And that, of course, is exactly what happened. We won a splendid trophy, Sean allowed himself the luxury of a smile – and the rest of Doncaster, myself included, have been smiling for him ever since.

It all seemed so far away when we started out on our Johnstone's Paint journey back on 17 October in front of a meagre 3,629 at Huddersfield Town's impressive Galpharm Stadium. The first-round tie came barely a month after we'd appointed Sean as manager and with us still staggering in the bottom third of League One. We already knew much of what to expect from the Terriers, having played out an entertaining 0-0 draw in Sean's very first match in charge, and a hardy 450 or so souls from Doncaster turned out to cheer their heroes.

Huddersfield enjoyed the balance of play early on before Rovers took the lead after 25 minutes. Lewis Guy cut the ball back to Jason Price whose finish did nothing for the health of home goalkeeper Matt Glennon. He was subsequently taken off injured.

That old war horse Andy Booth levelled just before the hour and the last half-hour saw the pendulum swing to and fro with both sides missing good chances and the prospect of the dreaded penalties increasing with every such gaffe.

But with just three minutes to go we got the goal that sent Rovers fans home happy. JJ this time returned the compliment by setting up Lewis Guy and we were home and dry 2-1.

That brought a famous football name to Belle Vue for the northern quarter-final – Accrington Stanley. The clash was the first between the two clubs since 1962, the season in which the Lancashire club first crashed out of the Football League. But the romance of the occasion was certainly lost on Sean McDaid whose screams of pain could be heard for miles around after an horrific first-half incident. Adding insult to a knee injury that was to keep him out for a couple of months was the fact that the referee didn't even award us a free-kick – he re-started the game with a dropped ball.

The detractors of fielding a strong side in what they saw as a second-rate competition were in full voice that night as Steve Roberts also took a fearful knock. But the consolation came in the fact that we sent the fans home celebrating a 2-0 victory.

Both goals were created in the first half by Jonathan Forte who first set up Paul Heffernan for a turn and shot, and then Sean Thornton to net from the edge of the area. The visitors were belatedly reduced to ten men in the second half when Shaun Whalley was sent off. Many were left convinced, however, that the biggest wally was dressed in black.

That meant we could put the competition to bed until the new year. Ordinarily, a draw against Darlington would not have been greeted with enthusiasm, but this tie meant a quick return to Donny for Dave Penney.

The irony wasn't lost on the media that Penney may well have expected to lead Doncaster into the new era of the Keepmoat Stadium, yet here he was with only the third visiting team to play on the sacred turf, preparing to do his best to knock us off our perch. The attraction of Penney's return helped to produce a remarkably good crowd of 8,009 on a none-too-warm January evening – a figure that also confirmed my idea that Rovers fans were beginning to warm to this competition, after all.

Poor Dave had obviously taken on a difficult task with the League Two club as they came to the Keepmoat on the back of seven successive defeats, but they competed well enough, particularly in a scoreless opening 45 minutes. The breakthrough came shortly after half-time, courtesy of a pinpoint cross from JJ Price and a cool finish from Paul Heffernan. There was, realistically, only one team in the contest after that, although it took until three minutes from time for JJ to drive us into an unbeatable 2-0 lead. He may have been a beaten man that night, but Penney rightly got an excellent reception from Rovers fans and left with our genuine wishes that he could turn around the north east club's fortunes, which he duly did.

By the time we approached the northern area final against Crewe, a fascinating question was on all our minds. And it wasn't whether we could improve on that 8-0 drubbing Dario's boys handed out in the LDV Vans. The new Wembley project was stuttering towards its conclusion and there was still a chance that the winners would play in the final at the new stadium. It could even have been the ground's curtain call. Sadly, further delays meant that was not possible and Cardiff's Millennium Stadium remained our holy grail.

Talking of holy grails, they don't come much purer in football terms than Dario Gradi and Crewe Alexendra. The bloke is a legend of the lower leagues for his ability to unearth young diamonds and play great football, not to mention the mutual loyalty shared between him and his club whilst managerial casualties reached epidemic proportions elsewhere. I doubt whether you could arrange a match between two teams more committed to playing football the right way than Rovers and Crewe Alexandra.

By this time, I was virtually smelling Johnstone's Paint and desperate to see us go all the way in this competition. But there was still to be many a twist and turn before we could begin to think about Cardiff.

In the first half of the first leg at Crewe, it looked like a stroll in the park as we swept into a two-goal lead through a coolly-taken penalty from Heffs and a Stockie effort after 40 minutes. But this must have been one of Gradi's most effective team talks because the home side came out after the break looking more like Real Madrid. It took them around 15 minutes to wipe out our advantage with their striker Luke Varney among the scorers and we could so easily have been on the rack. Yet Heffs settled our suddenly jangling nerves by giving us a 3-2 lead before that flash of lightning Varney levelled it all up again five minutes before the end. Wow, what a game and it was still all to play for at the Keepmoat.

All thoughts of that memorable night were a million miles away by the time we actually came to host the second leg. In fact we were in such a sick state on the day before the second leg against Crewe that we only had eleven senior players fit to play and requested a postponement. Our version of squad rotation wasn't quite the same as Manchester United, Arsenal or Liverpool. It was more a case of our lads taking turns to visit the doctor. But, save for a plague or earthquake, Sky Sports insist the show goes on and so it was a case of roll your sleeves up and hold onto your sick bags. The rules dictated that we had to name 15 players, but there were never going to be many substitutions that night – getting the lads on the bench was hard enough, getting them off it and onto the pitch might have been a step too far.

It was already going to be a difficult night for yours truly for completely different reasons. I had arranged to be away in South Africa and so could only listen to 90 of the most nerve-racking minutes of my life on the internet – or more like 89, as I'll explain in a moment.

We would have welcomed some early encouragement in such an hour of need, but instead everything seemed to go against us. Young Varney struck again after we'd dominated the first half-hour without reward and it was 2-0 by half-time – and therefore 5-3 on aggregate. We weren't as sick as parrots – for some of the lads that would have been an improvement.

Lesser teams would have thrown in the towel, but the next 45 minutes went against all known medical science. Heffs, one of the stricken players, found enough energy to pull a goal back after 63 minutes and suddenly the pressure was well and truly on the visitors. Minutes ticked agonisingly by and with just ten left it looked as if Crewe might just hold on to their by-now slim advantage.

Suddenly we were awarded a penalty and Heffs ran up to slot it into the net. My frustration even from so many miles away was totally unprintable as the referee somehow awarded a retake. Could Heffs stand up to the pressure and do it again? Could he even stand up? You bet he could and now it was 2-2 with a shoot-out almost inevitably on the cards.

There I was glued to the internet broadcast when unbelievably my phone went – what kind of idiot would dare to phone me a couple of minutes from the end of a cup semi-final? You'd be more likely to get a sensible answer from Nick Hornby in the middle of an Arsenal match. But, for some strange, reason I actually answered it. "Congratulations, we've done it," was the tone of the excited message. "What are you on about?" was a translation of my response. "We've won 3-2 – Jason Price got the winner!" came the increasingly incredulous reply. Would you believe it? My broadcast had been a couple of minutes behind all evening and I'd missed the goal that eventually took us through to the final.

As I was to see for myself countless times afterwards Copps did the spade work and we had one of those heart-stopping 'and-Jason-Price-must-score' moments. His first effort was blocked, but the big name scraped in the rebound and the vast majority of the 12,500 fans were in South Yorkshire dreamland. JJ had an uncanny ability to mishit his shots and this was one occasion on which we were more than grateful for just that.

I couldn't have been more proud of the team for that victory. Believe me, there was no-one in Donny using the phrase 'only the Johnstone's Paint Trophy' after that epic. Everyone was talking about Cardiff – the FA having by this time announced that the new Wembley would NOT be ready in time – and the final against League Two Bristol Rovers on April Fool's Day.

But first we had some very important league games to deal with, as we were still extremely close to the play-offs. Nobody would have thought Rovers were suffering from an energy crisis as we entertained play-off rivals Swansea City the following Saturday in what was a thriller of a football match. To cover our walking wounded, we brought in the vastly experienced Alan Wright on loan from Sheffield United and he was given a hell of a time by that one man box of tricks Lee Trundle. Akinfenwa – who else? – gave the visitors an early lead before JJ, by now finishing as if he was shelling peas, levelled just after the half-hour. Trundle got his name on the scoresheet from a spot-kick just before the break and Heffs levelled again shortly afterwards. Both sides went for it hell for leather in the final half-hour but neither could get the goal that would have made all the difference to our respective campaigns. Nevertheless for the second time in a week the Keepmoat faithful had been superbly entertained – this time by a 2-2 draw.

Behind the scenes we signed on young Sam Hird from Leeds and Neil Sullivan returned for another spell as we went down 2-1 at Crewe, who got some revenge on us by scoring an injury-time winner.

Spirits raised again on the Tuesday night as we gained our first ever victory at Nottingham Forest's City Ground and therefore our first double over the Trentside club. It wasn't a particularly sparkling 90 minutes against a home team by then spluttering towards the play-offs. But the winning goal was a very memorable one as Stockie produced one of his eye-catching specials from fully 35 yards. Mark McCammon saw his season ended when he dislocated a shoulder and JJ Price successfully shielded the ball near the Forest corner flag for most of the last four minutes of added-time. Maradona couldn't have made a better job of it. I swear that if the referee hadn't blown his final whistle, the great man would still be there now.

Sadly, our striker crisis got even worse as we went down 4-0 at Oldham, with JJ suffering an ankle injury. And a pretty dreadful end to March saw us go into the cup final in tenth position, as successive Keepmoat defeats at the hands of Cheltenham Town, 2-0, and second-placed Bristol City, 1-0, meant we'd seen our colours lowered four times in seven starts on our own turf.

The consolation was that we could travel to Cardiff totally focused on the cup, as it now assumed even greater importance with our promotion hopes up in smoke. What an occasion it was – the first-ever national cup final that dear old Donny Rovers had ever appeared in. Time again to take stock and appreciate that it was for occasions such as this that we had saved our football club from the scrap heap.

After our Carling Cup epics, it was a strange feeling to go

into a major cup-tie as favourites but we knew that League Two side Bristol Rovers, who had eliminated neighbours City in their area final, would be very difficult opposition. Remember also that the Pirates had twice as many fans as we did in the magnificent Welsh capital.

No thoughts here of teams not putting out their best sides. We had the might of Paul Heffernan, James Coppinger and the inimitable Jason Price all coming back from injury for the occasion, although sadly it came all too soon for Mark McCammon. What followed was, in some ways, a near re-run of the classic clash with Dagenham and Redbridge when we won back our place in the Football League.

All the pre-match talk about settling down in the early minutes went totally out of the window as we went 2-0 up inside the first five minutes. In fact I'd scarcely had time to sit down and take in the magnificent view when I was up from my seat and celebrating. The official timing of Jonathan Forte's goal was just 51 seconds. Heffs, who had done so much to get us this far, made his first major contribution of the final by robbing the Bristol goalkeeper Phillips and rolling the ball into the path of the on-loan youngster. Forte may have missed out on playing Premiership football with Sheffield United, but he'll always remember the feeling of scoring the first goal in a cup final. From my seat, I can tell you it feels pretty damned good.

We would gladly have settled for that as a tonic start, but a few minutes later came a second and potentially killer blow for the underdogs. Sullivan fired a monster of a kick straight down the middle and Heffs latched onto it to rifle a shot low into the bottom corner. After all the football we'd played under Professor O'Driscoll, it looked like we'd taken the quick and shortest route to cup glory.

The rest of the first 45 minutes was comfortable enough viewing. We were happy to keep Bristol chasing the ball and that meant they rarely looked like getting back into the game. With just a little more ambition we could perhaps have got the third goal to put the tie beyond the Pirates – and how we came to regret that.

Bristol needed a boost in the second half and they got a massive one from their first real attack after 49 minutes. Sean McDaid committed a foul on Sammy Igoe and Richard Walker kept his cool to roll the ball past Sullivan from the penalty spot, despite the great man's noble attempt to keep it out. Suddenly the momentum of the game was completely changed and, roared on by 40,000 fans, I just knew Bristol Rovers were in with a real shout.

Just after the hour mark, Walker found some space for a cross and, with our defence suddenly at sixes and sevens, Igoe calmly levelled the scores. I don't mind admitting I was having kittens at this stage as Bristol looked the more likely side to win the tie, the momentum having turned fully in their favour.

Craig Disley juggled the ball past two defenders and had a golden chance to put Bristol in front, but fortunately the midfielder sliced his shot wide. The Pirates were now exerting near constant pressure and we needed a couple of excellent saves from Sully to prevent our ship from sinking completely. The veteran produced a flying one-handed save to keep out a Walker free-kick and then tipped a 30-yard drive from Igoe over the bar.

But we somehow survived the onslaught and, as extra-time approached, started to make openings of our own. Forte broke away but, rather selfishly, opted to shoot when a pass to Heffernan would have been better. Chance lost. Lee then saw a far-post effort blocked by the goalkeeper's legs at a corner and Heffs could so easily have won it in the final seconds but, after twisting past defender Steve Elliott, the striker turned his shot wide.

The game hung on a knife-edge in extra-time but, with just ten minutes remaining before the shoot-out, we edged our noses back in front again.

I can still envisage in my mind's eye Sean Thornton swinging over a tempting left-wing corner and Graeme Lee, our skipper, pulling away from his marker before planting a header into the back of the net. This time my extra-time joy had to be tempered – just for a while longer. For unlike Sir Francis Tierney's 'golden' goal, the game was still on for ten more nerve-racking minutes. Bristol pushed men forward in a valiant attempt to rescue the tie yet again, but this time we proved shipshape and held out for a memorable victory.

Fireworks, fanfares, and champagne filled the air as we celebrated at the final whistle. It could have been the Champions League or the World Cup – the feelings, I assure you, are just the same.

Finally, after 127 long years, Donny Rovers had won a major trophy – and it was my team that did it. There was to be no late miracle in League One that season as we duly finished outside the play-off places, but this was a day nobody could take away from us.

I still have mementoes from the Johnstone's Paint Trophy in my sports room at home; the memories will last forever. Another part of my dream was fulfilled and the next question was: could we use this as a launch pad to make it all the way to the Championship in 12 months time?

9

*

STEP FIVE: WEMBLEY WINNERS

Doncaster Rovers 1 Leeds United 0,
Wembley Stadium, League One play-off final, May 2008.

PAUL GREEN, popular midfielder who made 277 appearances in Rovers' meteoric rise from Conference to Championship, says: "John Ryan is one of those chairmen who comes and talks to the players week in week out – whether it's to congratulate you or wish you better luck next time. John has been fantastic for the club when you think where we were and where we are now. It has been an amazing achievement."

KEVIN BLACKWELL, Sheffield United manager and former Leeds United boss: "The Doncaster Rovers story has been about the meeting of minds. John Ryan has been terrific for the club and has come together with the likes of Mickey Walker, Dave Penney and now Sean O'Driscoll and taken them on an unbelievable journey. When people look back, it will sink in just how far they have come from bleak Belle Vue to a state-of-the-art stadium at the Keepmoat, and from the Conference to the Championship. John is at the head of what is a very well run football club."

THIS part of my dream could so easily have ended before it began.... during the summer, I received a serious offer for Rovers from Adam Pearson, who had recently sold up at Hull City and was looking for another club. He offered to buy my shares for between £3m and £4m. In some ways it would have been easy enough for me to decide that I had taken Rovers as far as we could realistically go and bow out safe in the knowledge that I'd be fondly remembered by our fans for all that we had already achieved. But this decision wasn't about money, or about my legacy, but what I genuinely felt was in the best long-term interest of the club I still loved. I knew that I hadn't yet delivered the most distant and daring promise I'd made to Rovers fans – promotion to the Championship.

In my view, the club was still better off in the hands of folk who were genuine Doncaster fans. I say that with no disrespect at all to Adam, for whom I have a personal high regard and who has since gone on to Derby County and then back to Hull City. But it's strange how these things turn out. For Adam's offer indirectly, at least, helped get things moving in a different direction and one which, I believe, is hugely significant for our future.

I'd been thinking for some time that we needed to spread the responsibilities a little wider in the interests of the club. My links with Terry Bramall and Dick Watson developed one bleak Saturday afternoon when Rovers and Blackpool played out a dreary scoreless draw at Belle Vue. I knew that Dick, who'd long since been a faithful follower of the club, was watching the match from one of the cabins we pitched behind the Town End goal. These cabins weren't exactly the council's cup of tea; at first they labelled them a health and safety hazard and threatened to postpone our opening League One game of that particular season. But they certainly did us a favour in allowing me to introduce myself to Dick, who then put me back in touch with Terry. The great result was that both joined the board. This was shortly after they had sold Keepmoat, the social housing business, for a very large sum. I asked them to join with me in taking what amounted to a 29 per cent share each in the club. To achieve this, I sold my shares to the duo at favourable rates. Naturally, it took a while to complete the transaction and it was only in September that we were able to officially announce the deal. Since then Terry and Dick have proved to be massively helpful to me and to Doncaster Rovers both financially and in terms of their unstinting support. So Adam's interest led, as it happened, to the creation of the three Doncaster musketeers.

Also during the summer I had to reflect on where we wanted to go on the pitch The reason we replaced Dave Penney with Sean O'Driscoll was to further our ambitions as a club and that meant promotion to the Championship. As I've been at pains to point out elsewhere, this is no implied criticism of Dave who has his well-deserved place as one of the true Donny heroes in our revival, both as a player and then as an extremely successful manager.

Our spell in League One had been enjoyable and consolidating our status had been a reasonable outcome, but it was undeniable that the main heights we had reached had been in the cup competitions - the Carling Cup and the Johnstone's Paint Trophy. Rovers fans, however, enjoy the big one-off occasions and our success at Cardiff over Bristol Rovers had, I believe, cemented Sean's place in their hearts. I had been under a great deal of pressure to address the situation after we failed to click into gear before Christmas, but they were beginning to smell the coffee.

What I wanted on the eve of the 2007/8 campaign was for Rovers to get over the largely self-imposed handicap that seems to afflict us each season. I think I'm going to suggest to the Doncaster council one day that we celebrate Christmas in August – for we never seem to click into top gear before the festivities have died down. It's not for the want of trying nor a lot of thought, I can assure you. Being renowned slow starters is a big handicap, for it merely heaps more pressure on the club after the festive period.

This time, more than any other, we kicked off with a squad looking equipped to put that weakness right. I was delighted to see Richie Wellens signed from Oldham Athletic in the summer. In my opinion, he was one of the biggest stars shining at League One level; he just had to be a Championship - or even Premiership - hero in disguise. A skilful ball player who fitted the Donny mould perfectly, he first caught my eye a few seasons previously and I, for one, was very anxious that we should do all we could to snap him up after his contract with the Latics expired. Sean O'Driscoll usually turns the other way whenever this chairman goes off on one about some player or other. But when I gave him my speech about a very talented young man whom Oldham had just allowed to flee their nest and put a telephone into his hands, the maestro was equally sold on the idea. He never regretted it.

Another interesting new boy was young Martin Woods from our neighbours Rotherham United. Keepmoat fans will probably never forget the quality of his goal here for the Millers and it wasn't the only spectacular goal he scored. Here's another lad with a great future. He's got a left foot to die for and can give goalkeepers nightmares from the sort of distances others can't hope to reach. Again he came here for free – and that had got to be no money extremely well spent!

We got something old and something new from our mates at Elland Road. Neil Sullivan had already shown our fans just how good he still was during his loan spell here and I honestly think that his permanent transfer was 100 per cent our gain and Captain Birdseye's loss. Another player out of contract at Leeds was young Sam Hird, a central defender with more than a touch of class about him. We quickly marked him as one for the future. Gordon Greer arrived from Scottish club Kilmarnock after impressing in the pre-season friendlies and, most significantly of all, we lashed out a record fee of £200,000 to bring in James Hayter, from Sean's old club Bournemouth. A thorn in our side on more than one occasion, Hayter joined Brian Stock in furthering our Bournemouth connection and the bookies quickly made him 14-1 against to become the league's top scorer. I didn't know about that but, if he was the bloke to deliver us the proverbial 20 goals to help get us promoted, he'd have been well worth that transfer fee – and perhaps a few pennies more!

Looking at Rovers in pre-season, a build-up that included Keepmoat defeats to both Manchester City in Sven Göran Eriksson's first game in charge and Manchester United in front of Bobby Charlton *et al*, caused me to make another of my famous public predictions. I boldly told the press this was going to be the season in which our dream of Championship football was fulfilled. The fact that Leeds United kicked off with a 15-point handicap – a decision announced on the eve of our friendly against the Red Devils – only added to my sense that this had to be our season of destiny. Logically, Leeds simply had to get themselves promoted sooner rather than later, so clubs such as ourselves were duty bound to make the absolute most of this opportunity. Although decidedly disappointing over the previous two seasons, Nottingham Forest were also too large a club to stay at this level indefinitely. I had reason to feel that on the pitch, if not off it, we compared favourably with both of these former giants.

The pessimists soon had reason, however, to think that

this time JR had shot his mouth off too far. We took just a single point from our opening three games, including a home defeat by Bournemouth that obviously hurt Sean and Richard more than a little. The early pressure lifted with a notable 2-1 win at ten-man Swansea City on 1 September, with Wellens scoring two well-taken goals. Thoughts that the victory would kick off a promotion push were a little premature, however, as a mixed month saw Rovers lose to a Mark Bunn-inspired Northampton at our place, just come up short in a five-goal thriller at Southend, yet dispose of both Crewe and Cheltenham Town comfortably enough at home.

If anyone still harboured a misconception that success would be anything but very hard earned, it came from the visit of Walsall in early October. Goals from Matt Mills, whom Sean had taken on loan from Manchester City, and Lewis Guy put us totally in control during a one-way first half. Yet the battling Midlanders hit back to eventually win 3-2, an insult made into an injury by Copps fluffing a late penalty and Guy talking himself into a sending-off.

It was still early in the season, but a section of the fans had already seen enough. The protests urging me to 'SOD out' – a play on the initials of our manager – were very vocal and quite upsetting. It's so easy to trot out phrases such as 'he doesn't know what he's doing', 'his tactics are all wrong' or 'he's lost the dressing room' – but how many really know the true picture? I had picked out Sean for his tactical prowess – a factor that had taken us to our Johnstone's Paint triumph just a few months previously. Also I was in a good position to know that his relationship with the players was very strong and positive. The only remaining issue in these circumstances is whether the man himself has had enough – in which case you can't really blame a manager if he wants to escape the criticism. But that also wasn't the case. Sean was resolute in his view that we would turn the corner and I totally agreed with him. The show had to go on....

The rest of the month was to have its fair share of encouragement on the pitch and a very important development off it. Sky Sports cameras chose just the right time to visit the Keepmoat as they saw us in tip-top form against Huddersfield Town. Goals from Stockie and Mark Wilson scarcely did us justice as 2-0 was the very least of our dominance.

It was on the following Wednesday (17 October) that I was able to release a very important piece of news. Terry Bramall and Dick Watson officially joined me as equal controlling shareholders. We celebrated this with a hard-earned and ultimately well-deserved point from a scoreless game at the City Ground, against a Forest side who had moved into third spot after an uninspiring start of their own. I'm not saying we were denied a late penalty, but if the ball had been finger-printed afterwards there would have been compelling evidence against defender Kelvin Wilson.

There was a great Sunday afternoon for that jack-in-the-box Jason Price, as we eventually overwhelmed leaders Leyton Orient 4-2 in what was a second-half classic. It was 0-0 at half-time when Price came on for Sean McDaid and netted within seven minutes. The visitors turned the tables with two quick-fire goals of their own before big Jason levelled, Hayter smashed in a brilliant bicycle kick and Wellens made it safe. Phew, what a thriller!

Fans then had to wait more than a fortnight to see us in home action again, by which time we'd been on our travels no fewer than four times. Four points from away games at Swindon and Gillingham was a fair enough return, but we ran into FA Cup trouble when fellow League One side Oldham Athletic led us 2-0 inside the first 49 minutes at Boundary Park. That man Hayter paid two more installments on his huge fee by single-handedly rescuing our FA Cup hopes, as we fought back for a 2-2 draw. That's just the sort of result that tugs at the heart strings of a fans' chairman just a little. My celebrations at staying in this great competition when we had stared an instant exit in the face were tempered a little by the realisation that replays could only add to the demands on our squad in murky November. But emotions were completely the other way around as our hold on the Johnstone's Paint Trophy was relinquished in our area quarter-final tie at Grimsby Town. Again, you could argue that the result was small fry (if you forgive the Grimsby pun) compared with our League One mission, yet we could scarcely deny our feeling for this competition after all the fun and glory we had enjoyed just a few months back. The manner of defeat put a strain on me too. We levelled twice through Lewis Guy and Paul Heffernan before eventually bowing out in the dreaded penalty shoot-out. I say dreaded because that is exactly what it is – yet the soccer gods had been kind to us in previous shoot-outs, I suppose.

Our welcome home could have been a lot better. After getting out of jail ourselves, we lost a lead in the Keepmoat replay against Oldham as they staged their own comeback to put us out 2-1. Good job we were just beginning to fire in the league. A fine 3-1 victory at Port Vale extended an unbeaten run that was beginning to reach very promising proportions by the time our 'bogey' team Yeovil came to town. Needless to say that was enough to signal a first loss in eleven as that old war horse Marcus Stewart sealed a 2-1 away victory. It raised the hackles of Sean's detractors, too, but then home defeats are never Top of the Pops with any club's fans, particularly with so much to play for.

Yet it was a happy Christmas – a very happy one – as we hauled ourselves up to fourth spot by the end of the year with successive and largely emphatic victories over Crewe

4-0, Northampton Town 2-0 and Southend United 3-1. Maybe we are not so bad before Christmas after all. Nevertheless, I had to admit that Leeds had been the team of the season so far. I, like most observers I suspect, figured that their 15-point handicap would at least rule them out of contention for an automatic promotion place. They set out needing around 90 points – usually title-winning form – to make the play-offs and I didn't fancy Dennis Wise's chances of instantly putting together a successful side. Yet that is exactly what happened as Leeds began with a long winning run that weekly cut the gap between them and their potential rivals. Without apparently playing that well, they developed the very useful habit of scoring winning goals in the last five minutes – one I wouldn't object to at the Keepmoat. Amazingly, they even went to the top of the division for a few hours over Christmas and were right up there in the mix with the likes of Carlisle United, Swansea City and Forest.

Call me crazy, call me a visionary, call me what you like, but I had a very vivid dream about going to Wembley and beating our rivals Leeds United – it could only be the play-off final at the end of the season. Anyway, I was mad enough to put my neck on the block and tell the *Yorkshire Post* about it – so I went on record as predicting we would get promotion through the play-offs (p.s. I still wanted to be in the top two though).

Our New Year resolution to turn frustrating draws into victories lasted just 73 minutes as that side Walsall equalised a Jason Price goal to earn themselves a 1-1 draw, before Hayter settled a cracking game against Carlisle United with the only goal seven minutes from time to put us on Cloud Nine again. That set the stage for our first meeting with Leeds, who were just beginning to wobble a little. Stockie's superb free-kick gave us a deserved first-half lead and we matched our hosts punch for punch after the break to earn a priceless 1-0 success. I will also always recall this special day for laying a wreath beside the statue of the great Billy Bremner.

I have been in the game long enough to know that just when you think you've cracked it, you're likely to come a cropper and that happened the following Friday. A hugely impressive Swansea City side came to the Keepmoat and smashed us 4-0. They may have rubbed our noses in it with a couple of late goals but the Swans were already well in control before Steve Roberts saw red for a professional foul. This was the night we realised that Swansea, not Leeds, were the team to beat in this league and that was going to be no easy task as they now held a ten-point lead. We ended January in second spot after a 2-0 win over Hartlepool, but Hayter now needed an operation for a hernia and I was pleased we were able to bring in good cover in Gareth Taylor, from Tranmere Rovers, and Stuart Elliott, on loan from Hull City.

The Swansea game apart, it was now getting more and more difficult to get past Sully; the veteran oozed confidence between the sticks. Three more successive clean sheets followed and, most importantly, we cashed in at the other end to convert those into nine precious points. Millwall were taken to the sword at the New Den. There was little sign of their opening day resistance on this occasion as we ran away with a 3-0 success, courtesy of Pricey, a thunderous shot from Copps and Greenie in time added on. A couple of spot-kicks sunk an unhappy Bristol Rovers before Pricey showed he does like to play beside the seaside by netting both goals in a revenge victory over Bournemouth.

Once again, we were on a roll and couldn't wait to bring on the Leeds at the Keepmoat. The game was due to kick off at high noon on the Saturday but a big overnight freeze meant the pitch wasn't fit for play. Leeds threw out their dummies and called us a Mickey Mouse club, but we were just as disappointed as they were – if not more so – because we were looking forward to claiming another three points. It was then our turn to lose another excellent tussle with Carlisle by a lone goal and we ended February edged out of the ultimately crucial second spot on goal difference by Forest. The victory ensured the Cumbrians were also nicely tucked in just a point behind us, with Swansea frankly out of sight.

Two games a week meant a hectic and vital start to March. Injuries were piling up and the going was hard but we won a backs-to-the-wall fight to hang on to an early lead at play-off hopefuls Tranmere Rovers, then repeated the 1-0 act in a stormy match at Bristol Rovers. When we saw off Gillingham 2-1, we'd even closed the gap between us and Swansea temporarily to six points. Was it asking too much for us to go up as champions? The answer unfortunately came in the next two away games as we lost out 1-0 in an even game at Brighton and then went to Yeovil Town on Good Friday and found a new way of losing to them. Already one-nil down, we were deflated when Sully inexplicably tried to dribble past one of their strikers and instead presented the home side with a gift second goal. Heffs' goal after 75 minutes started the charge of the Rovers brigade but, as usual, we couldn't blow their house down.

Another difficult examination by Oldham Athletic – who this time held us to a 1-1 draw at a snowy Keepmoat – meant suddenly we were trailing Carlisle by five points and desperately in need of victory against Friday-night visitors Nottingham Forest. I say Friday night because I went to see my mother during the afternoon and she took me a bit by surprise with her hearty congratulations. "Great result today," she said. "What do you mean?" I replied. She then insisted that she'd been watching Sky Sports News and had seen the scoreline Doncaster Rovers 1, Nottingham Forest 0. Well, she's always had a bit of a psychic or intuitive side has mum and that was in my mind as we put Colin Calderwood's men to the sword throughout the night whilst struggling to turn domination into goals. Paul Smith in the Forest goal had an inspired night until finally being beaten when Gareth Roberts fired in a 74th-minute free-kick via the inside of a post. So there we were, just as she said, priceless 1-0 winners. Forest were then nine points adrift of us in fifth spot.

Trust April Fool's Day to put a fly in the ointment. The re-arranged game against Leeds followed much the same pattern as we piled on the pressure. But this time we were destined not to score and Alan Sheehan rifled in a free-kick to keep Leeds in the play-off reckoning. Again the squad was fast becoming depleted with injuries and we needed to roll up our sleeves just to stay in the hunt. The trip to Huddersfield Town showed us that character-wise we were onto a winner. Gareth Taylor got us back in the game after the Terriers had dominated to lead 1-0 in the first half but, after Matty Mills was sent off and Holdsworth had restored the home side's lead from the free-kick, our backs were firmly against the wall. Yet we defended with our lives and two minutes from time grabbed a point with what was a very big goal – Copps fed Greenie and he struck firm and true for a point that was almost as valuable morale-wise as a victory.

We were now entering the home straight with Carlisle looking firm favourites to join Swansea as the promoted two. Our 43rd game was on the Friday night and we managed to get our strikes in first as goals from Sean McDaid and a Stock penalty were more than sufficient to see off visitors Swindon Town. We don't normally expect Leeds to do us any favours but that's just how it turned out on the following afternoon as they beat Carlisle United 3-2 at Elland Road. Carlisle were now three points clear – a useful, but not decisive advantage – with Forest a further three points adrift of ourselves despite stringing some results together.

Our trip to Leyton Orient yielded a Mark McCammon goal and a single point but we ended the day optimistic enough as stuttering Carlisle lost at home to Southend United. Forest won again and were now just a point behind us. Ominously, perhaps, Leeds won at Millwall and now looked a fair bet to reach the play-offs. Our task in game 45 was straightforward enough. We needed to defeat already relegated Luton Town at the Keepmoat to give us a shot at automatic promotion on the final day. The Hatters creditably gave their all but Mills and McCammon eased us to a 2-0 victory, made all the more significant by Carlisle's potentially devastating 3-0 defeat at Millwall.

It was time to get out the calculators and work out the permutations. With Swansea already up, we were a point clear of Forest and Carlisle in that order. We had seven days to contemplate what we now considered as probable automatic promotion. For if we could overcome Cheltenham Town away from home, there was nothing that either Forest or Carlisle could do to stop us. It was a nervy, but exciting week. For so long in the season, we'd been on the coat tails of the top two and in recent weeks the play-offs had seemed to be a far more likely outcome as Carlisle piled on the pressure. But I had my personal doubts about the Cumbrians and wasn't too shocked by what happened. When we lost 1-0 at Brunton Park, I'd formed the impression that promotion might be a bridge too far for them and its strange how often this can become a factor. I chatted to the lads on the way to Cheltenham; the mood was positive and

I put my dream as far to the back of my mind as possible. Logically the odds were now running in our favour. Granted, the home side still needed a point to ensure their survival at the other end of the league, but you'd expect the promotion-chasers to triumph more often than not.

Such afternoons are loved and hated in equal measure by fans all over the land. This was the sort of day when the scores from other games inevitably get communicated to the fans – and therefore everyone else – and you can end up feeling you are fighting a number of different battles all at the same time. For us, however, the focus was simply and totally on winning the game. That would be good enough. The game kicked off with Rovers doing most of the running, yet failing to make an early breakthrough. In contrast, we were quickly told that Forest were one goal and then two goals up against Yeovil – since when could we expect The Glovers to do us a favour! That scoreline had become 2-1 by the time Richard Gillespie struck a blow to our hearts by giving Cheltenham the lead after 24 minutes. The odds, if anything, had switched into Forest's favour, although we still had plenty of time to hit back.

Our problem could be put in a two-word nutshell - Shane Higgs. The Robins goalkeeper was in outstanding form and he kept us at bay until half-time with the home side still leading 1-0. The news from the City Ground was that Forest were now 3-1 up, so we kicked off again assuming we would need to take all three points to get promoted. The second period was an extension of the first, only even more one-sided. Chances came and went or more accurately were denied by Higgs and his over-worked defenders. With each miss people who have watched half as much football as I were beginning to think it would not be our day. Then came a major breakthrough. Jason Price flicked the ball on and Greenie lashed his shot joyously into the net. There were still

14 minutes to go - time that would slip by very quickly, but might well have seemed like an age in Nottingham.

Still, we poured on the pressure and, still, Higgs and his gallant defenders somehow prevented us from adding to our score. There were five minutes left on my watch when the unthinkable happened - the goal did arrive, but at the wrong end. Our need to throw players forward inevitably gave the home side some space on the break and when Richard Keogh crossed into the penalty area, Paul Connor got the decisive touch to send the ball past a stunned Neil Sullivan. Time stood still. My disappointment was total. Surely, it was asking too much for us to score TWICE in the last five minutes and bury 85 minutes of frustration. As you might expect, those minutes flashed before me and yet, in all honesty, we did create openings and Higgs again stood in our way. The final whistle went – we had (somehow) lost 2-1. All that remained was to get confirmation of Forest's result. Yeovil had pulled a goal back late on, but Forest ended up 3-2 winners.

You've got to be big in these circumstances and I needed to set an example. I told the players and officials that this war was far from over. We may have gone into the Cheltenham game putting all our emotional and physical energy into getting promoted automatically, but now we had to raise ourselves up again for the play-offs. There was interesting news as I looked at the other results. With Carlisle failing to win their final game at home to Bournemouth, we were third and it looked likely that Leeds would finish sixth and meet us in the semi-final. That would have made my dream of beating our rivals at Wembley null and void. But fate had produced another twist in the piece. Leeds actually overtook Southend United and moved into fifth as the Shrimpers surprisingly were unable to defeat relegated Port Vale at Roots Hall. So, instead, we would be the next visitors to Essex whilst Leeds tackled Carlisle. I phoned Mark Arthur at Forest to congratulate him on his club's achievement. They had won their last six matches to sneak into second spot and if anyone was going to pip Donny, I was genuinely pleased it was them. My sentiments were genuine enough as was the Forest chief's reply that they hoped that we were successful in the play-offs.

Our players were totally gutted and decided against a Sabbath rest. Instead they held a team meeting the following day to discuss their disappointment and get their minds round the challenge that lay ahead. The days that followed leading up to Friday's visit to Roots Hall dragged enormously. I gave out the rallying call that we could still make our dream come true and chatted with Sean who was pleased with the way the team was responding in training. On the road to Essex I chatted to as many of the lads as possible to give them words of encouragement. We knew full well that Southend had limped over the play-off line themselves but expected them to be grateful for one last crack at promotion

Teams like Donny don't play many two-legged ties - we don't get into Europe very often, other than on holidays - but there was never going to be much prospect of us changing our gameplan. As always we set out to try to win the match, but this proved to be a very hard-fought contest with a fair splattering of chances at both ends. With the second leg in mind, a 0-0 draw was a reasonably good result for us, although our upbeat mood was offset by the realisation that Paul Heffernan had ended his own personal season by getting himself sent off in the closing stages. Watching Leeds play Carlisle brought mixed emotions. Logically, we would have fancied ourselves even more strongly against Carlisle after their poor end to the season but then there was that inviting prospect of an all-Yorkshire final and you know what. Carlisle took a two-goal lead at Elland Road only for Leeds to net in injury-time to give themselves a chance of redemption. Their second leg was played before ours and I've got to say I wasn't too surprised when Leeds completed their comeback act with a resolute 2-0 victory after extra-time.

The following night – an atmospheric Friday under the Keepmoat floodlights – saw us attempt to fulfil our side of the bargain. It turned out not only to be one of the most important nights of our season, but one of the best. The evening started well and just kept getting better and better. Big Jason Price quickly made a nuisance of himself and won us a penalty when he was brought down after just minutes. Stockie stuck away the spot-kick to put us ahead on aggregate. Jason got his head to a cross after 20 minutes to claim a second before Copps took over. He's a lad who probably under-sells himself goals-wise considering his flamboyant abilities but, on this night, he produced a virtuoso performance all of his own. The 13,000 Keepmoat crowd were in raptures six minutes before the break when Copps cut in from the right and netted with a stunning shot from 20 yards.

When you're 3-0 up at half-time, it's strange how often the second half pales in comparison, but this certainly wasn't the case – Copps made doubly certain of that. Just four minutes into the half he ghosted past three Southend defenders and rolled in a cool finish before eventually completing his hat-trick with a spectacular free-kick into the roof of the net. It was one of the best trebles you could possibly wish to see and on such an important occasion. Southend pulled a goal back to lose 5-1 and, despite the scoreline, took some credit from the night. This was an occasion when we were firmly in top gear rather than our opponents performing poorly.

So the Leeds United finale was definitely on and we had nine days to prepare for the most important game for many a year. Given the friction between the two clubs earlier in the season, it was always going to be a feisty occasion and there was plenty of verbal jostling in the build-up. Leeds already had a bigger allocation of tickets than us, which wasn't surprising considering the relative sizes of the two clubs. But, in addition, we had to deal with the problem of Doncaster-based Leeds fans who bought tickets for our section. Fortunately, the situation became public knowledge soon enough and we were able to address it so there weren't hooligan problems on the day.

Ken Bates used the time to tell all and sundry that he was expecting Leeds to claim their rightful promotion, particularly after failing in his bid to get the 15-point penalty rescinded. That wasn't a problem, but I did take some offence at Mike Parry, of Talk Sport radio, ranting on that Donny had no right to be on the same pitch as a club as mighty as Leeds United and that the result was a virtual formality. I can't answer everything that is said about my club in the media, but this was one occasion when I wanted my say. So I phoned Mr Parry and told his listeners my side of things – explaining how we had matched Leeds on the pitch during the season and that I was very confident that we would get the better of them at Wembley. I rung off by saying that perhaps the broadcaster would care to eat some humble pie when Rovers proved him wrong.

I wasn't just shooting my mouth off, I believed every word. I not only expected to win, I thought we'd do so convincingly. We'd been the better side in both our League One clashes and I expected Wembley to suit our more expansive style of football just fine. Leeds gained a victory in the pre-match point-scoring stakes when we tried to book our hotel and found that our first choice was already the province of our opponents. No worries, I thought, we'll go elsewhere and have a great time.

The day before the game produced the ideal aperitif. In the afternoon Hull City won their place in the Premiership with a 1-0 victory over a Bristol City side, including our old mate Michael McIndoe. Interestingly, the winning goal - an absolute cracker of a volley – was netted by the veteran Dean Windass, a player whom I have admired for years. Perhaps that was another good omen for us? The same evening also saw another occasion which was very special for me personally. We held a directors' dinner at the Grand Wyndham Harbour Hotel, at which my fellow directors stood up and thanked me for all I'd done for the club over the past decade. I won't pretend that I didn't feel very emotional. There's something wonderful about being honoured by your peers, the people who know best what goes into the running of a successful organisation. Their message that night was that it was time to celebrate how far we'd come, whatever the outcome of the following afternoon's big match. But I was inwardly very confident that we'd give ourselves something more to toast before we went home.

Matchday was also an extremely emotional time, even before kick-off. Seeing the large Doncaster contingent in a crowd of just over 75,000 brought a huge lump to my throat. More often I've looked around with pride at our loyal followings at small and often dilapidated football grounds and here we were at the home of football taking part in a match many Donny folk would remember forever. To add to my joy, the Ryan clan was here in force. Alongside me was my lovely wife Lynne and attending, too, were my five children and my sister Janet and her family. What an occasion, too, for my brother Philip, the club's photographer. I spared more than a thought for my dear departed father who would so dearly have loved to have witnessed such a day as this – perhaps he did.

I was sat within yards of Ken Bates, who was his usual cocky self. But this day was only going to be a party for one of us – and I was in the mood to celebrate. During the presentations just before the game, groundstaff brought out two huge sausage-shaped balloons onto the pitch. When they were in position, one in each half of the field, they allowed the balloons to rise unfurling two huge banners, one bearing the Rovers emblem, the other that of Leeds United. They rose into the bowl of the Wembley air, rising at exactly the same rate and to the same height. They emphasised to me that at this point in history 'minnows' Doncaster Rovers and mighty Leeds United were now exact equals. Forget comparative trivia such as finances, points deductions, club histories and gates - we were here because we were every bit as good as a club that had reached the semi-finals of the Champions League only a few short years ago. In fact, in my mind even better. Soon the balloons were removed and out onto the stage came the players of both sides, loosening up and soaking in the atmosphere. Did they realise at that very moment they were carrying the hopes not only of 75,000 fans but everyone who was tuned in anxiously to the radio, watching on Sky TV or perhaps on the internet? In a way, I hoped not. I wanted the players to be focused, but relaxed. If only we could just play our normal game on the biggest of stages, I was confident we could pull it off. Looking around, the Leeds supporters were more visible and more vocal, but we could cope with that. After all, we beat them in a much more partisan atmosphere at Elland Road.

Finally, it was time for the talking and hype to stop and the match itself. I'll always remember those first 20 minutes. During that early period we took the game confidently, fluently, almost effortlessly, to Leeds and created a series of openings that could easily have decided the tie before Leeds had drawn breath. Barely seven frantic minutes had gone by before Greenie did a trick or two to dance to the by-line and pulled the ball back for JJ around six yards out. Anything can happen in such circumstances but this time the great man's strike was sweet enough and would have sailed into the net but for a nick off a Leeds defender that carried it over the bar. We came forward in waves and United's defence parted like the White Sea. Poor old Captain Birdseye alongside me didn't have a prayer – but he did have a goalkeeper by the name of Casper Ankergren. Mere mortals had become heroes over 90 minutes through their acrobatics between the sticks to keep Rovers at bay this season – this guy went a long way towards cult status inside the first quarter. First Copps, then James Hayter weaved their way into goalscoring positions only for the Leeds guardian to dash smartly off his line and literally snatch away their moments of glory. Leeds defenders knocked the ball a little ponderously around at the back in a bid to quell the pressure and turn back the red and white tide, but even they must have been wondering what was hitting them.

Thrilled as I was with the way we'd started, anxious thoughts inevitably started to creep into the back of my mind –we've played like this without getting a goal, is this a day when we're going to regret our generosity? I looked at Ken Bates again. Would it worry him if his side got away with daylight robbery? Not a chance.... The pace inevitably settled down and Leeds came more into the picture. The game was now much more even in terms of possession although we kept that potentially deadly duo of Jermaine Beckford and Dougie Freedman at arm's length. Nothing yet to unduly alarm the mighty Neil Sullivan.

Half-time provided 15 minutes to soothe the frayed

nerves and thumping hearts. Everyone had an urgent view on what they'd already seen. The half had been ours on points for sure but, with no goals on the scoreboard, the immediate destiny of both teams was still very much in the balance. It's either you or I, Ken Bates, this league ain't big enough for both of us.

Two minutes into the second half and suddenly the moment we'd been waiting for arrived. I'll cherish it for the rest of my days. Tenacity wins a corner on the right and over goes Stockie to take it. His delivery is driven and accurate and arrowing onto the head of one James Hayter, the £200,000 man. Unmarked and 12 yards out, there's still plenty to do. The header is true and bullet-like, rocketing downwards into the space on the line between the stranded Ankergren and Neil Kilkenny. The net bulges, a split second to take in the enormity of the moment, and Rovers are ahead in one of the most important games in our history. Had the world ended right then, I would have sworn I was in paradise. A great goal, punching the air, with the woman of my dreams celebrating alongside me. Who says football is a daft game? I wouldn't swap it, not now anyway. You could even have added another couple of noughts on that cheque for Hayter and I would not have objected. But, hold tight folks, there was still 43 minutes to go.

Naturally it seemed like hours. Leeds poured forward in droves, without seriously testing Sully with a direct effort. Young Sam Hird was doing a great job in defence – what a time for him to get his big chance. These were times when you need your goalkeeper to inspire confidence – or just to keep the chairman sane. More than once big Sully came off his line, jumped like a gazelle and clutched that ball securely to his chest. Thou shall not pass was written all over it.

Both sides gambled with their substitutions. Leeds were committed to do-or-die all out attack, Sean looking to keep what we had, but we would be short of firepower if this agony extended into extra-time. Suddenly, there is room for us on the break and Copps threatens to make the most of it. But a great tackle by Jonathan Douglas denies the in-form winger just as he is about to pull the trigger. Our players are tired, almost out on their feet, I feel sure that otherwise Copps would never have been catchable.

And then the fourth official holds up his board: FOUR minutes of added-time. Four minutes too long from my perspective, but is it long enough for Leeds to find an equaliser? The pattern continues with Leeds pressing forward but our lads on the pitch look a lot less nervous than some of us up in the stands - until the moment of triumph. Everything I had dreamt about for 50 years – and more specifically the last ten since I had taken the reins at Rovers – is suddenly encapsulated into the shrill sound of a referee's whistle. We are in the Championship folks and my feet won't touch the ground To his immense credit, Ken Bates is one of the first to congratulate me. "You deserved it today," he says. Those were four brave words and I admire him for that.

Everywhere I look I see red. Jumping, dancing, waving, folk who have probably never met before kissing and hugging like long-lost lovers. The lads go to the fans to lap up the moment. Sean famously says he's off for a cup of tea – he knows how to live it up. Make mine a double.... I wasn't going in the dressing room, but the photographer Steve Uttley takes some standing up to and this isn't the time or the place. I'm just about through the door with the biggest smile that ever lit up a human face when I'm drowned with champagne. I feel like I've won Formula One, the Premiership and the Eurovision Song Contest all in one go. Who cares now about falling at Cheltenham, when we've tasted glory at our grand national stadium?

I could almost feel sorry for Gary McAllister and his men. Like Dagenham and Redbridge before them, they have fallen victim to our prowess at sudden-death football. The full consequences of what happened at Wembley couldn't possibly be absorbed in a single instant, no matter how many times I'm slapped on the back and congratulated. That will happen during the next three or four months when we prepare once again for Championship football and Leeds contemplate at least 12 more months in a division they surely should never be in. I've worked throughout my life for moments like this. It matters not whether the initial celebrations are raucous or otherwise, the immense satisfaction and anticipation I can take with me on my summer holiday is what it is really all about. I can almost see Jimmy Hill and Bobby Robson dancing through our defence all those years ago at Belle Vue and my fellow fan's teeth chattering away in celebration. We were back in the second flight of English football at long last; my fourth and final promise thrillingly fulfilled.

PART THREE: THE PROMISED LAND

10

*

JOHN RYAN'S DIARY OF CHAMPIONSHIP SEASON 2008/09

ADAM LOCKWOOD, Doncaster Rovers' club captain 2008-9, says: "John wears his heart on his sleeve and the football club is a major part of his life. He is a chairman who wants to be involved in everything, even though he is a very busy man. We see him at both the Keepmoat and the training ground and he always tries to pop into the dressing room before kick-off to wish us all the best. You can't underestimate the risks involved in putting your life and money into a football club but the success we have had at Donny Rovers has been unbelievable. He also just happens to be a really nice guy; one of the lads. Typical of him is when he came down to the training ground, saw us playing table tennis and challenged us all to a game. Needless to say he is better than all of us!"

BACK home, I pause my video at the crucial moment. James Hayter's header hits the back of the Leeds United net for the 1,000th time this afternoon. Cue commentator Alan Parry. "Now Doncaster Rovers can dare to dream," he shouts at the top of his voice. Now that's an interesting phrase – it will come in useful one day. If life was perfect, I would have whisked Lynne off for a fantastic holiday and continued the celebrations for a couple of weeks – and then some. But I'll tell you exactly how long the euphoria actually lasted – two days.

On the third day I had a meeting with Steve Denos, Paul Green's agent. The lad was now out of contract and there was going to be no hesitation on our part in offering him another one. Greenie had been with us almost since time began. I'd seen his rise from Conference player to one of the most highly-prized assets in League One. He scored the header that set us on the way to that most important victory of all in the Conference play-off against Dagenham and Redbridge; he got the breakthrough in the game that clinched promotion from League Two the following season against Cambridge United. But more than even his heroic deeds, Greenie's a great lad. Cut him open and he'd bleed for Doncaster Rovers, I thought.

Steve knows his moments to begin negotiations. His client had just had a very good game at Wembley and was therefore on a personal high. He hit me with a thunderbolt I could barely take in – Greenie was heading to Derby County. It was a done deal, *fait accompli*, nothing anyone could do about it. I couldn't believe it. Money had torn asunder a part of my dream. Greenie had accepted a £6,000 a week deal to join the newly-relegated side. If it had been £5,000 we would have come up with a package to compete with it. I'd definitely have offered him a testimonial that would have netted a popular player such as him a cool tax-free £250,000 or so. But I never got the chance to talk to Greenie. Denos had, in my mind, done the dirty on me. How ironic. The same man who did us the greatest of good favours by pointing Michael McIndoe in the direction of Belle Vue from Yeovil had now helped to turn the head of another Donny favourite and guide him out of the exit door. I'd have loved Greenie to have stayed with us in the Championship.

Continuity has always been a big theme of our rise through the leagues – look at how long the likes of Andy Warrington, Tim Ryan, Simon Marples, Dave Penney and a few notable others stayed with us after our Conference days. Greenie would have been the only one to make it all the way from Conference to Championship. And I genuinely think he would have been much better off as a player. I'm not one to stand in the way of anyone's career path, but another season with Donny would only have added to his value and standing in the game. His silky skills and passing were totally suited to and part and parcel of Professor O'Driscoll's system. But how would he fit into the more up-and-at-'em-style of Paul Jewell and Derby County? I realise that the level of loyalty in this game is very low and that we have got far more than our fair share of it at Doncaster Rovers. But, yes, I was angry, very angry that we lost Paul Green to Derby County. Not angry with the player so much, whom I've spoken to on several occasions since. But angry with the way that money can and does so often win the day.

Losing Greenie the way we did took the edge off our triumph, but taught me one very important lesson – the fight to make it in the Championship had begun months before a ball was kicked. Obviously going up a division makes increased financial demands on any football side and one of our most important decisions was always going to be over the playing budget. The previous season's figure of £3m put us among the better payers in League One, although well behind the likes of Leeds United and Forest. But even increasing that to £5m did no more than put us among the poor men of the Championship. The players were put on a ceiling of £4,000 a week, with the express intention that we were not going to bust that for anyone we might add to the squad.

It makes me chuckle when I hear fans talk about money

supposedly coming into football clubs and wondering where it all goes. Well, to put you in the picture, we budgeted for a LOSS of about £2.3m. Such figures are, of course, dependent on variables such as our estimated income through the gates and other totally unknown factors including monies from runs in the Carling Cup or indeed the very lucrative FA Cup. So what happens to the deficit? The three Donny musketeers, as I call us, then have a responsibility. Each season we undertake at least one share issue to cover the losses with the three leading shareholders taking the lead. This means that the club runs on a sound financial footing without the major debts that are run up by almost all of our competitors. This is, of course, given much less priority by the fans than the 'sexier' tasks of bringing in players and winning points – but is becoming more and more vital with each and every season that goes by.

This 2008-2009 season, Luton Town and Bournemouth, whom 12 short months ago were kicking off alongside Donny in League One, have been plunged into instant and very real danger of losing their Football League status come the end of the campaign. I'm not going into the rights or wrongs of their penalties, but Luton start with minus 30 points and will almost certainly remain in the relegation zone all season. Bournemouth have been penalised a hefty 17 points and, if Sean's old club is to achieve redemption, it will probably be at the expense of our near neighbours Rotherham United who have exactly the same handicap. All of these deductions are the result of financial difficulties the clubs have encountered. Basically, any side that goes into administration, for example, is assured of being heavily penalised.

Who knows whether even at Championship level we will see the same kind of problems beset one of our competitors? It could conceivably be that the issue of relegation is decided not just by skills on the field but the way figures stack up off it. The other point to make is even more important. Debts can threaten the very existence of our clubs, as we know all too well from the dreaded Ken Richardson era. I've always promised to look after Donny Rovers during my tenure because the club was here before I took over – and will continue, God willing, for a long time afterwards. I take very seriously my responsibility to eventually hand over Rovers in good shape, both on and off the field. So that means that I will not countenance busting the bank in a distant hope that it might takes us a few more places up the table. And I honestly believe most of my fellow supporters will agree with me.

Some fans may have expected more hectic activity in the transfer market than actually took place. Sean was adamant that he wanted to bring in John Spicer, a talented midfielder from Burnley, as his replacement for Greenie. He got to know the lad at Bournemouth and was convinced that he could again do a very good job for him. The deal was agreed and we got our man. The other signings were to boost our defence. Matty Mills had already spent a couple of successful loan spells with us and we beat off competition from Southampton to land him for a club record fee of £300,000. Money definitely well spent. We also finalised a deal to bring Stuart Elliott, who had been on loan with us from Hull City, on a permanent deal and later in the summer added a Dutchman to our ranks. I liked the look of Jos van Nieuwstadt from the very start. An elegant footballing type of defender, he obviously fitted the O'Driscoll prototype - here's to total football at the Keepmoat.

The rest of the business we conducted behind the scenes probably didn't grab the imagination of the general public, but those who know Rovers will hopefully appreciate that it was just as, if not more, important than new signings. We agreed deals to protect our engine room and one of our most outstanding talents from the prying eyes of jealous competitors. After losing Greenie, we didn't want to risk Richie Wellens, Brian Stock, James Coppinger and James O'Connor going into the shop window. All signed three-year deals to stay at Doncaster Rovers and I sincerely hope that they see out their contracts with us.

There was also the huge matter of improving Sean's terms. He signed a new three-year rolling contract along with his assistant Richard O'Kelly. I'll tell you this right now. Whatever happens to us in the coming season, Sean O'Driscoll will remain our manager – unless he decides that he has had enough, of course. I speak with Sean four or five times a week and I know and appreciate his complex character better than most. People see his public image and most notably his downbeat press conferences and often ask me – how does such a man motivate his players? There is definitely a side to Sean O'Driscoll that those who don't work directly with him – or know him personally – are unlikely to see. I know from first-hand experience that his relationship with the players is absolutely top class. I was aware from the recommendations I had on his behalf when I recruited him that he was the type of manager who was loyal to his players and expected the same in return. He fills players with confidence, both in their own abilities and the system he loves to play. A highly intelligent guy in his own right – hence my calling him the professor – he enjoys dealing with intelligent guys out there on the pitch. We may be trying to win football matches rather than joining MENSA, but I think you'll gather the soundness of his thinking.

In the chats we had during the summer, Sean continually stressed the fact that he wanted to give the players who had done so well for us in League One the chance to play for us in the Championship. It wasn't just blind loyalty, but confidence in their ability and togetherness as a unit and he was talking to the converted, as far as I was concerned. I was also convinced that we should keep all the lads at the Keepmoat and see how it went. We decided that we would do just that and review the situation after ten games or so.

So this is it, folks! Ten years ago I raised eyebrows when I forecast that dead-on-our-feet Doncaster Rovers could once again compete in the second flight of English football, just as we did when I first became aware of football at my beloved Belle Vue. Now we are ticking off the days until we can start living that dream.

These days the Championship, or good old Division Two as it was when King Alick was setting out, is a major league – and not just because it's the doorway to the promised land of the Premiership. This is the third most watched league in the world – deferring only to the Premiership and the German Bundesliga. And when I look at some of the famous clubs taking part this season – and the resources they have at their disposal - I, of all people, begin to appreciate just how far little old Donny Rovers have come. Birmingham City, Wolverhampton Wanderers, Sheffield United, Sheffield Wednesday, Nottingham Forest, Derby County, Queens Park Rangers, Charlton Athletic, Coventry City, Reading – just some of the clubs that have graced the elite league in recent seasons, but how many of those could you be certain of finishing in the top half this term let alone challenging for promotion?

I read the newspapers, listen to the radio pundits and balance them against my own convictions. Whichever way I look at it, this is going to be an uphill task. Only Southampton, widely rumoured to be in deep financial strife, and Blackpool, a club that has risen above its means in the last few seasons, are in our league financially. Both clubs may well struggle, then there's a similar financial question mark hanging over our neighbours at Sheffield Wednesday that could conceivably draw the Owls into the relegation equation.

But, in all honesty, predicting the top six and the bottom three in The Championship is virtually an impossible mission. And that's why, in my view, this division is currently a lot more interesting in many ways than the Premiership, dominated so thoroughly by the so-called Big Four. The bookmakers come up with their predictable verdict – and I'm secretly delighted. We are installed virtually across the board as favourites for 24th and bottom spot in the league and instant demotion back to League One. All that rings some kind of bell, doesn't it? We were regarded as probable relegation fodder in our first season back in the Football League, again after coming up via the play-offs. Then we defied all the odds to dominate League Three and gain promotion along with our friends from Hull City. I can't promise the same thing again, although naturally I'm a little envious as well as thrilled by the fact the Tigers, led by chairman Paul Duffen, are now kicking off in the Premiership. Perhaps the dream isn't quite fulfilled yet.....

One of the many exciting aspects of the season ahead is that I genuinely have no definite idea how we'll fare - for the first time in years. I'm confident our pure football will make us better than a bottom-three side, although at this stage I'll secretly shake on a deal for 21st spot and another go at the learning curve in 2009/10. As you may appreciate, our knowledge of this league is a bit rudimentary. We've been concerned with League One for three seasons - and that was, of course, where Sean managed before he took the job here. So we're going to have to learn – and learn fast. In the meantime, I'd like to defer to my old mate Neil Warnock, now at Crystal Palace, who confidently tells me that we'll be okay. But there again I'm too long in the tooth to ever take 'too good to go down' as gospel.

It might not seem amazing to followers of bigger clubs but I was thrilled with 8,000 season ticket holders. Again, it means we are among the sparsest supported sides at this level and that we'll have to work extremely hard to fill our 15,000-capacity Keepmoat, except for the most attractive of visitors. Yet all things are relative and you have to remember the progress we've already made. The season ticket figure is the highest in our history and a full 3,000 up on last term. We've started to turn Doncaster red and white again and turn the Leeds United invasion back at our borders. Gone are the days when I drove into Doncaster and could have been forgiven for thinking that I was on my way to Elland Road. So much water has passed under the bridge at both clubs in recent seasons. I recall some friendly banter with Leeds fans who recognised me at an airport this summer and talked about the play-off final. We are in the Championship now and Ken Bates and co are in League One – life can't be bad!

I enjoyed a summer holiday in Miami – although June seems a long time ago now – and watched a fair bit of English cricket. Even as a Yorkshire supporter, I was relieved when Michael Vaughan stood down as the England skipper. He has been living on his past reputation batting-wise and, sadly, no longer seems to be worthy of his own place in the team. For some time, I'd been secretly advocating that Kevin Pietersen, a good friend of mine, would make a very good skipper and was delighted at his appointment to take charge in time for the last Test of a losing summer against South Africa. I first met KP a few years ago when he was at the same event as Paul Collingwood, the England and Durham batsman, whom I also know very well. I immediately took to him because, quite apart from his outrageous personal talent, he is a man of vision and drive – the ideal captain in my view.

Anyway, enough of all that, this is no longer cricket but time for the beautiful game to take over. Let the talking and speculation subside and the football begin. I feel like a born again teenager.

Derby County 0 Doncaster Rovers 1, Saturday 9 August

EVER wondered whether that cranky old fixture computer, with its nasty habit of sending you to the back of beyond on a freezing Tuesday night, has some well-disguised sense of humour? How else could you explain John Ryan opening his Championship account with a 'double D' clash at Derby County? Only a joke, of course and not even my own, but the comments of the Radio Five Live commentator go down well when we get the privilege of being the commentary match on a day when the Premiership stars are still in mothballs. More relevant, of course, is that this means an instant reunion with Paul Green. My initial anger is beginning to subside A LITTLE by now, although I still wish he was playing in our shirt this afternoon.

There is more than a bit of *déjà vu* about the whole occasion. As 3pm approaches, eager anticipation turns into a few fluttering butterflies in my stomach. I don't normally get too nervous at football matches, but this is a big occasion for us. I think back to Leyton Orient and our first match back in the Football League a few years ago. There we were back in the 'big time' and expected by many of the neutral public to get a bit of a thumping. We won 3-1 that glorious, boiling hot afternoon and it set the tone for the whole season. The weather is also pretty kind today and I'm quietly confident that the gulf between the two clubs, who have been light years apart until recently, has now totally disappeared.

Derby created records in the Premiership, but none that they'd care to remember – fewest wins, hardly any goals, a handful of points. I have plenty of time for their chairman Adam Pearson but, as I glance across to him, I'm glad I'm not in his seat today. There's a sense of a complete new start at Pride Park and who knows when or even if the various pieces will fit together? In contrast, we're a settled enough side – I could have picked nine of the players myself without fear of contradiction – and our style of football is equally well established under professor Sean. There's a crowd of around 33,000, including a healthy section from Donny, and looking around I've got to say that Pride Park is absolutely superb – a real credit to Adam Pearson and co. I have an interesting conversation with Greenie in the tunnel. I tell him that I wish him well generally, but he's going to be on a loser today.

The opening skirmishes are even and my stomach starts to settle a little before one incident gets me up off my seat in exasperation. Derby forward Rob Hulse clearly handles the ball as a cross comes into our penalty area and deflects the ball onto our post. But no free-kick is given. It would have been 1-0 to the home side and our protests would have fallen on deaf ears. Equally alarmingly, in my view, Lewis Guy is brought down in the penalty area by Alan Stubbs, the former Celtic and Everton defender, but Andy D'Urso waves play on. I reflect on certain conversations I had in the summer – here's the first evidence that, as a comparatively small club, we are likely to be on the receiving end decisions-wise in the Championship. I play back the incidents endlessly afterwards when I watch the highlights on ITV and my suspicions are totally confirmed. Here comes my first letter of the season to David Allison... The match turns out, by the way, to be Stubbs' last in professional football as he is retiring through injury. He hasn't always had the best of good fortune in the game, particularly health-wise, so I wish him all the best for the future.

On the plus side, I like the way our clever forward Lewis Guy gets into space and creates a couple of half-chances. Just before the hour, I'm up from my seat again – this time in joy. Guy has sneaked unguarded into their penalty area for the umpteenth time and finished off a quickly-taken free-kick. Derby County 0, Doncaster Rovers 1 – we're back in dream land again.

The next half hour is nothing like what I expect. I thought Derby would throw the kitchen sink at us – but obviously that's one thing they've forgotten to buy in the summer. Instead we pass the ball around confidently to the delight of a large Rovers contingent and the dismay and despair of the rest of a packed Pride Park. The final whistle goes – we've won! I feel totally ecstatic; we could not have asked for a better start. I catch a glimpse of the Derby chairman and, half jokingly, ask whether we can take Greenie back on loan. The look on his face suggests he has more urgent things on his mind.

Notts County 1 Doncaster Rovers 0,
Carling Cup first round , Tuesday 12 August

SEEMS strange after the high excitement of our League Cup run a couple of years ago, but this competition is not at the top of our current agenda. Having said that and appreciating the fact that Sean will take the chance to field some of the lads who didn't make Saturday's starting line-up, I firmly expect us to beat Notts County. After all, most clubs have in recent years.

The last decade hasn't been a happy one for Nottinghamshire football - and that's an under-statement. Driving into Meadow Lane, I instantly feel that this is a

League One ground at the very least, yet manager 'Charlie' McParland was struggling to keep the Magpies in the Football League at the same time as we were aiming for promotion to the Championship. In the end, they just managed to edge clear of their neighbours Mansfield Town, who are now beginning life in the Blue Square Premier.

The plight of the Stags brings back some chilling memories of Donny at our lowest ebb. Booted out of the Football League; fans trying desperately to get rid of a chairman whom they see as being the root of all their ills; and having to start almost from scratch with a new manager and a totally new team. Only two years ago we were delighted to get a last-minute goal to stay in the FA Cup at Field Mill when the protests against chairman Keith Haslam were beginning. How quickly things change – now there are three divisions between us. Just before the season started, I did an interview with the *Non-League Paper* comparing our two clubs and wishing Mansfield Town well.

I can't help but notice the floodlights of their neighbours, Nottingham Forest. How will they fare this season after taking the often underestimated step up from League One? I note they've spent £2m or more on Rob Earnshaw from Derby, and another million on Joe Garner from Carlisle, a lad I quite like. It's alright for some, Nigel Doughty, but will you finish higher than us?

I won't waste too much time on the 120 minutes that follow – they weren't really worth watching to be honest. If ever a game had 0-0 stamped on it, this was the one. We have all of the ball, Notts defend in depth – the night drags on and on. Gareth Roberts clubs a shot against the bar after about 20 minutes, but generally our shots are coming from distance and not worrying their experienced goalkeeper Kevin Pilkington. Paul Heffernan obviously would love to score against his old mates, but his shot goes wide and the stalemate continues. Extra-time begins and my mind is already straying to whom is likely to take our penalties. But, then, a night of unending frustration takes a step for the worse as the Magpies' lively sub Myles Weston plays a one-two on the edge of our box and finishes well to put the home side in front. The blow comes one minute into the second period of extra-time and we don't look like equalising in the minutes that remain.

Was it any consolation that it was 'only' the League Cup? I'd be a liar, if I said that's how I'm feeling as I inch my way back to Cheshire. Nobody likes getting beaten and you can put me at the head of that queue. But, yes, if pushed, I'd rather go out of this competition tonight than lose three points in the Championship - oops, I'm beginning to sound like a Premiership chairman already.

Doncaster Rovers 1 Cardiff City 1, Saturday 16 August

A MIDWEEK defeat leaves me looking forward even more to the weekend - and our first Championship match on home soil at the Keepmoat. This is, after all, what it has all been about, bringing Championship football back home to Doncaster and it will be interesting to see how our fans react. It was a difficult task to gauge our likely home attendances before a ball was kicked, but it's not really much of a surprise when I check in the days leading up to this one and discover that a sell-out is very unlikely.

In the event we are more than 3,000 short with a crowd of 11,874 welcoming the players for the first match at this level for 50 years - and, with Cardiff being well supported, 2,200 of those have made the 200-mile plus trip from South Wales too. Am I disappointed? My cautious answer has to be yes, but you won't find me being scathing about Donny fans whom, in many ways, have been among the most loyal in the business.

Going back to the last time these two sides met in 1997 there were just 1,004 fans at Belle Vue for the League Two fixture - a game, by the way, that ended in a 1-1 draw. We've got eleven times that number today and are more than grateful for it. To get the Keepmoat swinging from the rafters we are going to have to play the kind of football that keeps this dream moving forward.

Today is a good test of our new-found credentials on the pitch. The Bluebirds were one of the teams of last season - a campaign when so many dreams seemed to come true. From the unlikely beginnings of a nothing-to-gain third-round tie at Chasetown in Staffordshire - a team in the Midland Division of the Southern League and creating their moment of history by reaching that stage, Cardiff had then flown all the way to Wembley, making themselves popular with Donny fans in the semi-final by ending Barnsley's fantastic run that had taken them past giants Chelsea and Liverpool. Today therefore sees a return to Yorkshire for Peter Ridsdale, the former Leeds and Barnsley chief, who is now their chairman. He's a man who has his critics, particularly after Leeds hit the financial rocks so spectacularly, yet personally I've found him very likeable.

The game itself simply can't live up to the hype and is a fairly quiet affair, at least as far as clear-cut chances are concerned. Rovers fans sing 'Play up Pompey' to remind our visitors of their 1-0 FA Cup final defeat to Harry Redknapp's lot but, generally, the atmosphere is a bit muted. Half-time comes and goes with barely a sniff of a goal, but it's better after the break - and there's something for the Rovers fans to cheer. A hundred or more intricate passing moves may have failed, but a route-one ball from Matty Mills does the trick. Lewis is the prize Guy again as he races down the middle to smash the ball joyfully into the Cardiff net.

There's just over 20 minutes left and I've got visions of

looking at the TV in the directors' lounge and seeing Donny Rovers at the top. Certainly, there's reason for optimism because we now seem very comfortable even after Cardiff boss Dave Jones switches to 4-3-3 in a late bid to get something from what seems like a pointless afternoon. The clock ticks uneventfully onto 88 but then there's an unlikely - and totally farcical - sting in the tail. Mark Halsey is one of my favourite referees, but on this occasion he inadvertently does the visitors a favour. A pass from one of the Donny players clips him on the back of the heel and sets the Bluebirds on the attack. Until now, we have been calmness personified at the back but, for some reason, goalkeeper Neil Sullivan and defender Adam Lockwood get into an almost comical tangle going for a routine long ball. Jay Bothroyd joins in the fun by miskicking but there's Ross McCormack, of all people, to roll in the equaliser. Three seasons ago he spent some time with Rovers on loan, today he is the man who has prevented us from starting our campaign with successive league wins. That's football. A draw against the FA Cup finalists doesn't look too bad on paper, but just at this moment feels like a kick in the proverbial teeth. Time on the way home to remember that my glass is of the half-full variety, methinks. Anyway, four points out of six ain't that bad.

Queens Park Rangers 2 Doncaster Rovers 0,
Saturday 23 August

THE strangest things remind you of how far we have travelled... today it was some of the familiar roads on the journey south towards London. How easy it would be to take the road off towards the likes of Woking and Kingstonian, whom we visited in the Conference. Or, for that matter, set the sat nav for Leyton Orient, Brentford or even Millwall.

But, no, this time we're playing at Queens Park Rangers, one of the richest clubs on this planet no less. It's our first match at Loftus Road for 50 years, so we might as well enjoy it folks. I remember saying at the beginning of last season that the era of multi-millionaires bankrolling Premiership clubs was virtually at an end - they have been putting a few extra zeros at the end of their cheques for a few years now. But today we're on Billionaire's Row in the Championship. First lightning bolt was the sudden appearance of Formula One giants Bernie Ecclestone and Flavio Briatore on the scene. Strong rumour has it that they'd have liked to have put their stake in Chelsea, Arsenal or Roma before settling, if that's the right word, for comparatively mundane QPR. Then, if that's not enough, along comes steel baron Lakshmi Mittal, labelled as the fifth richest man in the world with an estimated fortune of £20 billion. So, from counting the pennies, it's suddenly loadsamoney time at Shepherd's Bush. Will the real folk that matter, those supporters who have gone through hoops for this club, really get a better deal now they have big names and big egos in their engine room? It will be interesting to see...

The aim today is to give Rangers something to think about. If we can keep the home team at bay for a while, the patience of fans expecting their side to go from zero to hero status straightaway may wear thin. Instead we give away a terrible goal after barely five minutes. On-loan Real Madrid lad Daniel Parejo lifts a routine free-kick into our box and there are no Spanish eyes or even English ones on Dexter Blackstock, unmarked in the six-yard area, who supplies the simple finish. That gives Rangers the lift they want and the afternoon takes on a sombre look just before the half-hour. Sully again looks like he has run out of friends as we suddenly have no defence to a long ball through the middle. This time Emmanuel Ledesma, a 19-year-old Argentinian, does the rest, with the aid of a fairly blatant handball, I have to add.

For a few minutes I fear the worst as Sully saves well from Damion Stewart's header and keeps out Ledesma's bicycle-kick. Then, thankfully, the siege is lifted and a strange form of slow death takes over. They don't look like scoring again but, more critically, neither do we. A James Coppinger shot that goes just wide is the closest we come as we go down to our first defeat of the league season. To add to our collective pain, defender Matty Mills, already looking a find, goes home with a broken jaw. Not a good day at the office, even if it was a luxurious one.

Would I swap places with QPR? Not an earthly. I read a rather amusing article in *The Sun* after the game that compares my expectations for Sean and my lads to those that QPR's mega-rich backers must be loading on Iain Dowie. No, I can't promise we'll finish above Rangers this season, but I will guarantee this - we'll make more friends than they will and we'll show Rangers some good traditional Yorkshire hospitality after Christmas.

Doncaster Rovers 1 Coventry City 0, Saturday 30 August

TODAY represents yet another early landmark in this adventure playground of a season. It's years and years since we've faced Coventry City, a club who seemed to be perennial survivors in the top league until finally giving in to gravity a few seasons back. I may have been sent to Coventry a few times in my life, but I can't recall us ever playing them.

Since dropping back down to earth, the Sky Blues have got a spanking new ground, the Ricoh Arena, but enjoyed precious little, if any, success on the pitch. Instead they've been shedding managers like there's no tomorrow - and that's always a sign of problems. It's too early to know what to expect from Chris Coleman's side this season, of course, but today should provide us with a clue or two. Young Coleman did a great job at Fulham, so I hope he gets a fair crack of the whip in the Midlands.

Interesting, too, to see the crowd is 11,804 - almost exactly the same as our first home game against Cardiff and therefore a reasonably accurate estimate of our support. Even selling out the Keepmoat for every game wouldn't guarantee us breaking even - but it's in our interests to get as close to that as we can.

There's plenty of pleasing-on-the-eye possession football in the early stages today, but not many incidents to get me off my seat. That is, until, Richie Wellens produces a moment of outstanding quality on the half-hour. I defy any Rovers fan to stay on their backside as a 25-yard rocket lands in the top corner of Keiren Westwood's net. How I love Richie Wellens! Always rated him while he was at Oldham, but Sean, being a southerner, hadn't seen so much of him. But now he wouldn't want to be without the man.

Back to the match and 'Copps' misses a chance to add a quick second before Coventry reply with a flurry of late first-half corners. But there's little for the visiting fans to cheer - or yours truly to worry about - after the break as Rovers stack up the chances. Lewis Guy, Gareth Taylor, James Hayter and Adam Lockwood should all have scored. On another day no doubt they would have done. Football's a fickle game and we would all be rueing those misses now had City been a little slicker and nicked an equaliser. But, trust me, that wouldn't have happened if we'd played until midnight. Our defence is looking good at the moment and there are no late dramas from Sully and co this time.

I make my way back to the directors' lounge well satisfied. It's a case of smiling faces all round as we raise our glasses to seven points from four matches and a position just outside the top six. Here's to the international break!

Birmingham City 1 Doncaster Rovers 0, Saturday 13 September

WE'VE had two weeks to wait for this one - although that's not long when you think we've spent precisely 53 years trying to catch up with the likes of today's hosts. One of the side-effects of promotion is that we're more subject to the eccentricities of 'international breaks' than we were in League One. Most matches in the latter league go ahead unless any team has too many players called up for the various squads, but there is no programme at all in the top two leagues. Just seems so frustrating that when we've barely started, we have a two-week lay-off. At least it's given us plenty of time to soak up the joy of a healthy looking league position.

Nearest we got to the internationals was watching England on TV, not too exciting a prospect it has to be said, although Fabio Capello is beginning to turn things round. Then there's a practice game against our friends from Darlington. We win 7-0 behind closed doors with Jason Price making a welcome return from injury with a couple of goals. Wonder what Dave Penney made of that?

There's a sense of real sadness among the players, however, as they are trying to come to terms with some very bad news. John Dodsworth, who has been our main driver for several years, has just passed away. He was a friendly character who enjoyed a good relationship with the players and they are clearly shaken by the news, as are Rovers officials. Happily, we believe that John's son will take over and that our link with the company will continue but, for now, it is little consolation.

Birmingham have gone close to establishing themselves

in the Premiership in recent seasons, but here they are back in the second flight once again under the stewardship of Alex McLeish. Mind you, St Andrews has most of the marks of a top stadium and is another indication, should we need it, of just how far we have come at Rovers. The occasion gives me the chance to meet up again with a couple of good friends in David Gold and David Sullivan, who have long since been driving forces behind the Blues.

There's no sign of any inferiority complex when the game kicks off - but plenty of what we might be up against this term. I get out of my seat for three cast-iron penalty kicks in my view - none of which are given. I'll certainly be looking closely at the DVD after this one. The game appears to be turning in our favour in the 24th minute when Birmingham's Mehdi Nafti is sent off for a crude two-footed lunge at James Coppinger. But nothing is simple in football and ten men can often be as difficult to break down as eleven. Teams normally just withdraw a striker and can galvanise themselves, particularly if they think they have been victims of an injustice. The other injustice of the half, however, is that somehow the teams go in level. Goalkeeper Martin Taylor produces a string of saves to keep us out. The home crowd boo Birmingham off at half-time and we have reason to think we're in the box seat.

But it takes just a few seconds after the resumption to prove me wrong. It's route one stuff and Cameron Jerome produces the finish to put the home side in front. They then have a short spell of pressure before normal service is resumed. We knock the ball around like Arsenal and have Brum anxiously on the back foot. Darren Byfield lets fly with a scorcher only for that man Taylor to tip it onto a post. The final whistle goes and we're left scratching our heads.

Karren Brady writes afterwards that we were one of the best footballing teams to visit St Andrews in 2008 - not bad that when you consider they were on the same field as Manchester United and Chelsea a few months ago. But compliments don't bring points - and without points, there's no chance of prizes.

Doncaster Rovers 0 Charlton Athletic 1, Tuesday 16 September

HAVING looked at the DVD from Saturday, my views on the main incidents from St Andrews are unchanged. In short, I think we should have had not one, not two, but THREE penalty-kicks. But what did we get? Not a sausage. I send off a complaint to referees official David Allison about the refereeing of Gavin Ward. Personally, I don't think he was up to officiating at this level.

Yet if Saturday was daylight robbery, this was living proof about the thief in the night. What's that old saying about a boxing match? If matches were decided by possession and shots, this one would have been stopped at half-time and Rovers declared the winners. Yet you can batter a team for almost all the 90 minutes - and that we surely did - and still get beaten in this weird and wonderful game of ours.

I was really pleased we had a match so quickly after the Birmingham trip to get some of that frustration out of our systems – but this was much, much more painful...Gareth Taylor and Lewis Guy nearly scored inside the first minute, then in the third came what turned out to be the tamest of killer blows. Jonathan Fortune lumped a harmless-looking free-kick forward and Andy Gray looped a header over Neil Sullivan. There's no doubt we're a bit weak at defending set-pieces at the moment.

The rest of the night sees us launch wave after wave of attack at Nicky Weaver's goal. Credit to the goalkeeper, the lad saved everything thrown in his direction. But this was the kind of night where if we'd got one goal, we might well have ended up with six. Okay, we weren't creating clear-cut opportunities with every attack, but you'd think we'd get a break somewhere along the line. Instead it's a long tale of blocked shots, last-gasp clearances and 'if onlys' in the London side's penalty area.

I tell you what the Addicks offered - virtually nothing. Alan Pardew's going home with three points tonight, but I wouldn't be too sure about his side's prospects.

Bristol City 4 Doncaster Rovers 1, Saturday 20 September

THERE are occasions when you genuinely wonder how level this football playing field really is. I've spent time on the phone this week talking with Mark Halsey, a referee I genuinely admire. On Saturday he sent off the Chelsea and England skipper John Terry during their 3-1 win at Manchester City. These days, of course, you can look at incidents like this at your leisure on TV - it was a justifiable decision. Terry was the last man, but was surely dismissed for the nature of the foul itself.

But now we have an incredible furore going on and I can't help but ponder whether there would be this amount of fuss if one of our own Rovers players had been the man in the dock rather than our national captain and one of the highest paid stars in the Premiership firmament.

Halsey is clearly shaken by the hostility aimed in his direction and I assure him of my support. I phone up the *Yorkshire Post* and they air my views about the controversy. Part of the reason for the hysteria is that Chelsea are due to host the other Manchester lot on Saturday and they'd much rather have Terry keeping an eye on United's finest. The 'experts' predict Terry's appeal is doomed early in the week but come the announcement on Wednesday and you've guessed it - Terry and Chelsea are off the hook and Halsey is

Above: Time stands still as 'Sir' Francis Tierney prepares to strike our golden goal against Dagenham and Redbridge.

Above: Me pictured with our dynamic duo of Mickey Walker and Dave Penney.

Above: Yours truly pictured with my daughter Gemma and Michael McIndoe, who joined Rovers after a 'private' chat!

Above: Our new Keepmoat Stadium – a magnificent sight.

Above: Richie Wellens and Darren Fletcher during our prestigious friendly with European champions Manchester United.

Above: Skipper Graeme Lee heads our winner in a rollercoaster Johnstone's Paint Trophy final against Bristol Rovers at the Millennium Stadium, Cardiff.

Above: We've done it! Celebration time with my wife, Lynne.

Above: Rovers' match-winner James Hayter wheels away to celebrate as we defeat Leeds United at Wembley. *Photo: Philip Ryan*

Above: Our joy bubbleth over: In the firing line after the Wembley victory over Leeds.

Above: Pick that one out! Spot-on on my very own football pitch.
Picture: Mark Robinson, The Sun.

Above: Our big day - getting married to the love-of-my-life Lynne.

Above: Lynne and I relax at home in Cheshire.

Above: With fellow Musketeers Dick Watson (*left*), Terry Bramall and my good friend Neil Warnock.

Below: A touching moment with Manchester United boss Sir Alex Ferguson, who presented us with a gift to mark the opening of the Keepmoat Stadium.

Pictured: Views of home. *Above*: Centuryan House, which I had built 12 years ago in Cheshire.

Above: My property by the sea in beautiful Cape Town, South Africa.

seemingly hung out to dry. Needless to say, I am more disappointed than surprised. When first appointed into his position at the FA, I thought Lord Triesman could be a breath of fresh air. But this week's experience has left me far from sure. I try to contact him to let him have the benefit of my views, but despite his PA saying he would get back to me, I hear no more about it. It's fairly easy to brush off the chairman of a club like Doncaster Rovers, methinks.

Anyway, back to the real football world. You know that when you're down you can rely on an old friend – to kick you in the teeth. Michael McIndoe was the darling of Belle Vue as we stormed to the League Three title, then took on the high and mighty during our Carling Cup run. There's been a fair bit of water under the bridge since then and, after a temporary move to Derby and spells at Barnsley and Wolves, he pops up in opposition to us for the first time this afternoon, playing for Bristol City.

And, you've guessed it, he has a big say in what turns out to be our biggest defeat of the season to date.

Again, we are well in the game during an entertaining, but ultimately scoreless, first 45 minutes. Lewis Guy goes closest to providing us with an interval lead with a shot that sails inches wide and he gives Bradley Orr such a going over on the flank that City take him off at half-time. So now, without their regular penalty taker, it is McIndoe who steps up two minutes into the second half to give City the vital breakthrough from the spot. I often complain about penalties – have you noticed? – but not this time as Sullivan clearly bundled over Nicky Maynard.

Credit Bristol for the way they turn the screw. Two more goals fly past Sullivan within the next 15 minutes and that, to all intents and purposes, is it. But there's time for a Richie Wellens special – a spectacular blast from just inside the box – and for McIndoe to add a second to give the scoreline an unflattering look from our point of view. The league table's not looking very flattering either – we need to get ourselves moving again soon.

Doncaster Rovers 0 Southampton 2, Saturday 27 September

I strongly fancied us to beat Southampton. The mega problems off the pitch at St Mary's are well documented and the Saints have made a poor start, fuelling concern they will end up in the relegation mix. After three defeats on the spin, this would be a good time to get lucky – or so I wish.

When things aren't going for you, you can even find new and unlikely ways to lose. On this occasion an own-goal and a penalty do the damage, much of it self-inflicted. We had our chances early on. Jason Price shoots straight at Kelvin Davis and Darren Byfield gives the Saints goalkeeper a better test of his undoubted athleticism with a header.

But we just can't seem to get in front at the moment and when the opening goal comes, it's at the wrong end. Former Saint Matty Mills turns sinner by turning a shot from David McGoldrick into his own net midway through the first half. Don't talk to me about penalties – Wellens is very harshly adjudged to have brought down Adam Lallana eight minutes later and Andrew Surman knocks in the spot-kick. A bad day at the office could easily have got even worse when the referee again pointed to the spot ten minutes from time. But this time Sully makes the save. Ironic isn't it? Having been denied stonewall spot-kicks at both Derby County and Birmingham City, here we are being penalised twice on our own pitch.

Maybe I'm a little bitter because for the second time in successive Keepmoat matches, a poor side has left with all three points.

Doncaster Rovers 0 Sheffield United 2, Tuesday 30 September

AS I've said before, I've got plenty of time for Sheffield United; the Blades' visit here was one of the first fixtures I looked out for when the list came out. It will ensure a good gate at the Keepmoat, be nice to meet up with some good friends and colleagues and, fingers crossed, could be the ideal way of breaking our recent bad run.

Radio Sheffield are making the most of it and I happily do a pre-match interview expressing my positive feelings towards United – yet stating my confidence we'll do well tonight. There's confusion before the start when midfielder Brian Howard is named as one of United's substitutes only for the Blades to change their minds and give Nathan Dyer the shirt instead. Apparently, Howard's loan move from Barnsley hadn't yet gone through.

The night starts promisingly with us having far more of the ball and pouring enthusiastically towards Paddy Kenney's goal. Sean's made a few changes with defender Sam Hird and striker Lewis Guy out and Adam Lockwood, Martin Woods and Mark Wilson making their first starts of the season. Copps isn't playing – he's unwell. But it's the same old pattern with Darren Byfield shooting inches over the bar before we score in our own net for the second successive home game when Gareth Roberts turns in a shot from Danny Webber.

We now crank up the pressure to fever pitch – Adam Lockwood's header is saved, Stockie hits the bar with a thunderbolt and Jason Price misses a great chance from the rebound. We all have our views on Jason and I love him to bits. He's one of the nicest lads you could wish to meet and did extremely well for us in League One. But can he score goals for us in the Championship? I sincerely hope so, but the jury's out, as they say.

An interesting fleeting thought – where would we be in the league if James Beattie and Billy Sharp were in our side? But this is the real world… The pattern continues after the break and I still think we can get back into this. But then the Blades hit us on the break; Beattie slides a ball through to James Quinn and it's goodnight Rovers.

Defeat is not easy to take when you've actually played very well and that was the case against the Blades. Kevin Blackwell trots out the usual line of a professional job well done – football-speak when an apparently bigger club gets the rub of the green. Truth was we could have been out of sight by half-time tonight.

Barnsley 4 Doncaster Rovers 1, Saturday 4 October

WE said we'd give it ten games and see where we were going and there were meetings with Sean and Richard before the trip to our South Yorkshire rivals. It's difficult to believe it, but I heard one fan on Radio Sheffield actually liken the current goal famine to our *annus horribilis* of 1998. Come on, mate, smell the coffee! But there is plenty of support from the fans for Sean too. The majority, I say, realise we are not a big club at this level and the Championship takes some adjusting to. Also, we are playing far better than our bleak results suggest.

Chairmen pull the trigger far too early and far too often and that's not on the cards. Not at all. I convince myself we're going to beat Barnsley. After all, we ALWAYS beat Barnsley. The other season we smacked them twice in League One and scored five with a reserve side at Oakwell in what is now the Johnstone's Paint Trophy. Just three reasons they don't seem to like us.

All we need, I tell myself, is to get the opening goal, then our patient, possession football will come into its own. I take my seat at Oakwell confident, but wary. The pre-match talk is that Barnsley boss Simon Davey is walking the tight rope – how ridiculous. You often don't know whether these things are actually true, but the word is that the Tykes boss will get the boot if they lose to us today. And, yes, this is the same bloke who guided them to safety from a perilous position two seasons ago and took them to the FA Cup semi-final, beating Liverpool and Chelsea a few short months ago. Not only is this a cruel game sometimes, it can be downright nasty. I've been treated to a fair amount of abuse at Oakwell in the past and a Barnsley fan says on the radio phone-in that he hopes they can knock that horrible smile off my face. Smiling costs nothing and I'll apologise to no-one for it.

Anyway, I've reason to smile as we score after just eleven minutes. Still we can't get a striker on the scoresheet, but Brian Stock's penalty is more than welcome. We proceed to dominate the first half as the venom aimed at the Barnsley manager reaches unacceptable proportions. Still, the consolation is, this must be working in our favour and we need the points just as badly.

Five minutes after the interval comes what well-spoken managers these days call a 'defining moment' – and it should, in theory, be in our favour. Lewis Guy is sent through the middle and our former war horse Darren Moore hauls him down. No one wants to see a true pro like Darren get his marching orders and I would have preferred to see Guy get his chance. There's more than a hint that 2-0 would have shattered the home side's fragile confidence.

Chants of 'We want Davey out' are raining down from the stands and history looks likely to repeat itself. We've not lost this fixture for 29 years and don't look like getting beaten today. But then Stephen Foster thumps home a header and it puts a few doubts in my own mind. Surely, we're not going to throw it all away against ten men?

There then comes the sort of moment that either has you dancing in the aisles or tearing your hair out – depending which team you're backing. Jamaican international Jamal Campbell-Ryce drifts past two tackles – or should I say non-tackles – and releases a shot from just outside the box that Sully would save nine times out of ten. Instead it creeps into the corner and we're 2-1 down. Mickey Walker talks about our heads going down and he's right. Our lads look stunned, they don't know what's hit them. Oakwell's suddenly a different place. Davey gets a pat on the back from Jon Macken after the substitute bangs home number three and then Iain Hume smashes another bolt from the blue high into our net for an unlikely fourth. The late introduction of substitute Reuben Noble-Lazarus, already the youngest player in Football League history after his midweek appearance at Ipswich, completed the home celebrations.

I'm not so much dazed, more raw with anger. I usually try to bite my tongue and keep a perspective on things, but today I just can't manage it. I pour out my morbid thoughts to a *Yorkshire Post* journalist, saying that I'm thinking of resigning because I've taken the club as far as I can. At the time I mean it – every word. It's the fan in me raising his voice again.

Back home, I carry out some personal soul-searching. Worried Donny officials want to know whether I was quoted correctly and indeed I was. But, having slept on it, I reassure them that I have no intention of going. In turn, the support I receive from them is great to hear at such a crucial time. I honestly believe that John Ryan has more to offer my club – if, in my heart of hearts I'd thought otherwise, I would have quit there and then. No doubt about it, this weekend will prove a watershed in my personal season.

Doncaster Rovers 0 Blackpool 0, Saturday 18 October

PERHAPS this international break was good news for Donny. It has given a few of us time to reflect and regain a sense of perspective on what has happened so far. Yes, we need to improve but, on the other hand, have much reason to believe that will happen. Even our most vehement accusers would probably agree that our points total to date has not flattered our performances.

It's looking good for England as they predictably thrash Kazakhstan 5-1 on the Saturday, before earning a much tougher three points on the road to South Africa with a 3-1 success at Belarus in midweek. You'll have to forgive me but just at the moment I'm not too worried about England. I suppose it's a mixture of the continual disappointments over recent years and the way the team has been run under successive managers.

We've been hit for six - literally. We've been unable to turn possession into goals and when we've made mistakes at the back, we've been ruthlessly punished. Today's visitors Blackpool provide us with a good example of what we need to achieve. Promoted through the League One play-offs after a fantastic run, they battled tooth and nail to stay clear of trouble in the Championship last term - and they managed it. What a brilliant job Simon Grayson has done beside the seaside. I'm delighted for them as they are a small and friendly club - just hope we can put one over on them this afternoon.

The first half is a carbon copy of much of the season so far. We're well on top, but simply can't get the goal we need. Jason Price runs his heart out up front, yet is symbolic of what I'm beginning to think. Perhaps the move up from League One is too much for some of our lads - the style of football is fine, but perhaps it's the pieces in the jigsaw that no longer fit.

Well organised and resilient, Blackpool make a better fist of it after the break when the play is far more even. Steve Kabba, the former Blade, goes close a couple of times and there's a serious appeal for a spot-kick in our box - well, we're due a penalty decision in our favour. Then, with the game meandering towards a seemingly inevitable 0-0 draw, comes a furious finish. Martin Woods hits a great shot from 25 yards that smashes against the woodwork - just inches away from turning an average day into a special one. Then James Hayter goes through with seconds left, but the Blackpool goalkeeper saves with his legs. Possibly the two highlights of the whole afternoon have been squeezed into those last couple of minutes and provide us with more to discuss as we go back into the boardroom.

It may still be early in the season, but already the results from other games are relevant. Forest's 2-1 defeat at QPR – their sixth successive reverse on the road – at least saves us from being bottom of the Championship.

Reading 2 Doncaster Rovers 1, Tuesday 21 October

THERE's nothing like a football fan for optimism. Here we are near the bottom of the Championship, without a win in our last seven games, travelling to face a side I think could be the best in our division. And on top of that, the home side have a 100 per cent record in their own stadium. Reading were a touch unlucky not to stay in the top flight last term and have a great manager in Steve Coppell who plays the game the right way. Yet stopping off in the motorway services as I travel down to the game with Dave Parker, I enjoy some great banter with Rovers fans and honestly think this might be our night.

Usually when you're struggling you might want to duck and dive from the fans - but that's not the case here. They're great people with Donny Rovers in their hearts, and they know I'm just as desperate for things to turn as they are. It reminds me just how worthwhile this job is - I'm chairman of a club that many folk hold dear and if we can do anything to make their lives more enjoyable that can't be a bad thing, can it?

One of the first things that impresses me about Reading is a tremendous friendly welcome to what is a fantastic stadium. Steve Uttley, our media manager, says afterwards it almost reminds him of the Keepmoat in that the media are treated really well and not with the cold suspicion that sometimes happens at other grounds.

The match itself gets underway and I'm quickly reminded that, football-wise, we have every right to be here. Sean, who has pretty well stuck to his guns so far, makes no fewer than five changes and switches to a 4-4-2 formation to try to shore things up a bit. I'm pleased to see the Dutchman Jos van Nieuwstadt making his league debut in defence. I must admit I liked the look of him when we played Newcastle in a pre-season friendly and I'm surprised he hasn't featured before now. But that's all healthy stuff - I've got my opinions just like any other fan and Sean shouldn't take too much notice - and he doesn't.

Talking about Steve, I'll definitely be in touch with him to see the DVD after this one. Both Reading goals have me tearing my hair out in exasperation. The first is from a free-kick after 18 minutes that I am convinced is suspect. The tackle is regulation and surely not a foul and it's just our bad luck that André Bikey gets up to nod Stephen Hunt's kick past Neil Sullivan. We're suspect from set-pieces - that's granted - so we can do without the referee awarding our opponents gift free-kicks.

The game is generally well contested and is bound to win us some more favourable reports in the national press. We look just as likely to equalise as Reading do to add to their lead and I'm off my seat punching the air 16 minutes from time when that super Dutchman nods home a cross from Copps. Told you, Sean!

But there's barely a minute to enjoy the prospect of a great away point - and here's another variation on the officials' wall of shame. This time, there's no argument about the free-kick. But the DVD shows the ball being moved forward and re-angled to allow a more precise delivery for Kevin Doyle to head the winner. I just can't believe it. We've lost again when surely we deserved something from an enterprising display.

Norwich City 2 Doncaster Rovers 1, Saturday 25 October

LYNNE and I fly to South Africa the day after the Reading game. My wife has been looking forward to this break for months and I must admit I could do with some kind of rest. The last few weeks have been emotionally and physically draining, with virtually nothing to give us a lift. Being a football man, it's not going to be all enjoyment, of course. I'm acutely aware that there are a couple of very important games taking place in my absence.

Still not quite sure how my dear wife managed to whisk me away from a clash with our beloved Barnsley on Tuesday night, but first of all we've got Delia Smith's infinitely more homely Norwich City to deal with. Does anyone enjoy listening to their team on the radio or over the internet? I very much doubt it. It's just one of the hardships of being a true fan. If I wasn't listening (and kicking) every ball, what would I be doing instead? I'd only be imagining in my head every pass, tackle and shot until plucking up the courage to switch on and find out the real truth. The thing about a commentary is that you are often on the edge of your seat for little reason. Each and every time the commentator raises his voice you hope for the best - or fear the worst - and 99 times out of 100 it comes to nothing. It's like being on a rollercoaster with your eyes closed.

Today, as I settle down nervously in my apartment, there's not too much to raise the heartbeat in the opening 45 minutes. It sounds like a fairly average and evenly-matched game - what we'd expect really against a side that aren't too far ahead of us in the table. I allow myself the luxury of a cuppa to celebrate a scoreless first half - perhaps this is going to be our first away point since the opening day at Derby.

Thoughts of a draw suddenly go out of the window - the commentator virtually demands a penalty as Jason Price gets into a tangle with Dejan Stefanovic and it's given. I could see from here, ref, honestly! In my mind's eye, our great man stumbles into the penalty area and hits the deck like a drunken seaman. He can usually trip himself up - no slight on his character, but if you've seen Jason Price play very often, you'll know exactly what I mean. There's that usual heartstopping wait for 30 seconds or so whenever a penalty is about to be taken and suddenly 'it's in the back of the net! Stockie has made no mistake from the spot and we're in front. Instinctively I check my watch - a bit unnecessary really when we're here in a different time zone - but the commentator reminds us there are only 13 minutes left. Only 13 minutes.....the great Brian Clough said it only takes a second to score a goal, so there's plenty of time yet. But I'd imagine that the very least we'll get from here is a draw.

I'm counting down the minutes - ten, nine, eight... - has time ever moved so slowly? Well, apart from the last 20 minutes against Leeds, has time ever moved so slowly...? I can't believe it. The roar of the home crowd tells the tale a split-second before the commentary. Sammy Clingan has a shot charged down and it falls perfectly for Antoine Sibierski to nod beyond Sully. My disappointment is instant - it's like a stab in the heart. But at least we haven't lost. All points, particularly away from home, must be gratefully received I suppose.

But, no, this is too bad to be true, surely! The crowd's gone mad again and Leroy Lita has put Norwich ahead in injury-time. I picture Delia Smith clapping her hands in joy - she's a nice woman, but just now that's little consolation. A cuppa is no good, I'm going to need something stronger.

Doncaster Rovers 0 Barnsley 1, Tuesday 28 October

AM still in South Africa lapping up the sunshine, but dark thoughts are turning fast towards Barnsley. As a fan who knows his statistics, it's 40 long years since the Tykes have won at our place, so that's as good an omen as I can come up with. The bad news is that we are without both Richie Wellens and Brian Stock – and you don't have to be a detective to know how important that duo is to us. I get more and more hyped up as the day progresses and, by the time I settle down for the broadcast, I feel like I've played two or three matches myself.

Sounds as if we have made a bright enough start with Jason Price twice going close and Copps firing just wide. But that livewire Campbell-Ryce is buzzing and, as you can gather by now, an accident is always just around the corner. Just before half-time – and a soothing drink – comes a potential turning point of my evening. Jon Macken puts Barnsley into the lead and it's difficult to feel too optimistic. We haven't scored more than once in any game this term so far, so what Price a couple in the second half tonight? Just now, one would be nice.

Again, the best chances apparently fall to Jason and

again they don't end up in the back of the net. Poor lad, he's putting in a lot of effort this season, but just can't get that first goal. I look at my watch constantly as the minutes tick by. It's incredible how fast a game appears to go when you are losing. The final whistle sounds and we've lost – it's ten matches without a win now and, for the first time, we are rock bottom. Wish you were here? I bet you do but, right now, it's hard to enjoy my holiday as much as I'd like after a double setback.

Doncaster Rovers 0 Swansea City 0, Saturday 1 November

I HAVE heard so many accounts of the Norwich and Barnsley matches now, I honestly think I must have been there. Opinion is split between two camps at the moment. There are those who believe we're still playing genuinely well and that, almost by the law of averages, the goals and the points must follow eventually. Meanwhile the 'half-empty' merchants are trading on the idea that a natural goalscorer is the answer to our problems – but, without one, we'll probably go down.

I'm not a fence sitter, but I'm probably some way between the two. I've witnessed the quality of our football and find it hard to think there are 40-odd better teams in England than Donny Rovers. A quality forward would be beneficial but let's consider the practicalities. Virtually every club in the country is after a striker and how much would such a player cost, most particularly in terms of wages. The player I'd like to see at the Keepmoat is Dean Windass of Hull City. It's no secret really. The ever-green (or ever-grey!) player did so much to get the Tigers promoted, including the classic winning goal at Wembley, but now appears surplus to requirements at the KC. I can envisage him doing a job perhaps just behind the front men, giving us a better link between midfield and attack. But I'm not the coach and I'm not the manager and Sean will have his views.

What I won't do is completely go against the wage structure at this club on a whim and I know the manager is fully behind that policy. It's important that the club is financially viable, especially in days when the media is highlighting the effects of the credit crunch more and more. As far as I'm concerned, we go back to the dark days of 1998 over my dead body – and certainly not before.

My mind is now focused on Swansea City and, forgive me for saying it, but it's yet another difficult task. The Welsh side were outstanding in winning League One last season and have started much better than either ourselves or the other promoted side, Nottingham Forest. They play expansive, entertaining football – rather like ourselves – and although I'd like to forget it they thumped us 4-0 at the Keepmoat last season.

Confidence shows in the early stages as Swansea make a swift start. Not many sides have us chasing shadows on our own pitch. But, thankfully, we weather the early storm and start creating chances. Jason Price, inevitably, goes close to breaking his season-long duck. How appropriate it would be if he could bang one in against his former club. Time then appears to stand still as Lewis Guy is sent clean through the middle. This could scarcely have fallen to a better finisher (sorry, Jason!) and I'm convinced the net is about to bulge at last. But, no, he fires wildly wide and I hold my hands to my head in exasperation.

Cometh the hour, cometh Jason and another good effort that flashes just wide, but there's another massive moment to come. All seems innocent enough when Brian Stock goes off after 73 minutes – that was always likely to happen on his return from injury. But when James Hayter gets a push in a goalmouth scramble, where's our penalty taker when we need him? The task instead falls to Paul Heffernan, starved of first team opportunities so far and only on the pitch for a matter of minutes in place of Lewis Guy. Paul's a good finisher and I'm pretty confident as he steps up to take the spot-kick. But, unaccountably, he fluffs his effort and the Swansea goalkeeper could have put his cap on it, as the football proverb goes. Missed penalty? It feels more like a kick in the teeth. That gaffe was the difference between a great result and a merely reasonable one - not good enough to take us off the bottom. I feel for Paul as he trudges off disconsolately and I feel for all our fans.

Sheffield Wednesday 1 Doncaster Rovers 0, Saturday 8 November

NOW back in England and having some fun with Sky this week. They are following a football chairman preparing for the 'big match' and they've chosen me. They come to my home in Knutsford to do some filming. I show them my football memorabilia and chat to them about my life as a fan. They seem to be enjoying themselves. Then for some serious stuff. We go out onto my football pitch and I take a few penalties. I slot the first half-a-dozen away Ronaldo-style before finally missing the target. Wonder which one they'll use for the piece?

They want to know my thoughts for Hillsborough and I'm genuinely optimistic. I tell them that we're playing well – and the results will come. That's not spin, I honestly believe it. I begin the two-hour drive to Sheffield, such a familiar journey. Sad to say the famous old ground isn't in the best of states these days, but it's still quite a stadium and I've got the whiff of an exciting game in my nostrils. Wednesday aren't playing all that well at present and Brian Laws wants a result – but surely not as badly as we do. The rumours and counter-rumours of a takeover at Wednesday are rumbling on and on and there doesn't appear to be an end in sight. I could have told them months ago that Geoff Sheard didn't have any money.

You're not going to believe this, but we're by far the better side today. Sam Hird, Richie Wellens and Matty Mills all go agonisingly close in the opening stages as Wednesday struggle to live with us. Yes, there are chances for Wednesday, too, in what is turning out to be a thriller of a first half. Sully saves spectacularly from James O'Connor and more routinely from Leon Clarke and Marcus Tudgay before the inevitable happens - Clarke gives the home side a 43rd-minute lead.

I do a quick half-time interview in which I say that if we keep playing this way, I'm still confident we can get a good result. You could run that interview to cover virtually every game this season - except perhaps for QPR and a bad 20 minutes at Bristol City - and yet time after time we've left disappointed.

There are plenty of second-half chances as Hird again goes close and Sean sends on Lewis Guy and James Hayter to give us more pep up front. John Spicer is also unlucky before, with Wednesday fans biting their nails and wishing their lives away, Hayter fires in a low shot that is brilliantly tipped away by Lee Grant - the goalkeeper Owls fans have been complaining about recently.

So we've lost again - but it's difficult to be too down after seeing what I'd describe as a magnificent Donny Rovers performance. This was probably one of our best 90 minutes to date and Wednesday know they have been fortunate today, even though Lawsy points out that they had a few opportunities themselves.

Doncaster Rovers 1 Ipswich Town 0, Saturday 15 November

I'M beginning to see the Championship for what it is. We didn't know exactly what to expect before we kicked off and I can't say that the skill level has been out of our league. It's been the sheer pace and competitive nature of the games that has impressed me. Most games are extremely entertaining, even though there has been an obvious shortage of goals. Bystanders might think we're a dour side, trying to hang on for a point and getting beaten by the odd goal. But that's never been Donny Rovers' style in the last decade and it's no more the case now. We're playing the same possession football, taking the initiative against most of the teams we're facing.

What is obvious is that the defensive qualities of Championship teams are much higher than in League One. One criticism labelled at us in the division below was that, considering the territorial advantage and the sheer number of opportunities that we created, we didn't cash in royally enough. But that didn't really matter when we wasted a dozen openings yet still went away with a one or two-goal success. Now, it's comparatively harder to open sides up. Almost all our opponents have been extremely well organised and forcing chances from open play is no mean task. Add that to the undeniable fact that we have lacked the killer touch in front of goal when we have needed it.

It's good sometimes to have some more witnesses to what is going on - and that's one reason I'm delighted that this is our first match being screened live on Sky TV this term. A wider audience should be treated to a genuinely good game of football because Ipswich have a similarly good reputation to ourselves. It kicks off at 5.25pm by which time all the other sides around us in the table have played their games and the need for points is even more obvious.

Heffs, one of the forward lads still searching for his first goal this season, sees an angled shot deflected agonisingly wide as early as the fourth minute. The fans have different views on Heffs, undeniably one of our top marksmen in recent seasons. For whatever reason, he didn't quite look himself early in the campaign and there had been talk of a loan move that might provide us with room to bring in another striker. But that hasn't happened and he could still be a Donny hero if he can just find his radar tonight.

The crowd have an obvious pantomime villain to boo as Ipswich midfielder David Norris gets stick every time he goes near the ball. The lad did a controversial goal celebration at Blackpool a week ago when he indicated his support for his former Plymouth Argyle mate, goalkeeper Luke McCormick, who was jailed after admitting killing two young boys while driving with excess alcohol in his blood. Naturally, this isn't my fight, but the jeers inevitably make me think. I get someone to drive me whenever I know I'm going to have a drink after a game and sometimes stay over at my apartment in Doncaster after night matches. Nobody supports drink driving and the results can be absolutely disastrous, as this tragic instance shows. But I also understand, especially from my visits to Doncaster Prison, that we are all fallible human beings and it's much harder to judge when you know the person concerned. I'm sure the player can appreciate the feelings he stirred up among the friends and relatives of the two boys - yet he was trying to lend some support to a person he cares about. His primary guilt, I reason, is the way that he did it.

Talking of Norris, he comes closest to giving the visitors the lead after Richard Naylor's header comes back off the bar midway through the first half. Then he misses a bit of a sitter and I begin to think this really could be our night. That feeling grows a thousand times just before the break when at long last the Keepmoat celebrates a Rovers goal. Again, the breakthrough illustrates the importance of set-pieces. Stockie swings over a free-kick, Matty Mills nods on and there's Shelton Martis, a young lad on loan from West Brom, heading in from close range. The crowd goes wild - and that includes J Ryan. It makes for a happy half-time interval in the directors' lounge - albeit a slightly nervous one as we have forgotten what it feels like to be defending a lead. Unbelievably it was our first Keepmoat goal since 28 August and that Wellens special against Coventry.

Sure enough there are plenty of thrills and spills in the second half when I'd gladly settle for a quiet night. Sully makes a fantastic save from a left-foot volley from Darren Ambrose, who'd just come on as an Ipswich substitute. But he's not the only former international keeper in form. Richard Wright, who has England caps to his credit, shows just why as he gets his fingertips to a Martin Woods special. It's heart-in-mouth time as Spanish sub Pablo Couñago has a header saved with his first touch in the 71st minute, before he misses the kind of chance I'd have tucked away in my prime - well, probably - six minutes from the end.

Great match, great watch, plenty of entertainment and the final whistle goes. We're still bottom of the table but tonight that scarcely seems to matter a jot. After 12 winless matches, we've done it - three points feels all the better for having to wait so long. The only way, I say, is up...

Burnley 0 Doncaster Rovers 0, Saturday 22 November

ANYONE who has been involved in a relegation scrap knows that once you're down there it takes more than one good result to get out. The victory against Ipswich is already just a happy memory, but if we can build on that with two or three more victories, it will improve our outlook no end.

I took a gamble in midweek in trying to get another striker into the Keepmoat - but it didn't pay off. We've been linked with a move for Dean Windass for weeks and not all of it has been wide of the mark. Rumour has it that he has fallen further down the pecking order at the KC after a training bust-up, so I make a discreet call to Paul Duffen, the Hull City chairman.

We said we'd meet up at some stage during the season, so I could have a look at their stadium, which is the prototype on which the Keepmoat has been built. But I'll drop Deano into the conversation and see how it goes. It turns out he has no problem with us approaching Dean about a loan move and soon enough I'm in possession of Dean's number. I'll always back myself as a salesman and a few minutes of chat are enough to establish that the veteran is indeed interested. I tell him that we're playing great football, without a finishing product and that a move could have benefits for both sides. Any goals he scores for us can only help with his aim of playing first-team football and, who knows, it could be permanently with us. Basically, a deal has been agreed in principle to take Windass for three months, with us paying a sliding scale of his wages.

I've chatted with Sean about this before, but now it's come to the crunch. I phone him to say that if he really wants Windass, I'm sure the pieces are in place for us to get him on loan. It's now up to Sean to phone the player and possibly tie up the deal. However, it falls through as Windass asks whether he would be an automatic choice for the weekend and doesn't get the assurance he wants.

So we arrive at Turf Moor with what we've got and in pretty good spirits. There's no question about Burnley's credentials - they are having a very good time in both the league and the Carling Cup - so a draw would perhaps not be a bad return. It's freezing in bleakest Lancashire and

Burnley, who had unbelievably knocked out mighty Chelsea at Stamford Bridge on penalties ten days previously, struggle to get into their rhythm early on.

You'll have to forgive me but the sight of Steve Bennett in the middle doesn't usually fill me with anticipation and joy, but this time things seem to be working in our favour. An early clash between Matty Mills and home striker Steve Thompson results in a yellow card apiece. Fair decision. Then, on the half-hour, the same Claret is seeing red after a naively late challenge, again on Matty. Only decision the ref could make.

Burnley will be down to ten men for an hour - surely their jug is half-empty now. Ever the chess player, Sean makes his move. He's started with three central defenders but sacrifices young Sam Hird for James Hayter as we look to cash in on Burnley's misfortune. Lewis Guy might have done better than mis-cue wide from a James Chambers cross before a howler from goalkeeper Brian Jensen presents us with a golden chance in first-half injury-time.The hero of the Bridge shoot-out heads Richie Wellens' centre straight into the path of Jason Price 30 yards out. I wait for the stewards behind the goal to duck - sorry Jason, mate - and sadly I'm not far wide of the mark.

Don't know whether the ref failed to tell Burnley to turn around after half-time, but they are rarely seen over the halfway line again. Wave after wave of Rovers pressure heads towards their end - and we know that one goal will probably win it. If Jason is the blundering bludgeon, Stockie's the crafty creator - a dink out of the blue sends Jensen backpedalling furiously towards his goal only for the Burnley keeper to redeem himself with a tremendous tip-over save. It gets even better in injury-time for the by-now restored guardian as he saves not once, but twice from a head-scratching James Hayter.

A point is not a bad result, but you can understand my emotions after the final whistle. Driving back home, I listen anxiously for news of Forest's home match against fellow strugglers Norwich, Sky's late kick-off match tonight. Once again there's an ironic twist, with the Canaries going down to ten men - also in the first half - and this time coming out with all three points from a 2-1 victory.

Forest's defeat takes us off the bottom of the table and is a real kick in the teeth for Colin Calderwood's men - especially as they are due at the Keepmoat in a few nights' time.

Doncaster Rovers 0 Nottingham Forest 0, Tuesday 25 November

IT'S always interesting to measure our progress against Forest - and not least because of the position we both find ourselves in tonight. Put bluntly, we are second from bottom with only Forest below us and the down side of Norwich's victory at the City Ground is that a little gap is appearing just above the relegation zone. Thinking about the 90 minutes ahead, a draw would not help either side particularly. We haven't quite got into the must-win stage of the season yet, but it's clear that when you are in the drop zone, a multitude of draws spells danger.

Victory tonight would give us a four-point cushion over Forest and that would be a reasonable advantage. With the return match at the City Ground due as soon as Boxing Day, I'd love six points from this quick double - but four would also be highly satisfying. Forest were shocking at the Keepmoat in March - if ever there was a 1-0 thrashing that was it.

Tonight they have a new face between the sticks, Lee Camp, on loan from QPR, and already responsible for saving last-minute penalties at both Derby and Bristol City.

But here he is beaten within two minutes and only the width of the bar saves Forest. It's a superb curler from Copps that rocks the away fans and leads to a determined early assault. Gareth Taylor twice goes close to getting a goal against his former club before the game starts to even out. Joe Garner, a lively striker who is now in the Forest side after injury, goes close twice and then there's another heart-stopping moment when Nathan Tyson races down the middle. Having seen him on several occasions now my views on the Forest forward are decidedly mixed. His lightning pace makes him look an obvious threat, but there doesn't seem to be much end product. One thing's for sure, when a lad is motoring like him, it only takes the slightest contact to get a defender in trouble. I thank my lucky stars for common sense refereeing when James Chambers gets just a yellow just before half-time.

The second half is fairly tame by comparison, but the talking point of the night is yet to come. Camp may be in good form, but he butter-fingers a shot from Copps towards his own goal. I say 'towards', but the truth is it goes a yard and a half over the line! Yet, you've guessed it, neither the referee's assistant, nor the referee are in position to give it. It's a massive call and one that could very easily have an influence on how the two clubs finish the season. To be honest, I'm totally furious and hardly impressed when a quick viewing of the DVD confirms what most folk in the ground probably thought. Even the Forest fans were singing the praises of the referee afterwards.

I'll always talk my views through and the assessor explains why, in his opinion, the goal wasn't given. The officials have to be sure that the ball has gone over the line and neither the referee nor his assistant was well enough placed, as they had been taken by surprise by a snap-shot from 25 yards that Camp inexplicably juggled. But if ever an incident backs up my call for goal-line technology it is this one. It would have helped us *and* the referee - as he will be marked down for getting the key decision of the match wrong. If it had been at Liverpool or Manchester United, you'd have seen the incident a thousand times over. Because it was at Doncaster, only our fans – and relieved Forest supporters - will probably remember it.

There's still time for Camp to have another red-faced moment as substitute Stuart Elliott lobs him from fully 50 yards - yet the ball bounces agonisingly wide of the post. So we stay just a point clear of our rivals when it could so easily have been much better. I speak quite openly with the Forest chairman Nigel Doughty who doesn't seem too impressed with his side, although happy enough to take a point. There have been more calls for Calderwood's head, so it will be interesting to see how that goes.

Watford 1 Doncaster Rovers 1, Saturday 29 November

BEWARE the fickle finger of fate... just a few days ago we were so close to being four points clear of bottom spot, tonight we're back in wooden spoon position again. Yet we tried our level best to defy the football gods this week. We knew that James Hayter had taken a knock in the Forest game and would be out for a while, so Sean brought in Steve Brooker on loan from Bristol City. Rather like Windass, the newcomer was offered a place on the bench - but this time he accepted it.

Sorry to bore you with talk about six-pointers, but this one almost qualifies for that title as I make my way to London. Watford's poor start has landed Aidy Boothroyd, who not so long ago was being hailed as the best thing since sliced bread, the order of the boot. In has come Brendan Rodgers, formerly a coach at Chelsea, and new manager syndrome spells BIG DANGER! So often teams greet their new boss - permanent or temporary - with an opening day win, but we can't afford to be the victims.

The Hornets are in the all-important fourth-from-bottom spot and it would sting us not a little should they extend their advantage over us by another three points. The game is frankly an advertisement for disappearing down the yellow Vicarage Road. There isn't a lot to recommend it, although Watford goalkeeper Scott Loach raises my hopes by pushing a cross from Richie Wellens against the underside of his own bar. We've touched wood so many times this season, surely one will go in soon?

Instead it's that wily campaigner Tommy Smith who gets the breakthrough for Watford after 31 minutes - a potential hammer blow on a day like this. Six players get yellow cards in a strange 18-minute spell. Well, at least it keeps the referee's hands warm. Can't say the same for mine, I'm afraid. News that Forest are leading Barnsley 1-0 at the break doesn't make my interval drink taste any better and it's going to be a very nervy second half.

Chances are at a premium before Sean gives Brooker his chance midway through the half. A few minutes later it's a case of David Fairclough eat-your-heart-out (readers under 40 probably won't remember Liverpool's original carrot-topped supersub) as Brooker comes to the rescue. John Spicer takes a lot of credit for his determination down the right and Brooker shows a predator's instinct to squeeze between two defenders and do the business.

A 1-1 draw is a reasonable return and we can't expect Barnsley to do us too many favours - their failure to score at Forest relegates us back to 24th and final spot. Never mind. Our results are what really matter and we're getting more and more difficult to beat.

Doncaster Rovers 1 Plymouth Argyle 0, Saturday 6 December

THIS week we welcome - if that's the right word - frosty December and icy blasts all round as we continue our Championship battle. Unfortunately we said goodbye to our new signing Steve Brooker in midweek. As we suspected on Saturday, the loanee suffered an injury towards the end of the Watford game and it has proved serious enough for him to abandon his one-month spell and go back to the treatment table at Bristol City. Shame that; one mini-game, one goal and Brooker was among our leading scorers. Never mind, I don't think we've seen the last of him yet.

A clash with Paul Sturrock's Plymouth Argyle isn't likely to set the pulses racing too much. But therein lies a feature of the Championship - unfashionable they may be, but Argyle still take a lot of beating. Indeed they have won more than they have lost on their travels, so this is unlikely to be an easy ride. It was virtually a case of last man standing as the team was selected for this game - injuries aren't exactly what you want when the squad is low on numbers.

Unsurprisingly, it's not the greatest of games with the action confined mainly to midfield. Martin Woods raises the temperature with a dipping shot just over the bar and Gareth Taylor is just unable to make contact with the goal at his mercy. But, just as thoughts of another unwelcome 'Doncaster Rovers nil' are beginning to surface, I'm out of my seat in wild celebration. Brian Stock unleashes a belter from 25 yards that has achieved the virtually impossible - hitting the opposition's woodwork, this time the underside of the bar, and bouncing into the net.

Argyle barely threaten Neil Sullivan but, on this sort of occasion, you just know they are going to have at least one big chance to score. That comes in the 62nd minute - one in which Sully again shows just why we rate him so highly.

Paul Gallagher, who is on loan from Blackburn Rovers, spectacularly flicks the ball over and beyond Matty Mills and sends in a pile driver from close range. I wouldn't want to be in the way of that, but Sully reacts brilliantly to turn the shot over the bar.

Five games unbeaten, four successive clean sheets at home and off the bottom of the table – I can almost feel my toes at the thought.

Preston North End 1 Doncaster Rovers 0, Tuesday 9 December

I'M in warmer climes when this one's taking place - and apparently I didn't miss too much. The game, according to everyone I spoke with afterwards, had 0-0 written all over it from a depressingly early stage. Main problem for us was that it didn't finish that way. Jon Parkin grabbed a goal for North End just eight minutes from time.

Preston had Paul McKenna making his 400th appearance, but there wasn't much hypnotic football on show. That puts an untimely end to our unbeaten run, with the main consolation being that Sheffield United won a similarly ghastly sounding game 1-0 at Forest tonight. We can only hope for better things on Saturday....

Crystal Palace 2 Doncaster Rovers 1, Saturday 13 December

I MAY have been thousands of miles away still in sunny Barbados, but this is one of those days I'm unlikely to forget in a hurry. It was always going to be an interesting date against Neil Warnock's side. Neil, as I've said, is a good mate and would do Donny a favour if he could. But today he's in charge at Crystal Palace and has concerns only for lifting the Eagles back up to where they think they belong.

My main memory of today, apart from the sheer torture

of listening to the 90 minutes on the internet, will be going over and over the incident that surely decided our fate. We got off to the best possible start after 15 minutes. The bets have been on whether it would be Heffs, Jason or Gareth Taylor who'd break their duck first - and today Heffs got his season up and running. Martin Woods sent over a free-kick and Heffs delivered the goods with a delightful header - delightful, I nearly knocked my tea over, as Sean would say.

We are sitting pretty after 25 minutes before one incident turns the tables in Palace's favour. Shefki Kuqi, the former Wednesday striker, goes through and Matty Mills slides into the tackle. Contact is made, but it's not a foul - not in my view in Barbados, nor on the video I scrutinise afterwards. Yet in the worst of all worlds, the official sends Matty packing and awards the spot-kick. Kuqi converts and suddenly it's all-square and eleven against ten in the home side's favour.

For consolation, I think back to the Birmingham and Burnley games when we had such an advantage, yet failed to make it count. Stuart Elliott goes close to giving us the lead again, but mostly it's a growing catalogue of chances at the other end. Every footy fan knows how time stands still in these circumstances when your team is holding on to what would be a very creditable draw.

Paddy McCarthy is stretchered off to add injury to the home side's frustration, but the worst pain (for us) is yet to come. Former Blade Paul Ifill crosses to Alan Lee, who used to play for Rotherham, and we've suffered a former South Yorkshire nightmare.

Neil is kind with his comments afterwards, pointing out how well we defended with ten men. But it's little consolation to us that on this particular day he didn't have to rant and rave about the officials.

Doncaster Rovers 0 Wolves 1, Saturday 20 December

STEPPING off the plane on Thursday was a case of 'out of the Caribbean frying pan and into the English fridge'. The winter is beginning to bite in England, although there's no fear of today's game being cancelled. We don't have the luxury of undersoil heating at Doncaster, but can cope with anything up to minus four degrees centigrade.

I certainly wouldn't want to miss this one, as it should be interesting to compare bottom and top of the league in direct competition. I may have reason to believe that we are in a false position, yet I can't say the same about our visitors. Wolves may not have been consistently outstanding, but Mick McCarthy's men have been good enough to be leading the pack. We have a few injury problems and few national experts would give us much of a chance - but I've seen enough of our boys to know there won't be too much between the sides.

My Christmas message to fellow fans in the programme notes is clear enough – despite our current position, I am more than convinced that we will dig ourselves out of trouble come May. There can be no better time than the season of goodwill to keep the faith, although I appreciate a fair few fans are expecting the worst.

It's a good, free-flowing game from the start. Wolves look threatening in the opening ten minutes or so before we settle down to a good first-half spell. Our best chance arrives after 26 minutes and once again it's the woodwork standing in our way. Paul Heffernan finds space on the right edge of the penalty area and strikes his shot near perfectly, only for the ball to crash against the bar. There's an amazing incident in the 38th minute that more than evens up the score luck-wise. Andy Keogh hits our woodwork TWICE, Stephen Ward has a shot cleared off the line and Sully parries an effort from

Richard Stearman. Great stuff for the TV highlights, but not quite so good on my nerves. Still, we can say with some justification that we've been the better side overall in the first half, and that can't be bad against a side of Wolves' quality.

A major moment in the 53rd minute - Wolves goalkeeper Wayne Hennessey appears to lose his bearings slightly and pushes Lewis Guy in the back. Penalty, I roar. But the referee inevitably waves play on. Nine minutes later Guy is sent sprawling again and this time I'm looking for a different form of retribution. It could - perhaps should - have been a red card for Wolves defender Neill Collins as he is the last man, even though our striker is veering slightly away from goal. You can sense the relief from visiting fans as the decision is a yellow.

Now we've played for 81 minutes and I'm beginning to think a draw would be a reasonable result when disaster strikes. Wolves win a free-kick just inside our half and when Michael Kightly curls the ball, it's Collins - who else? - who rises highest to nod the ball home. He was only playing at all because their regular centre-back Michael Mancienne was injured in the warm-up; he's only on the pitch now because the ref gave him the benefit of the doubt - and he's gone and scored the winning goal!

The remaining minutes fly by with Wolves playing out time quite impressively. One-nil to the Wolves is a sickener today. It's getting a bit late to take the compliments and yet have nothing tangible to show for it. So am I still confident we will get out of trouble, now another game has gone by? Based on what I've seen today, all the more so. We did enough to get at least a point against the league leaders, so I know we can pick up results in coming weeks.

Nottingham Forest 2 Doncaster Rovers 4, Friday 26 December

A happy Christmas is more than just a family get-together - it also has to include a Boxing Day football feast. Today's match beside the Trent is one that stood out when the fixture list was announced and has since taken on even greater significance. Forest and ourselves were neck and neck near the top of League One last season and have been in direct competition, it seems, for the wooden spoon in the last couple of months in the Championship. There have been signs of improvement from Colin Calderwood's side recently and they had a massive 2-0 victory at Southampton on Saturday which should raise their spirits again. That result means that, as we approach kick-off, Forest could get out of the bottom three with another success, providing the Saints lose to Reading.

Yet Calderwood is still walking a tightrope - an interesting contrast with our situation. Yes, there have been calls for Sean's head, but I've given him all the assurances I possibly can. I'm placing my confidence in the manager who took us out of League One keeping us in the Championship. Will Forest go the same way? The answer was to come a lot more quickly than I could have anticipated. We've had the better of our recent clashes and, surprisingly perhaps, Forest have failed to even score against us in our last five meetings. Mind you, they've got a useful goalkeeper in Lee Camp - he even saves shots that are a yard over the line! So I joke in the week that my prediction is a 4-4 draw.

Forest start brightly enough, but the 12th minute brings a great moment for me and one that will not be lost either on Paul Heffernan. Martin Woods curls a ball to the far post and there's Heffs to ensure there's no way back for Camp this time, with a downward header. The former Notts County man proves a point on his return to the city - he will have loved that.

It's a cause of great concern - not to say surprise - to me that we still haven't scored more than once in any game this season, but by half-time that record has been shattered. You can wait ages for one goal to come along and suddenly you've got THREE! Goal number two is a classic, probably the best we're likely to score all season. An intricate passing move has Forest chasing shadows before Woodsie flights a fantastic chip over the stranded goalkeeper. Even the Forest fans have to admit that was something else. We strung together 21 passes and then made it count – magical stuff.

Home fans were calling for Calderwood's head in the closing minutes at the Keepmoat, but this time they've made their minds up before half-time. Two-nil would have been nice, but a third puts us in dreamland. It's a set-piece this time as Richie Wellens takes aim with a bending shot that defeats Camp with the help of a deflection. Surely, we're not going to lose such a big lead. We've been defending well in recent weeks and Forest haven't been too much of a threat.

I'm almost getting sorry for Calderwood as two minutes into the second half he suffers another blow. He'd already brought on one sub in the first half when Kelvin Wilson was forced off, then made two more tactical changes at the break - now, one of them, Julian Bennett has twisted his knee and needs to leave the pitch. That leaves us 3-0 up and playing against ten men. We could get six or seven here. That thought looks even more feasible minutes later when, after John Spicer sees a shot cleared off the line, Heffs knocks in the simple rebound - Nottingham Forest 0, Doncaster Rovers FOUR.

How good does that scoreline sound? And all the more ironic when exactly three years ago we were getting beaten 4-0 in this same fixture, despite dominating the game almost as much as we have today. And there's significance too. Our goal difference is getting a huge boost and I begin to wonder whether we could be above Forest again tonight. Beware, however, the curse of ten men. Nathan Tyson, another of the half-time subs, makes a break down the left and, although his cross is nowhere near a Forest forward, Sam Hird inadvertently fires into his own net. Robert Earnshaw, who has had a miserable game, hits the bar and then suddenly it's 4-2. Chris Cohen curls in a free-kick and that jack-in-the-box Joe Garner gets on the end of it to flick home.

Surely there's no way my jokey pre-match prediction will come true? Thankfully, Forest's flurry comes too late to prevent us from getting the points, although it does take a layer of icing off our Christmas cake. If only we'd managed to hold our lead, we would have jumped above Forest as well as Charlton. Yet, in retrospect, that's a fairly minor annoyance at the end of such a brilliant day for us.

We travel home in triumph, but Forest can take no more. An announcement is made later in the evening that Calderwood has been sacked. Nice Christmas present for him. Forest owner Nigel Doughty was apparently in much warmer climes but made the dreaded phone call after hearing the result.

Suddenly both Forest and Derby, who are also struggling at the moment, are without managers while we can look forward with a lot more confidence.

Doncaster Rovers 2 Burnley 1, Sunday 28 December

THERE's no time to rest on our Forest laurels and here we go again 48 hours later at the Keepmoat. Needless to say, we need to build on our Boxing Day victory with further reward against a Burnley side still brimming with confidence from reaching the semi-finals of the Carling Cup. The value of back-to-back victories is immense, particularly when you are at the wrong end of the table and it's surprising how rarely that happens.

The fans are expectant and the early action matches the mood. Chris Eagles, the former Manchester United winger and also well known locally with Wednesday, presents an obvious threat for the visitors, but it's Rovers who should be in front. A first-time effort from Martin Woods tests goalkeeper Brian Jensen before the guardian has a luckier moment a few minutes later. Heffs, looking more confident with every game, fastens on to a long ball from Matty Mills and his shot looks goal-bound before bouncing off Jensen for a corner. Copps lets fly and I have to applaud Jensen this time for another important save. Robbie Blake hits the bar for Burnley. This is quite a game.

Then two goals in two minutes turns it firmly in our favour. Number one is gift-wrapped by Clarke Carlisle, the usually dependable Clarets defender. He picks the wrong beneficiary in presenting the ball on a plate to young Copps and there's no chance this time for Jensen. I'm on my feet again as Richie Wellens goes on one of his mazy runs - Wellens loses his feet and suddenly Burnley skipper Steven Caldwell is in the soup. I don't like seeing players get an early bath, but there's logically no choice - it's an instant dismissal and a Rovers penalty. Up comes Brian Stock... he doesn't miss these and this one is nestling snugly in the back of the net.

Unbelievable. Three-nil at Forest, 2-0 this afternoon... the half-time drink has never tasted as good. We won't count our chickens, however, as I'm reminded that Forest did slightly better with ten men and Burnley, of course, proved just as tough a nut to crack with a man short a couple of months ago.

The second half is tense, although Spicer goes close to giving us a decisive three-goal cushion. But we know we're in for a game when Martin Paterson throws his side a 62nd-minute lifeline by rounding off a quick break with a fine low shot. Chances ebb and flow as time stands still. I know full well that a draw would seem like a defeat now after being in such control at the break. But, fortunately, there are no further shocks and we hold on for a 2-1 victory that, all in all, we well deserved.

No mistake about it, Burnley are a fine side and to take four points off them is an excellent effort. Southampton lose and we're up to third from bottom. It would be even better but for Forest bouncing back under temporary management to win 3-2 at Norwich City.

Cheltenham Town 0 Doncaster Rovers 0,
FA Cup third round, Tuesday 13 January

LONG jump from 28 December to 13 January, so what's been happening? Unfortunately, as far as Donny Rovers are concerned, the answer in the words of Paul Daniels, is 'not a lot!' We were first due to go to Whaddon Road as long ago as Saturday 3 January, the original date for the third round of the FA Cup. But the big freeze meant there was never any realistic prospect of that match going ahead. Instead I spent my spare Saturday afternoon glued to the radio and the other ties. Amazing to think that Forest, whom we beat up so convincingly a few days previously, won 3-0 at Manchester City of all places. There's a bit of excitement for me the following day when the draw for round four pairs us at home to Aston Villa, who squeezed past League Two Gillingham with a late penalty. But that's all academic, of course, if we can't get over the hurdle of Cheltenham.

The following Saturday just added to our frustration. Prospects were reasonably good despite the cold until the Friday night when a severe frost left us hanging on for a Saturday morning inspection. Naturally when postponements like the Bristol City date happen people start talking about undersoil heating and whether we could have done more. We opted against such measures a few years ago and issue a statement a few days later explaining our point of view. Nevertheless the loss of the game is a blow and that just because we were looking to get our own back on a certain Michael McIndoe. There are four Championship games off in all but Forest's 2-0 win at rock-bottom Charlton widens the gap slightly.

Fortunately the forecast is much better for the Tuesday night when we, at last, get into FA Cup action. Seems a bit strange to have waited until January to be involved in this great competition. In recent years we have entered at the first-round stage and usually fallen before the big boys have even got stripped. The exception was a couple of seasons ago when our reward for a couple of wins was a 4-0 home thumping by Bolton Wanderers at the Keepmoat. Before that, of course, we had our spell in the Conference when we weren't even guaranteed to reach the first round.

There's a score to settle tonight, given Cheltenham's 2-1 victory that denied us second place and automatic promotion in the last league game in League One. It has been about eight months since and I still haven't quite worked out how we lost that day, although one inspired goalkeeper had something to do with it. The pattern looks eerily familiar in the early stages as our chances pile up. Heffs nods over from close range from a Martin Woods cross, before goalie Scott Brown denies the same player soon afterwards and then holds onto an effort from Sam Hird.

Cheltenham sense they are still in the hunt and nearly go in front themselves. Midfielder David Bird meets a right-wing cross from Andy Lindegaard with a downward header, but Rovers goalkeeper Neil Sullivan gets to it in the nick of time. The second half follows a similar routine with Doncaster seeing plenty of the ball without finding a way through a well-organised Cheltenham rearguard. Brown makes another couple of notable saves, from John Spicer and Sam Hird. Is there any way past a Cheltenham goalkeeper?

The answer nearly comes when Heffs turns sharply in the box, beats the guardian all ends up and sees his shot crash against a post. Frustration turns to relief right at the end when we could so easily have been out of the Cup. Bird's shot is blocked on the line and spins agonisingly wide of striker Lloyd Owusu, who is waiting for a possible tap-in.

Southampton 1 Doncaster Rovers 2, Saturday 17 January

THERE's much to celebrate in the build-up, not least my brother Philip's 50th birthday. We have a party for him and ensure he has a great weekend with us on the south coast, with our sister Janet joining the celebrations. Philip is also one of our photographers and a true Rovers fan.

The match itself is of the utmost importance, of course. Despite our previous two league victories, Saints still kick off just ahead of us in the table after their important 1-0 win at Barnsley last weekend. I've suspected all along that Southampton will be one of the bottom three and this is a trick that we can't afford to miss today - particularly as they beat us 2-0 at the Keepmoat.

To be fair, the home side throw a fair amount at us in the opening 45 minutes and Neil Sullivan has to be on his guard. But there are good chances for us on the break with Kelvin Davies confirming my good opinion of him with a great double save from Lewis Guy and Sam Hird and we go into half-time pretty optimistic.

Saints soon Copp for it in the second half as James Coppinger gets into top gear. I'm barely in my seat as he beats three players on a mazy run and his shot is deflected into the path of Martin Woods - 1-0 to the Rovers. That's enough to get the fans on the home team's back which leaves me with mixed feelings. If it makes our task simpler I'm all for it but, as a chairman, I'm bound to have some sympathy with Rupert Lowe for the abuse being thrown at him. As far as I'm aware it was the previous administration that ran Saints into the ground and now he is paying the price. A second goal arrives with ten minutes to go and, unsurprisingly, it's Copps who deservedly gets his name on the scoresheet after great work by substitute Gareth Taylor.

Saints reply in injury-time, but it's too late to give me any more than a minor attack of the jitters. The whistle goes and I get my mental calculator out. Norwich have beaten Barnsley to move out of the bottom three, but Watford have come a cropper at home to Sheffield United - so that's good. Charlton have lost yet again - this time to Sheffield Wednesday - and Forest have won again. We're still in the relegation zone but level on points with Watford, with a game in hand. It's frustrating not to be in the clear, but we've done all we possibly can this afternoon and made the weekend all the more enjoyable.

Doncaster Rovers 3 Cheltenham Town 0
FA Cup third round replay, Tuesday 20 January

SOME folk think tonight's game isn't quite so important as a league match - if only they knew.

There's even more than a fourth-round tie against mighty Aston Villa at stake as we try to put the record straight against 'Mad Dog' Martin Allen's lot. We try to keep to our budgets at Doncaster Rovers and spend what is in the kitty. Basically, we've agreed a £200,000 deal to sign Lee Hughes from Oldham Athletic but the money is only available should we continue our FA Cup run. There's £75,000 in prize money alone resting on tonight's game, plus the probability of a full house against Martin O'Neill's men on Saturday.

I'm confident it will be our night as we make the two-hour trip from Knutsford but there's always that nagging feeling that anything can happen over a mere 90 minutes - after all, Cheltenham were pretty close to knocking us out last week and then there is that match last season that we prefer not to talk about. Definitely taking it seriously is one Martin O'Neill because he is our guest in the directors' lounge. He arrives with his assistant and former Forest colleague, John Robertson, and I get introduced to the third member of his tribe who just happens to be an old hero of mine. Ian Storey-Moore was the king of the Trent End when I watched Forest in my university days and I've never met him in person before. We have a good time sharing some memories of those days in the mid and late 1960s, with Martin chipping in that Ian used to be his hero as well. All three are extremely complimentary about our hospitality - and they are very welcome. I just hope they will be coming back again in a few days time.

The match kicks off and there are just over 5,000 in the ground and a pretty quiet, almost flat, atmosphere. We're going to have to make our own running - and we're off to a good start. A curling free-kick from Martin Woods, who is in great form at the moment, crashes against the bar and Brian Stock is there to nudge us ahead. A second goal quickly arrives from defender Sam Hird but we can't quite relax yet. Our defence is having a shaky night and Cheltenham have one or two first-half chances themselves. Interesting words from John Robertson at half-time. He points out that the very uneven Keepmoat surface isn't doing our possession football any favours. But he seems impressed with what he is seeing.

The second half is a cavalier affair, although there's little chance of us losing our grip. Stockie half-volleys a cracking third goal from just outside the box and there are plenty of chances at either end in the last half-hour. I'm not sure what the Villa contingent are thinking as they leave 20 minutes from time, but I'd like to think they now know they'll be in for a game on Saturday.

Doncaster Rovers 0 Aston Villa 0,
FA Cup round four, Saturday 24 January

IT'S no-go for Lee Hughes as we consider the fall-out from the cup victory. We speak personal terms with the player for the first time and his demands are off our scale. We're not going to break our pay structure for him, I'm afraid. It's disappointing though as you'd think he'd have jumped at the opportunity to get back into the Championship for the first time since his spell in jail.

Steve Brooker is, however, nearing full fitness and due at the Keepmoat on Monday for a medical. It looks like we'll sign him for a fee dependent on the number of appearances he makes - the upper figure is £125,000. That'll probably be the extent of our January window business.

Meanwhile in the Championship another manager falls victim of the Donny curse. Colin Calderwood got the chop from Forest immediately after Rovers won at the City Ground, now Southampton have told Jan Poortvliet he is no longer their man, a few days after we won there. Can't help thinking that Saints' problems are a great deal more than just manager deep.

All manner of thoughts go through my mind as the big cup-tie approaches. We have a terrific record against Villa - only one defeat in ten previous meetings and victories in our last meetings in both the FA and League cups. King Alick scored a couple that great day 50-odd years ago. Wonder if he'll be looking down on us on Saturday. After we beat Villa 3-0 in the Carling Cup four years ago, I made a few headlines by saying the victory was even better than seeing Melinda Messenger topless. Just a few days ago I was watching Melinda progress through the first round of ITV's *Dancing on Ice*, so perhaps that's a good omen too.

I know we gave Martin O'Neill and co a fair bit to think about the other night and I honestly am pretty confident. Certainly I don't expect us to make as many defensive mistakes as we did on Tuesday.

I arrive at the Keepmoat early and the place, as you can imagine, is buzzing. The FA Cup brings with it an excitement all of its own and the countdown to kick-off is almost as tense as being at Wembley a few months ago – the difference being that this time we have far less to lose. Villa have been busy in the lead-up to the game, with Martin O'Neill bringing in Emile Heskey from Wigan for £3.5m. Shrewd move that, but the transfer goes through too late for the powerful England striker to face us today. Winger Ashley Young is suspended, but otherwise it's a full-strength Villa side. There's top quality in every department and I hope our lads aren't spending too much time thinking about the opposition otherwise they might be beaten already.

It's in these situations that Sean's down-to-earth approach pays great dividends. He will have been telling them that it's just another football match and it's our performance that matters, not Villa's. Whatever he's said seems to be working as we make an electric start. A brief glimpse of goal for Gabby Agbonlahor apart, it's all Rovers in the opening stages.

When we're passing the ball like this, there are few better sights in modern day football – and I'm not being biased. James O'Connor delivers a great cross in the seventh minute and there is Gareth Roberts, our left-back, up in attack. He fires just wide when he might have done better. Copps sends a crackerjack of a shot just over after a mazy dribble into the heart of the Villa defence and Richie Wellens, who is having a fantastic game, heads over the bar from a corner.

O'Neill is jumping up and down, looking agitated. Apparently he played down the importance of the tie – at least compared with the Premiership – when he arrived today, but you wouldn't think that by his antics. He wants to win and he can see this one slipping away. Villa hit back with Sully instinctively getting in the path of a close-range shot from Agbonlahor – boy, that lad's got some pace. But it's us who finish the half on top again as Woodsie clips the top of the bar from 20 yards and John Spicer and Stockie see efforts charged down.

I didn't want the half to end and the interval seems a very long 15 minutes in comparison with the 45 that have just flown by. I expect Villa to fight back in the second half – and I'm not disappointed. If anyone has any doubts that Sully is still a top-class goalkeeper, you should be watching this. A fantastic save denies James Milner on the hour before Sam Hird clears off the line from the ever-dangerous Agbonlahor. Seventy one minutes in and time stands still. Agbonlahor charges down the middle and there's nothing even Sully can do this time. The shot crashes past him but fortunately onto the bar. Touch wood we're still in the Cup!

Sean makes a couple of substitutions to try to stem the Villa tide. Big Jason Price comes on up front – what a time this would be to get his first goal of the season. The last 15 minutes sees a further twist in the piece. Now it's our turn to turn the screw and O'Neill's to plead for full-time. Wellens charges through only to shoot inches wide and Woods gets another crack at a free-kick in a very dangerous position. His effort swerves against the post and comes out to safety. A few days ago a similar effort came back off the woodwork for Stockie to score against Cheltenham. On such knife-edges Cup runs are made or ended.

There's time for one more Sully save that helps to tip the scales his way for man of the match. But there were a hell of a lot of good candidates in Rovers shirts today. The draw is THE result a lot of Rovers fans had been dreaming about – I would have loved the win. Still who is going to complain about going to Villa Park in ten days' time? The answer, it appears, is Sean O'Driscoll! I call him Mr Grumpy, but he doesn't seem to care. His post-match press conference causes the nationals to report that he didn't seem happy about the prospect of an extra game. Is he pleased with the result? "Ask the chairman!" he replies in his characteristic whisper. Well, actually, I'm more than content and not just with the prospect of more much needed cash. The FA Cup is a great competition and we have given everyone a lift today – not just our loyal fans, but fans of other teams throughout the country too. All in all, I'm a very proud chairman.

Martin O'Neill is the happier of the two managers and Mr Diplomacy himself. He lavishes praise on our "fine footballing side" and admits he is not too disappointed to get the chance to do it all over again, Also, as on Tuesday night, he mentions the state of the Keepmoat pitch. He doesn't think its bobbly nature is helping our flowing football and he's preaching to the converted, I can assure you. It'll be dug up in the summer but we'll have to put up with it until then.

Sheffield United 0 Doncaster Rovers 1, Tuesday 27 January

GOT to admit it, but Sean was spot on. Tonight's trip to our Sheffield neighbours is the BIG one, much bigger than the Villa cup-tie. And I say that as someone who doesn't like to see the traditions of the FA Cup devalued. Talk of fielding under-strength teams isn't really for me and I've been well pleased, for example, that we gave Cheltenham the respect they deserved by picking our best line-ups. The FA Cup is fantastic and we'll enjoy it all over again next week – but the Championship has been our dream and that's the way it must remain.

We've battled through three cup-ties, but it's taken 50 years to get back where we are in the league and naturally no-one, least of all me, wants to see that thrown away. We kick off tonight, as Sean has reminded everyone, third bottom of the league – and, if we are still in that same position at the end of the season, we'll be back to League One in August.

The challenge ahead at Bramall Lane could scarcely be tougher. There may be plenty of goodwill between us and the Blades, but we won't get any favours tonight, that's for sure. United are well-placed in fourth – a play-off spot – even though their fans haven't always been that impressed with what they have seen. They are also already in the fifth round of the FA Cup with a tasty Yorkshire derby against Hull City to look forward to. And there's another side issue at stake – I have a wager with BBC Radio Sheffield's Seth Bennett that Rovers will win at Bramall Lane, so this should be an interesting encounter.

The game's been heavily on my mind over the last two days when I've been in London on business. I get back to Doncaster in plenty of time, but the heavy traffic out of town is a late worry. I think back to the 2-0 defeat at the Keepmoat when we had enough chances, particularly in the first half, to bury them. We finally beat the queues and drive into Sheffield where we get a typically warm greeting. There's a large Rovers contingent behind one of the goals and the atmosphere generally is good.

The team news is highly interesting with us making four changes from the Villa tie. Sean goes with three centre-backs, including my favourite Dutchman, presumably to counteract United's aerial strength, and he gives Jason Price what could be a fairly lonely role up front.

Despite being set up fairly defensively, I see enough in the first 45 minutes to confirm my view of the two sides. We knock the ball around with confidence and style, whilst United lump it and hump it. It's not the kind of football I would ever want Rovers to play and I can understand the frustration of the home fans. An effort from Martin Woods flashes across goal, otherwise our slick moves end either with a last-gasp intervention or a final misplaced pass. Paddy Kenny remains untroubled in the home goal. Sully, on the other hand, watches a Billy Sharp effort go just wide and saves smartly from Danny Webber after a swift United break. All in all, I'm pretty satisfied with the evening's work so far.

Then it gets so much better... John Spicer makes an incisive break down the left side and squares invitingly for James O'Connor at the far post. He strikes his shot well, Kenny produces an instinctive block, but the ball squirms into the United net. The lads celebrate in a happy huddle near our delighted fans. This is potentially a very big moment in our season.

United go forward in search of an equaliser and we're on the back foot for most of the rest of the night. But there's plenty for me to appreciate as our defence holds up excellently, even without Sam Hird. Sully doesn't have a direct save to make, although the way he comes and claims a free-kick from a very dangerous position is top class. His calm authority is so important in these situations and it's notable how our defence refuses to panic amid the predictable assault from corners, free-kicks and long throws.

Jason goes off after 77 minutes – he's battled hard against that uncompromising customer Chris Morgan – and Darren Byfield takes the lone furrow up front. The closing minutes aren't as nerve-wracking as we'd imagine and we have a couple of much clearer openings ourselves. Nevertheless the final whistle is sheer music to my ears – followed closely by news that Norwich have squandered a two-goal lead against Southampton and Derby have lost 1-0 at Birmingham. It's our first ever win at Bramall Lane and we're out of the dreaded bottom three for the first time in months.

The journey back only seems to take about five minutes. There's nothing better to pass the time than a derby victory! Can someone get Seth Bennett on the phone, please?

Doncaster Rovers 1 Norwich City 1, Friday 30 January

REFLECTING on our great win at Bramall Lane, the reception we got from Sheffield United was terrific and that was extended immediately afterwards when Blades fans were very complimentary about us in their after-match calls to Radio Sheffield. It may seem a fairly small point, then, but it was a bit disappointing a couple of days later to hear their defender Matthew Kilgallon attempt to rally United support by saying they're surely better off backing the Blades than a Donny side who don't even know whether they will be in this league next term. I thought that was a bit unnecessary, although perhaps Matthew was revealing some of his former Leeds United colours with his comments.

More positively, there's good news with confirmation that we have signed Steve Brooker from Bristol City on a 30-month contract. I'm well pleased as I've been impressed with what I've seen of him at Ashton Gate. He was one of their top scorers during their promotion season and has always had something about him.

I'm counting each day to the transfer window deadline very carefully. Rumours have been growing for weeks about Matty Mills, with Birmingham City his chief admirers. It would also be little surprise to see clubs interested in the likes of Brian Stock and Richie Wellens to name but two. James O'Connor also attracted bids recently from Wolves. The truth, as I know it, is that our current squad are all happy to play for Donny Rovers and that means so much to me. This is a happy club and a highly unusual one. There's precious little loyalty in the modern game and we have more than our fair share of it here. Say no more…

There's no time to rest on our laurels with another crunch game coming up against the Canaries. It's on Friday night because of an important race meeting at Doncaster the following day, so it's a case of dusting the lads down and giving them as much recovery time as possible. I'm in demand from the press and my message is clear. There's never been a better time to be a Doncaster Rovers fan and I'd love to see the Keepmoat rocking tonight. Four wins on the bounce have given everyone hope, indeed expectation, that we can beat the drop.

I look at the table after 28 games and I don't think anyone is doomed yet. Charlton won on Tuesday night against Crystal Palace and I don't think we can take it for granted they will stay at the bottom. The other side most people are counting on getting relegated are Southampton, but they got themselves a great point at Norwich and have often come up with the unexpected away from St Mary's. I've said it before and I'll say it again – I expect Donny and Forest to continue to move away from trouble whilst the likes of Barnsley, Blackpool and Plymouth currently look more vulnerable. They've all got downward momentum and that's a very dangerous state of affairs for them.

Inevitably after the gruelling games against Villa and the Blades, much of the pre-match attention is focused on injuries and, in particular, Brian Stock, who is currently nursing himself through every game. Can he make a third massive effort inside six days? But there's more activity on the transfer front as we agree a deal to bring Dean Shiels to Rovers from Scottish Premier club Hibernian. Here is another Sean kind of player - an articulate young man who has plenty of ability on the ball. The sort you can readily imagine fitting into our fairly specialised set-up. Dean, just 24, started his career the right way with the Arsenal academy but certainly hasn't had life easy. He was blinded in his right eye due to a domestic accident when he was just eight years old and later had the eye removed. He has a reasonable scoring record at Hibs and can operate either as a striker or a midfielder. The deal is all agreed and is an initial £50,000 with payments to follow, depending on appearances. The ceiling figure is £160,000. The player will be at the Keepmoat on Monday for a medical when the formalities should be completed on what is the final day in the transfer window.

So, to tonight's game. I'd made a rallying call to Rovers fans after the Sheffield United match to get behind us and I'm delighted with their response. It was disappointing that we didn't sell out for the Villa tie. I know that the Premiership side didn't take up their full allocation, but we were 700 to 800 short of filling our section. One mitigating circumstance, apart from the economic climate, was that we had such a short time in which to sell the tickets. But to get just over 13,000 on a freezing Friday night at the end of such a busy week is extremely encouraging. I honestly think Doncaster folk are brilliant and support us all they possibly can.

We couldn't have asked for a better start. Matty Mills had just seen one effort cleared off the line before Heffs provided us with the major tonic of a 23rd-minute lead, His finish was a simple close-range header after Sam Hird had made a nuisance of himself at a corner. Sammy Clingan, the former Chesterfield midfielder who then played for Forest, is involved in a couple of the Canaries' chirpier moments but we reach half-time still holding on to our lead.

The second half, in theory, will be the time when the demands of the past week may well tell on our tired minds and bodies. I know full well that this will be far from a Delia Smith piece of cake.

Confirmation comes just after the hour. Norwich's big defender Jonathan Grounds rises high to nod the ball past Sully - the first to go past him in four games - and we're back level. It crosses my mind that Norwich could be favourites at this point but the response from Rovers is to play our best football of the night in the final quarter. Was James Coppinger pushed in the back by Gary Doherty in the 71st minute? Well, the referee didn't think so. Goalkeeper David Marshall then touches over a blast from Copps and Gareth Taylor shoots just wide. It all makes for a surprisingly strong finish that could have tipped the scales our way - but overall it's not such a bad point. I look at four points from the last two games and that is a pretty healthy return from a Rovers point of view.

Aston Villa 3 Doncaster Rovers 1,
FA Cup fourth-round replay, Wednesday 4 February

ALL goes well on transfer deadline day as we avoid what could have been a very significant departure. Promotion-chasing Birmingham City put in their third and final offer for Matty Mills. They began January by offering £500,000, upped it to £1m and then came back at the last minute with £1.5m. Sean speaks to Matty and so do I. Fortunately, he's a level-headed young man who is not too easily influenced by agents. As I've already said, I don't ever stand in the way of career progression and therefore I have to be careful. But I tell him that, in my opinion, it may not be the best move for him at this time. The Blues have been particularly unconvincing for most of the season, even though they are still in the top three. I believe Wolves and Reading will claim the top two spots, leaving Birmingham in the lap of the play-off gods.

So my advice is to keep playing here where he is totally appreciated and developing his game very quickly. The lad is 22 years old and there's more than a hint of John Terry about him - honestly. He's 6'3", strong and getting better all the time. Happily, Matty agrees and says he doesn't want to speak to Birmingham. I tell the media that the board's rejection of the offer - remembering that we paid £300,000 for Mills - is an indication of just how serious we are about progressing this club and that is exactly where I stand on the issue. A sum of that magnitude through the coffers would instantly wipe out more than half of the loss we are budgeting for this season, so would have been highly tempting. But I am committed - and Sean is committed - to keeping this squad together.

If we can get through this season still in the Championship, there is every reason to think that our young stars will improve still further and have us competing nearer the other end of the table next term. Rejecting that offer also says a lot about how much we value Matty at Doncaster Rovers. I've got to admit I was absolutely thrilled when the window closed. My biggest fear was losing one or more of the squad and there were inevitable rumours surrounding Stockie. But there were no other offers tabled, apart from the bids for Matty. The Shiels deal goes through as expected, so that means we have brought in two forward-minded players in the last week or so.

I've only been to Villa Park once before in the flesh and that was courtesy of their former long-serving chairman Doug Ellis about a decade ago. I met Doug in Majorca and we've shared a few trips on each other's boats, so I was delighted to accept his invitation to watch a Premiership match against Manchester United. The game itself wasn't that memorable, but what I do recall was the hospitality. Villa have long been up there with the very best and Villa Park is a terrific venue to watch football. It is one of the most atmospheric theatres in the game and it fills me with pride tonight that here we are at such a magnificent venue, taking on one of the best sides in the country. There are almost 5,000 Rovers fans among a crowd of about 26,000 and I am just disappointed for them that they don't see much justice. To be honest, when you face a Premiership team on their own pitch with a Premiership referee in charge, you can expect the worst – and Lee Mason certainly adds more credence to my oft-quoted theme of 'small-club syndrome'

The opening Villa goal is by Steve Sidwell from a free-kick that never was and the referee also turns a blind eye to Luke Young getting his hands in the way of a shot at the other end. John Carew adds a second goal within the opening 20 minutes and it's going to be an even bigger mountain to climb after that. I make my views clear to the official at half-time and he is a lot more even-handed thereafter. There's a moment to savour a few minutes after the restart when Jason Price manages to guide the ball into the Villa net from close range. The big man is off and running with his first goal of the season and we are back in the cup-tie.

We go agonisingly close to levelling the scores when a rising shot from Stockie is tipped around the post and, at this stage, the tie could go either way. But Villa then get a third goal through teenage striker Nathan Delfouneso just after the hour to make the final margin 3-1. That, I feel, hasn't done justice to the quality of our efforts on the evening. We have actually managed to look even more comfortable on the ball than Villa who, although they have rested a few of their stars, still put out a very strong side. The corner tally of 9-1 in our favour gives you an indication that we enjoyed spells of very good possession against top-class opponents.

The Villa experience lived up to my expectations in all respects. Once again the hospitality was fantastic – in fact, I would say it was even better than Wembley – and Martin O'Neill was a perfect gentleman with his positive comments about our performance. Naturally I'd have loved to have won – not least as the victors were guaranteed a live TV showing against the winners of the same night's replay between Everton and Liverpool. That would have brought in unbudgeted for money as well as being a great experience. Never mind. We'll have to defer such thoughts for another 12 months,

Blackpool 2 Doncaster Rovers 3, Saturday 7 February

I'VE got a soft spot for Blackpool and it was good as always to chat with Owen Oyston, who was there with his son Karl. Owen's hospitality has been a regular feature of our trips to the seaside in recent seasons, along with the joy of having fish and chips on the front and, in Lynne's case, taking the chance to get some time in on the skating rink. That's a pleasure she enjoys alone, I might add, as you wouldn't get me on the ice for anything. The nearest I get to it is watching ITV's *Dancing on Ice* which Lynne insists on seeing every week without fail – voting, of course, for Melinda Messenger.

This time we have to make do without the food and the skating, but the trip is made even more enjoyable than usual by the result. We've already created a number of 'firsts' on our travels this term – our victories at Derby County and most recently Sheffield United and Southampton were the first we'd ever achieved against those clubs on their own grounds and, again, Bloomfield Road has traditionally been barren territory for the Rovers.

In the first 30 minutes or so today I'm forced to accept that we are well and truly second best to a pretty lively Blackpool side, who have seen off Birmingham and Crystal Palace in their last three matches. David Vaughan fires the home side in front and they have a very good opportunity to make it 2-0 as DJ Campbell, on loan from Leicester City, makes a regular nuisance of himself. But then comes a break that gets us back into the hunt. Stockie latches onto a half-clearance 20 yards out and smashes in a superb shot. That is bound to take some of the sting and confidence out of Blackpool – for instead of being two goals up, they're back to square one.

Enter Professor O'Driscoll with another masterstroke. He pulls Copps back into midfield to stifle much of the menace of the Tangerines. The game is a lot different after that and in a hectic 15-minute spell after the interval we twice get our noses in front. The first is a sweetly-taken shot by our defender Sam Hird, a fine way to open his goalscoring account for us. DJ cancelled that one out within 60 seconds but, soon after that, Copps led the home defence a merry dance before driving us 3-2 in front with a terrific individual effort. A keenly contested game goes a bit sour as Charlie Adam, who has made a good debut, makes an awful tackle on former Blackpool player Richie Wellens and deservedly gets a red card. Wellens enjoyed a good reception from the fans at the start of the game but, now, they want to make him the villain of the piece. However the verdict was clear enough.

Facing ten men isn't our strong point, as I've already said, but this time it holds few terrors for us. The last few minutes see us looking more likely to add to our lead than Blackpool are to find an equaliser. This is another great result – our fourth successive success on the road in the Championship. It's difficult to over-estimate just how important these three points are. The continuing bad weather has prevented any of the bottom-four sides from getting out onto the pitch today, so in effect we've played one of our games in hand – and got full value from it. We're now up to 19th in the table, four points above Watford who are occupying the dreaded last relegation spot.

Time for me to put my mathematical hat on and estimate what we need to do to survive. I reckon that we are looking at a further FIVE wins from our last 16 matches. If we then pick up four draws that would take us to 53 points and almost certainly be enough – even though Leicester actually got relegated with 54 a year ago. The form table over the last half-dozen Championship games sees us top with five wins and a draw. In contrast, Paul Sturrock's Plymouth Argyle, who have been beaten 3-0 on their own patch by Derby County, look to be heading for trouble having taken just two points over the same period. That's an incredible 14-point change of fortunes between the two clubs and emphasises how so much can happen in a relatively short time.

Doncaster Rovers 1 Sheffield Weds 0, Saturday 14 February

I'M not a fan of the transfer window and this week's events have given me even more cause for scepticism. There are more developments on the Matty Mills front, even though we told Birmingham the deal was off on the supposed deadline day. The situation is this. The loan window will open in another week and Birmingham get around their predicament to try to twist my arm with an offer that is just about legal. Karren Brady rings me herself and offers a 'loan' fee of £1.5m with a view to a permanent transfer for a further £50,000

Now, we live in an age when loan fees do happen, particularly when Premiership clubs lend out their young stars to clubs from the Football League. But this sort of arrangement makes a complete nonsense of the idea of a 'window' and I'm still not playing ball. The other new factor involved here is the emergence of another agent. There's never been a problem with Matty's representative Warwick Horton but now another agent, Mike Morris, has entered the fray. As far as I know, he is not directly representing the player and, unlike Warwick, I get no sense that he has Matty's future at heart. His clear intention, it seems to me, is purely to feather his own nest.

Sorry, Birmingham, but you haven't handled this very well from the start. The first derisory offer of £500,000 immediately put my back up and therefore made their task all the harder. I also remember a conversation with David Sullivan when we were at St Andrews, in which he admitted how financially important it is for them to get promoted this season. They are surviving, rather than thriving, on gates of around 18,000 and it's not impossible to think that they could be struggling to maintain their current financial commitment. After all, we've seen big clubs such as Charlton and Southampton really struggle on the pitch due largely to the money problems they now have, so you can't take anything for granted in the Championship any more.

I am sure that Rovers fans will take a lot of heart from the fact that we have once again turned down a £1.5m bid for the player – who could have imagined that kind of thing happening just a few short years ago? But I am aware that we could face a battle to hold onto players who suddenly have become more visible on the radar of Premiership clubs. That, I fear, will be one of the unwanted spin-offs of taking on a high-profile club like Villa in the Cup. It just makes it all the more important that we win our current battle to remain in the Championship because it would be very difficult to keep our most highly-valued players back in League One.

Talking of money, Chelsea announce this week that they have lost £65m in the last 12 months, a figure that includes £23m in compensation for former managers José Mourinho and Avram Grant, plus five coaches.

It's not the way we run things at Donny Rovers. Although I suppose you could argue that I have been the club's 'Sugar Daddy' in the past – although never quite in the Roman Abramovich category – I do recognise the importance of making the club as financially viable as possible. And this is being done on average crowds of about 12,000 at the Keepmoat where fans are still watching their football at League One prices. You can get a ticket in one part of the ground for £15, whereas I noticed at Blackpool that the cost of admission went as high as £27. We also have great prices for youngsters – good for the future of the club but not bringing us that much immediate revenue. We always determine our season ticket prices in April, you see, and didn't gain promotion until 25 May, meaning we had to pitch the prices at League One level.

If Chelsea aren't quite in the same football world as ourselves, consider instead the situation at Leicester City whom, a few weeks ago, announced record losses of £23m. The Midlanders got away with murder a few seasons back when they somehow managed to defy a huge bill from the Inland Revenue and still retain use of their new Walkers Stadium. They are now reliant on their chairman and owner Milan Mandaric for financial survival and therefore operate just a heartbeat away from potential trouble. I wouldn't want Donny Rovers to be on such perilous ground.

It is international week and we do have some representation as new signing Dean Shiels is on the bench for Northern Ireland's comfortable 3-0 victory in San

Marino. I share a joke with Professor O'Driscoll after watching England get well beaten 2-0 by Spain. I tell him that he must have a second job, as the European Champions seem to be playing the Donny way with their sophisticated possession football.

Today's performance and result was another indication of how things are turning in our favour. A few months ago we dominated Wednesday on their own pitch and lost, this time we got our full reward – although it could easily have been by a wider margin.

The opening five minutes apart, it was all Rovers in the first half. Our passing was superb and we left the Owls chasing shadows. Heffs and Copps both had shots blocked before Heffs sliced a golden opportunity over the top in the 15th minute. Heffernan snatched at another chance in the 27th minute but made no mistake four minutes later when he headed home in fine style after latching onto a right-wing cross from Copps.

A brilliant tackle from Mark Beevers denied Heffs a second goal four minutes after the interval, before Martin Woods missed a gift in the 61st minute when he fired over the top from point-blank range. Not adding a second inevitably put us under a bit of late pressure and Leon Clarke almost pulled a point out of the fire for Wednesday five minutes from time, when he nodded a Jermaine Johnson cross against the bar.

But three points against Wednesday meant a very happy day for yours truly – our sixth win in seven league matches.

Doncaster Rovers 1 Bristol City 0, Tuesday 17 February

IT'S almost getting boring – yet another victory. Joking, of course, but you know what I'm getting at. This was billed as the clash between the two form teams in the Championship, so we can justifiably claim to be top dogs just at the moment. The winner came as early as the fourth minute and it was the Copps and Heffs double-act that did the trick again. The same duo who had opened up Wednesday for the winning goal struck when Copps split the defence and Heffs finished in style. Martin Woods volleyed just over before Sully showed his class with a superb parry to deny Gavin Williams an equaliser. City's Brazilian keeper Adriano Basso denied Woods and then John Spicer before the break.

The second half saw City with plenty of the ball but Rovers punching our weight on the counter-attack. Again it was great that we were able to sustain a late onslaught without too much panic. A look at the table has us up in a dizzy 15th spot.

Swansea City 3 Doncaster Rovers 1, Saturday 21 February

I WASN'T there at the magnificent Liberty Stadium to see our wonderful run come to an end – but the repercussions of this game rumbled on for some time afterwards. We were left licking our wounds and our reputation after Richie Wellens was sent off and accused of spitting at a Swansea player. The player assured us afterwards that he was not guilty of the offence and the charge was later withdrawn.

Insult may have been averted, but injured we certainly were as Copps was stretchered off and rushed to hospital for a brain scan in an incident that led to the controversial flash point between Wellens and Swansea midfielder Leon Britton. It had looked good early on when Copps gave us an 11th-minute lead but this time one goal wasn't going to be enough. Alan Tate went down under a penalty-area challenge from James O'Connor and Jason Scotland levelled from the spot 17 minutes later.

We began well after the break with Heffs and Sam Hird going close but Swansea always caused problems of their own. They went in front for the first time in the 71st minute when Scotland turned provider to set up Jordi Gómez. Wellens then saw red before Gómez netted again in injury-time to leave us empty-handed on our travels for the first time since Christmas

Doncaster Rovers 2 Derby County 1, Friday 27 February

THIS was a game I was particularly sad to miss – but the news winging over to Majorca made it a great Friday night. To complete a double against a side of County's tradition was yet another high spot in what is now becoming a memorable season. And to come from behind to see off Nigel Clough's men, who came to the Keepmoat on the back of four successive wins, was the icing on the cake.

Heffs had a couple of sniffs at goal in a first half high on pace but lacking in clear chances. Derby's Chris Porter shot over early on and then hit the bar just before the interval. Five minutes afterwards, Robbie Savage reminded the Keepmoat that he isn't just a wind-up artist by curling a spectacular free-kick past Sully and we looked in trouble. But good form gives you the belief sometimes to keep going in the midst of adversity and Heffs had us level within six minutes with a superb header from a Mark Wilson cross.

Heffs then had a good penalty claim denied before the tables were turned in the 71st minute when a corner from Brian Stock was only cleared as far as Wilson, who volleyed home from just outside the box with Bywater beaten.

The momentum had now swung in our favour and there weren't too many scary moments in the closing minutes despite a lot of effort from Clough's lads. Naturally it crosses my mind that we've got the better of Greenie's side twice this term and are well placed to finish above them. That's nothing at all against the lad, just human nature.

Charlton Athletic 1 Doncaster Rovers 2, Tuesday 3 March

TOLD you so. Charlton certainly didn't impress me when they somehow won at Donny and this defeat – albeit in my absence – has probably sentenced them to certain relegation.

We had to battle through a bit of a first-half blitz in which Tom Soares hit the bar and Jonjo Shelvey shot on sight but was unable to hit the target. That was the sort of ill luck that was afflicting us a few months ago. The turning point came four minutes after half-time when a clever backheel by Wellens gave Copps the chance to cut in from the left and open the scoring. Nevertheless, I was worried again in the 73rd minute when Nicky Bailey volleyed Charlton level from the edge of the area. Yet just three minutes later we got ourselves a valuable winner. Bailey brought down Wellens in the penalty area and Stockie stuck the spot-kick into the net - to the cheers of a very happy chairman a few thousand miles away.

Cardiff City 3 Doncaster Rovers 0, Saturday 7 March

BOY, what a holiday. Been soaking up the sunshine whilst Rovers have been piling up the points – an amazing 12 of them since I've been away. So you can imagine that we arrived back on Thursday with JR very much on a mission. It may be a long shot – long even by Cristiano Ronaldo standards – but we could just be setting ourselves up here for a crack at the play-offs.

The current table sees us nine points off the top six and if we could continue our winning run, then who knows? One thing's for sure, it's fantastic to be looking at the top half of the table for a change – remember we were rock bottom and being written off at Christmas.

There's hardly time for me to draw breath before I'm off

to Cardiff with the lads. This is one of those occasions when a Friday night stop-over is definitely called for. I give the team a rousing chat and, no doubt about it, the confidence among them is sky high. I also get the chance to chat to Sean and congratulate him more personally on our recent results.

But - and there's invariably a but in football – we knew full well that Cardiff away was always going to be a supreme test. They're sitting on the edge of the play-off zone, but still harbouring hopes of finishing in the automatic promotion places. Credit to Dave Jones and his team; they have built extremely well on last season's FA Cup glory and are known as one of the best footballing sides in the Championship.

There haven't been too many times this season when we've been well beaten by a better side – but this was one of them. The Bluebirds scored early through Michael Chopra and used that as a platform to dominate the afternoon. JJ nodded one over from a good position but, generally, we were under the cosh and uncharacteristically frail defending allowed Jay Bothroyd to double the home side's lead after 29 minutes.

Two-nil down at the break left us, as Sean admitted afterwards, with a mountain to climb and the possibility of getting a real hiding. We simply had to score the next goal if we were to stand any chance but, instead, Eddie Johnson added a third on the hour and, realistically, that was that. The lads never gave up trying and didn't allow Cardiff to rub our noses in it, but that was as good as it got on this particular trip to Wales.

I left Cardiff convinced that we'd played one of the sides who could well be in the Premiership next season, but I wasn't too disheartened. Losing is never nice, but it happens – and there are three intriguing home games to follow.

Doncaster Rovers 2 Queens Park Rangers 0, Tuesday 10 March

IF there was a match to give us a sense of perspective of how well we've done, it was the visit of QPR. Apparently one of the richest clubs in the world, it hasn't really happened for Rangers and they kicked off tonight in a disappointing mid-table position – as one of the sides we were looking to overhaul in the last few weeks. And when I tell you this was a fairly routine 2-0 win, it gives you some idea of our progress. In a way, it's the exact opposite of what happened at Loftus Road back in sunny August. This time we got two goals fairly early on and it was QPR who rarely looked like getting on terms after that.

Well, I suppose we should have expected a few comedy moments in Red Nose week, but the Keepmoat got a treat – courtesy of an horrendous mix-up between Rangers defender Damion Stewart and his goalkeeper Radek Cerny. In short, the goalie decided to come off his line and claim a harmless long ball; the defender thought he was still at home – and you can guess what happened to his header. All Christmas gifts gratefully received – even in March!

That gave us a crucial advantage after a relatively even opening and we got another major boost on the half-hour. Martin Woods delivered a teasing corner and Heffs headed yet another goal from close range. If you're looking for differences between Rovers when we couldn't score to save our lives and Rovers now, it's worth looking at Paul Heffernan. He didn't seem to be in ideal condition early in the season when he was mostly out of the side and we'd even considered the idea of loaning him out. There were question marks then over whether he was one of the players who'd struggle to make the step up to Championship football – but there are no doubts now. The lad has knuckled down, got himself as fit as I've ever seen him and looks to be in the form of his life. This was his eighth goal of the season and his third successive strike with his head.

On this particular evening, he could so easily have had a hat-trick as his strength and movement caused Rangers all sorts of problems. The big frame of Cerny was the only factor standing between us and an even bigger victory. In comparison, Sully had a quiet evening, so dominant was our defence. But when called upon, he produced a superb diving save five minutes from time. Pure quality.

I examine the table afterwards and that play-off dream, although distant, isn't over yet. Seven wins from the last nine might just do it. We've got 49 points - same as Rangers – and at a guess three more would see us totally safe. I know Sean will be looking at it that way for now.

Doncaster Rovers 0 Birmingham City 2, Saturday 14 March

SKY haven't exactly been regular visitors – but we'd like to think we've entertained them as well as anyone when they've been to see us. Also we have done pretty well on live TV results-wise over the last couple of years. We're always pleased to see the cameras, although Sean isn't that keen. They tend to want access to all areas on matchday and our manager would much rather get on with his job without the fuss. Not exactly John Ryan-style that, but that's probably why we work so well together. If the TV boys need a bit more, they always have a willing volunteer in yours truly.

Kicking off at 5.20pm isn't exactly a vote-winner, but then if you are on the box you have to put up with such things. At least it means there's a chance for me to digest the other results. Reading's latest home defeat by Ipswich will give tonight's visitors extra motivation no doubt whereas, at the other end of the table, Forest have slumped into big trouble by getting thrashed 5-0 at Burnley, particularly as

Norwich and Southampton have picked up valuable points. Barnsley, 1-0 losers at home to Blackpool, are in the bottom three for what seems like the first time this season.

Birmingham are a strange team – nobody seems to be that impressed with them and yet they have picked up the points. It's a chance once again to catch up with my old mate David Sullivan and, of course, the formidable Ms Brady. She has an interesting recollection of our chats over the Matty Mills transfer when she reports in her column in *The Sun* that I turned down their £1.5m bid in the interests of "further promotion under Dave Penney". Bit behind the times, love, and, by the way, I'm still not a "cosmetic surgeon". When will the message ever get across?

Being the supreme optimist and having a glass that isn't so much half but usually completely full, I'm still looking at the top end of the table as this game kicks off. Another seven wins and, who knows, we could not only reach the play-offs, but start them as favourites, given current form.

There's no reason to change my mind in the early stages as we more than match a Brum side who come with five players strewn across midfield, leaving that giant Cameron Jerome looking mean and lonely up front. Our closest to a breakthrough comes when we win a free-kick just outside the Brum penalty area. Woodsy curls in a delightful shot and goalkeeper Maik Taylor does well to turn it around the post. If there was an award for hitting the woodwork or even forcing great saves from opposition goalkeepers in this league, he'd win it hands down. Perhaps that's why we call him Woodsy.

The game is ticking along in a fairly even manner when, out of the blue, the visitors strike. It's a windy, hectic night out there and that may have played a part. I thought Sebastian Larsson's right-wing cross was going into orbit – it was in the air that long – but when it finally came down, it landed securely on the tallest head and, to be fair, it was one hell of a header by Jerome. After nine games without defeat on home soil, it suddenly feels unfamiliar to be a goal down.

We're still giving at least as good as we are getting but, on a night when we simply couldn't afford to make silly errors, we are in generous mood at the back. First Sam Hird slips up to allow Jerome to fire a fierce shot at our goal, then James Chambers makes an equally uncharacteristic hash of shepherding the ball back to Sully and Hameur Bouazza nips in to make it 2-0 from a tight angle.

It's always going to be a tough call to get back into the game after that against a side fighting tooth and nail for the points. But I'm reasonably pleased with the way we cope in the second half – we put Birmingham on the back foot for most of the time and, at least, don't end up routed.

Substitute James Hayter has a shot tipped round and a Mark Wilson blockbuster produces another competent Taylor save. I can see why this club wants Matty Mills, I don't rate Radhi Jaïdi, that big cumbersome centre-half, at all. Yet, somehow, we can't create any clear-cut chances and the result becomes more and more predictable. That old war horse Stephen Carr is busy at both ends, seeing an effort booted off our line before denying Matty Mills in similar fashion from a header.

I'm left with mixed feelings. Our promotion hopes are now probably over - a few days after they began – but I wouldn't wager too much on Birmingham's hopes in the Premiership, unless they spend very big.

Doncaster Rovers 0 Reading 1, Tuesday 17 March

THERE's no harm in making friends in this game and I think we made a few tonight - and in a good cause. This was Reading manager Steve Coppell's 1,000th game as a football boss and that takes some doing. Little did I know when I saw him running down the wing at Old Trafford as a skilful winger, who also won a place in the England side, that I'd be standing alongside this most articulate and pleasant of gentlemen in the Rovers boardroom, congratulating him on a feat that few managers last long enough to achieve.

Coppell has experienced the rough end of the stick – having no fewer than four spells in charge with Crystal Palace whom he took to an FA Cup final in 1990 – but has found a good club in Reading. He took them up into the Premiership, surprised a few folk whilst he was there and then, I'm glad to say, found a chairman who still believed in him when they were somewhat unluckily relegated last term. I hope he is celebrating at the end of the season – but not tonight, if we can help it.

Our staff are on their game and have come up with a commemorative plaque for me to present to Steve before kick-off. It's good to meet him again and interesting to hear him say that his long spell in management had never brought him to Donny before. The closest he came, he said, was bringing his Palace side into town for a pre-match meal. Apparently the bill came to £42 for 18 hungry folk. Must get a note of that place. I tell him that in a way he is cast in much the same mould as our own Sean O'Driscoll. You don't have to rant and rave when you've got a football brain and Coppell is another who has let his teams do the talking for him over the years.

Actually, the Royals have been misfiring recently and, after Birmingham's win here a few days ago, are in real need of three points to keep them in the hunt for automatic promotion. There are few early chances with the best probably falling to on-loan striker Dave Kitson who has a header saved by Sully. It takes us a while to get going, but there isn't much between the two sides and a blank half-time scoresheet offers us plenty of hope in the second half.

We're better after the break and probably have the best of it, without creating clear-cut openings. I'm more than interested to see Dean Shiels get his chance with half an hour to go and pleased with what I see. He shows plenty of promise, including a positive involvement in our best move of the game in which he and John Spicer tee up Stockie for a low shot that goes just past the post. Spicer also goes close, but in the 82nd minute the breakthrough comes at the other end. It may be a little harsh on the players, but I can't deny the quality – a superb curling effort from Kitson that gives Sully no chance.

Heffs forces a couple of saves in the closing minutes but this isn't our night. It's amazing how teams going for promotion tend to sneak these sort of results, but good luck to Coppell and his lads. My main regret is a bad injury to Copps midway through the second half. He is stretchered off after a foul by Kitson that could have warranted a red card. Paul Taylor, the referee, didn't even brandish a yellow. It could be the end of Copps' season – we'll just have to see how bad it is. By the way, an interesting point from our number one statistician, Tony Bluff. The last time we beat Reading at home was that incredible 7-5 game in 1982 when Ian Snodin scored a hat-trick. Remember it? As if it was yesterday.

Coventry City 1 Doncaster Rovers 0, Saturday 21 March

I'M thinking hard about the future and going to seek Sean's view on this. So far, we have resisted all Birmingham's overtures for Matty Mills, but we know that they want him – and want him badly. Alex McLeish has been to watch him on several occasions and he's no fool – perhaps, like me, he can see that Matty could be the next John Terry.

Our predicament is this. We'd probably have to double the

lad's wages to make him a realistic offer and we simply can't afford that. It's rumoured that Birmingham would pay him £20,000 a week so how could he say no? My idea is to make our terms loud and clear to Brum after I frightened them off with my tongue-in-cheek demand of £5m. We want £2.5m, plus a 20 per cent sell-on and a £500,000 payment when he wins an England cap. Because he will do so, believe me.

I chat to my fellow 'musketeers' and arrange to speak to Sean about it. But first I want another three points from our next two games, if we can, to make us all but mathematically safe. It would be great if we could ease any possible pressure on the club by getting those on brand new territory. Naturally we have never been to the Ricoh Arena; we haven't played at Coventry at all for 50-odd years.

I travel alone to this magnificent stadium and all is set fair for a good game of football – a superb setting, 18,000-plus in the ground and a lovely pitch to play on. Mind you, our lads won't be used to that after the bumpy Keepmoat. There are changes in our side with, as I expected, Shiels coming in for Copps who, thankfully, may not be as badly injured as we feared, but was never going to make this one. It's good to see James O'Connor back, even though he is just on the bench.

Mark Wilson forces an early full-length save from Coventry goalkeeper Keiren Westwood and I'm feeling reasonably comfortable before Sully comes up with one of his occasional calamities. He's a fantastic goalkeeper, as I've already said, but can invent new ways of conceding goals – ask David Beckham, who once famously lobbed him from the halfway line. This one is, in equal measure, both freaky and brilliant, depending on which side of the directors' box you're sitting in. Sully comes out of his area to the right touchline to clear but makes the cardinal error of kicking in-field rather than into touch. His clearance is picked up by David Bell 40 yards out and, to his credit, the youngster produces a superb lofted shot that gives the retreating Sully no chance of making amends.

We start to get a grip again just before half-time with Spicer denied one-on-one and Richie Wellens also forcing a good save. And it's much the same story afterwards as we play some delightful stuff without quite making the decisive incision. Again, there's plenty to enjoy about Shiels as he produces some skilful moments. It ended, however, as it started with Rovers on 49 points – and something to think about over the international break. We're eight points clear of third from bottom Forest with six games to go – close to the finishing line, but not there yet.

Doncaster Rovers 1 Watford 2, Saturday 4 April

ANOTHER quirk of the English season is that we generally have another two-week break when so close to the end of it – but I'm not complaining this time. The last three games have seen us fail to add to our 49 points and raise the outside possibility – one that as the chairman I can't ignore – that we could still be relegated, after all. One thing's for certain, I've now consigned that fleeting play-off dream to history.

It's been like a throwback to the early days of the season - plenty of possession and chances, a scarcity of goals and the odd, sometimes inexplicable, defensive lapse, all adding up to null points, as they say in the Eurovision Song Contest. This break gives us a time to reflect on where we are and double our resolve not to let this losing run continue and get sucked into a last-gasp relegation scrap.

The Matty Mills idea remains on hold as there's no way we can afford to be without our best players at this stage. I get the strong impression that the mood among the lads is still very positive, with one or two of them glad of the mini-break to rest tired or injured limbs. It looks very likely that we've seen the last of both Stockie and Copps for the season. I'd love to see Stockie get himself onto the pitch for one last hurrah, but we've got to be realistic. We're still nursing Steve Brooker, our new signing from Bristol City, with a view to next season, but there's no shortage of cover up front with Gareth Taylor returning after his loan spell at Carlisle United.

The loan deadline day sees us snap up an exciting 18-year-old winger from Newcastle named Kazenga LuaLua - I hope we see a copy of his brother's trademark goal celebration before the end of the season. Hopefully he can add a bit of pace and enthusiasm to us going forward.

There's cover enough to allow the incomparable JJ Price to head off to League One promotion challengers Millwall on loan. Talk about throwing him to the Lions. JJ is one of four or five lads who will almost certainly not be offered deals for next season, but we wish him all the very best for the future – joking apart, he's done a good job for us over the last couple of seasons or so and is a professional we could gladly recommend to many a club. He's proved a cult figure at Donny and won't lose anything in the popularity stakes should he help Millwall into the play-off final and score the winning goal against Leeds United. No harm in dreaming, is there? There was half a thought that Sir Elton John, reported to be returning to Watford, might be attending today's game but, as usual, I'm the most famous person there! The match itself pays testimony to the football fact that you can prepare for a game for weeks – and find all your plans go up in smoke within minutes.

We made a promising enough start with Martin Woods seeing a low shot turned away for a corner, But in the unlucky 13th minute the tide turns against us when Tamás Priskin gets away down our left-hand side and Sam Hird unluckily deflects his cross past Sully. Four minutes later it's a potentially decisive 2-0 as Cowie nods on a looping cross and again leaves our master goalkeeper well beaten. I say potentially decisive because the fact is that we haven't scored three times in a home Championship match all season, so 2-0 is a mountain rather than a molehill. Add the fact that we're trying to pick our way through a well-organised outfit on our minefield of a pitch and you get the idea that the odds are firmly against us.

Grumpy breaks the habit of a lifetime and opts for an early substitution to change the shape of our side. On comes Dean Shiels to further the good impression he has already made with some skilful footwork and flair on the ball. Overall, we react pretty well to the early body blows. It would have been all too easy to fold against a confident Watford who, understandably, seek to hit us on the break. Chances are, however, fairly rare until James Hayter comes on as a substitute and within a few minutes strikes a superb curling shot into the roof of the net for his first goal since his unforgettable winner against Leeds United in the play-off final. The goal sparks a late flurry but Watford hold on and we're stuck on 49 points once again.

I look a little more anxiously at the other Championship results and the 1-1 draw between Barnsley and Nottingham Forest is probably the day's best news. Plymouth, however, have taken a positive step towards safety with a fine win at Blackpool. Sean tells the press afterwards that we're in a relegation dogfight – probably a bit strong, but his heart's in the right place. Like me, he won't officially accept that we're safe until it is mathematically impossible for us to go down.

Ipswich Town 1 Doncaster Rovers 3, Saturday 11 April

SHOULD they or shouldn't they? That's the question facing the Football League at the moment – whether to dock cash-strapped Southampton ten points after their holding company went into administration last week or leave them in the hands of outrageous fortune. Potentially, this is the hot potato of the season – I can already envisage a series of Championship chairmen being up in arms if they rule that Saints have found a loophole and either decide against a points penalty or defer it until next season. It's Leeds United all over again, folks, with the prospect of the issue going on for months rather than weeks.

No doubt the League are hoping – not that they'd admit it, of course – that Saints go down anyway, so the heat can be taken out of the affair. From where I stand, however, that is a clear cop out – a firm decision needs to be made sooner rather than later and, in my view, Southampton are on very shaky ground. At the very best, they have found a loophole that will then need to be closed – just as Leicester City got away virtually scot-free from their massive financial crisis a few seasons ago and prompted the authorities to make points deductions for going into administration mandatory.

Poor old Luton Town, who are on the verge of losing their Football League status, were absolutely hammered with a 30-point deduction – action that began from the failings of a holding company. It was wonderful to see the Hatters have one last glorious day in the sun on Sunday when they defeated Scunthorpe United 3-2 to lift the Johnstone's Paint Trophy. Surely no-one, except the staunchest of Iron fans, will have begrudged them that piece of light at the end of a very dark tunnel. Well done, Mick Harford and Luton Town, and remember that going into the Conference may not be the end of the world, but can be the start of a new era. I genuinely hope that is so.

The trip to Ipswich seems to take a long time – we're desperate to get those extra points on the board, but a trip to the Tractor men provides no guarantees. Mid-table they may be, but they're still one of the best and most attractive teams in the Championship on their day. One good omen, perhaps, comes from our last meeting when we managed a crucial 1-0 home victory to end a long winless sequence. This would be the ideal game in which to stage a repeat.

Football does, however scientifically played, include the odd piece of sheer luck – and we get one in the opening minutes. Gareth Roberts goes down the left flank and puts in a very deep cross that floats over the Ipswich goalkeeper and into the back of the net. As Ron Atkinson once said: "What a great shot that over-hit cross was!" Ironically, Gareth was almost not here at all. Having missed the team coach due to an incident, he had to be grateful for the quick thinking ingenuity of Mickey Walker, who booked the plane that flew our full-back down to meet us. But none of us can celebrate for long. Owen Garvan raps in a low shot for an almost instant equaliser giving our hosts the early initiative, and they proceed to have the better of the rest of the half. Few complaints from me, then, when the referee blows with the scores still level at 1-1.

No-one knows why an interval so often changes a game, but in this instance who cares? We emerge for the second half as the more controlled and committed side and suddenly Ipswich are on the ropes. A draw would bring up our 50 points and be more than useful, but three would surely dispel any but the darkest O'Driscoll fears.

Suddenly we're in dreamland as Heffs reacts fastest after seeing his first header saved and slots us into a well-deserved 2-1 lead. It's all downhill from there and a really slick move involving James O'Connor and Martin Woods sees James Hayter score for the second successive game. A first double of the Championship season moves us up into 16th place and makes the long journey home seem like a hop. It's back-slapping time with everyone, it seems, convinced that we've booked our Championship survival.

Sean remains unconvinced, of course, but that's hardly a surprise, is it?

Doncaster Rovers 0 Preston NE 2, Easter Monday 13 April

WHAT'S the point in having your cake, if you can't eat it? Naturally I'd have loved ONE extra point to take with me on my end-of-season break to Majorca. For the second time in three days we raise ourselves to put in a good performance against worthy opponents but this is one afternoon when it just doesn't go for us.

Preston arrive with their play-off hopes in the last chance saloon – and overcome a bit of a battering to get themselves in front in the first half. James Hayter nearly completes a hat-trick of sorts –three goals in three games – with an early header well saved and I am in the act of celebrating Dean Shiels' first goal for Rovers when the ball comes back off a post with Andy Lonergan well beaten. Yet two minutes later we are a goal down and, yet again, it's a case of a player haunting his former club. Chris Brown, a one-time Rovers loanee, gets a firm head to an Eddie Nolan cross to halt our early momentum.

We step up the pressure straight after the break with Hayter going close with an overhead kick and Shiels just off target, but the equaliser we surely deserve fails to arrive. Instead, man mountain Jon Parkin sends in an innocuous looking shot that was going miles wide only for Neil Mellor to take control and stroke the ball beyond Sully. Defeat leaves us six points above third from bottom Forest who are in the drop zone with Saints and doomed Charlton. Just above them are Norwich and Barnsley, who are suddenly having a thin time of it at a very inopportune moment. Most of us have just three more games to play.

Everyone continues to assure me that we're safe – and our

staying-up glass must be 99 per cent rather than just half-full – but we're not taking anything for granted. I'll be listening to the match on the internet on Saturday as if it was the first game of the season. There's no peace for a football chairman.

Plymouth Argyle 0 Doncaster Rovers 3, Saturday 18 April

CLOUGHIE, famously, was in Majorca when his Derby County side won the then First Division title, so I suppose there was some consolation for me on the day when my Donny Rovers mathematically confirmed our coveted Championship status.

Most folk wouldn't think twice about exchanging another day in paradise for a visit to the wilds of Home Park. But that's where my heart was this afternoon as I listened intently to commentary of our 44th league game via the internet.

You don't get trophies, or necessarily even headlines, for merely escaping relegation – but let's put this into context. The struggles of newly-promoted sides including Scunthorpe United and Colchester United in recent seasons, and ourselves and Forest this term, have shown the gulf between the two divisions. For further evidence, note that Leicester City, who were relegated on the last day almost 12 months ago, have today booked their passage back into the Championship with scarcely a set-back all season.

Yes, getting into this league is one thing – consolidating that place is statistically nearly as difficult as a side making the massive leap from Championship to Premiership. Therefore I rate this achievement equal, at least, to beating Leeds United at Wembley that glorious day last May. All the more so when you consider that Rovers were the bookies' favourites to go down and were rock bottom going to Forest on Boxing Day.

The important point was that, in the immortal words of Corporal Jones in *Dad's Army*, we didn't panic. From the boardroom to the tearoom we kept our belief that we were doing things the right way– and that results would surely come. I can't praise Sean and his assistant Richard enough. It's no fun having your backs against the wall all season but, between them, they never budged an inch. Their collective calm helped to take some of the pressure off the players whom, in turn, have responded magnificently. Tonight we not only sit safe with 55 precious points, I don't think anyone would argue that we don't deserve it. We've played attractive, highly watchable football all season and won many new friends along the way, while defensively we've cut out the early errors and looked rock solid since Christmas.

How we would have fared if we'd been able to convert more of our impressive away form into points at the Keepmoat, we will never know. Certainly, the poor playing surface may have contributed to our failure so far to score more than two goals in any home match. We're an attacking football side but have looked more at home on some of the billiard tables we have played on during our travels. We will do our very best during the summer to put this issue right and begin to turn the Keepmoat into the friendly fortress that it needs to be.

Watching the goals on the DVD gave me huge pleasure. First we had Spicer's rocket of a 15-yard shot, then a fantastic cross from Gareth Roberts that produced a first-class header by James Hayter. Sully made one breathtaking stop but wasn't unduly troubled, and Heffs finished them off towards the end. Nervous times then still for Paul Sturrock's men but we can celebrate another double – and a guaranteed place in the Championship. Cheers!

Doncaster Rovers 2 Crystal Palace 0, Saturday, April 25

ARRIVED back in England on Thursday and, as usual after I've been away, there is plenty for me to catch up on.

The biggest Championship news of the week undoubtedly is the Football League's decision to take ten points off Southampton and therefore effectively relegate the Saints to League One. I don't have all the information at my fingertips but I thought from the beginning they were on thin ice with their stance that it was the holding company, rather than the club itself, which was going into administration. The only doubt in my mind was whether the penalty would come into force this season or next. Now Saints face the worst of both worlds. Should they go down, the penalty will be suspended until they kick-off in August. And they look pretty doomed going into the weekend's matches. I just hope this doesn't flare up into a long-running episode as in the Leeds United affair last season.

Other interesting news is that Ipswich have sacked Jim Magilton and replaced him with a certain Roy Keane. The Tractor boys won't admit it, of course, but this could be yet another victim of our curse on opposition managers. It's less than two weeks, after all, since we beat them 3-1 at Portman Road, although they have redeemed themselves with a derby victory over Norwich on home soil since then.

There are, thankfully, no such worries at Donny, although we do have problems of our own. As I speak with Sean, I'm beginning to wonder whether we'll scrape together a side for Neil Warnock's visit on Saturday. Adam Lockwood has been ruled out for the season following the injury at Ipswich and now Heffs is going into hospital for an operation, so he has joined a casualty list that also includes the likes of Copps, Stockie and Matty Mills. Shouldn't be too hard picking the team when there's only 16 fit players on our books anyway. It all makes Richard O'Kelly's comments that performances are more important than these last two results all the more understandable. Nevertheless, I don't like losing at any time and I want to give our loyal fans at the Keepmoat something to remember us by.

For someone as statistically minded as myself, there is actually plenty at stake. The league is so close that we could still finish anywhere from 11th – a position that would equal the best in our history – and something like 20th. Not everyone regards Neil Warnock as a friendly face, but then I can be an exception. It's good to have him here in our final game – I know he is admiring of what we have achieved here this season. There is an unfamiliar look about Rovers – and not just because of the composition of the team. We have decided to play in green hooped shirts to recognise the NSPCC and the charity's support of children.

In the first half we look more like our old adversaries Yeovil than Celtic. Palace run us ragged for most of the opening 45 minutes with Johannes Ertl, Neil Danns and Anthony Stokes all hitting our woodwork in a crazy spell of barely five minutes. With so many unfamiliar faces on view, it's not surprising that it is difficult to find our rhythm – but this is about the first luck we've had all season.

Having said that, young Kazenga LuaLua looked to have won us a penalty midway through, only for the referee to wave play on. We're thinking, however, about the sanctuary of the dressing room – or in my case the boardroom – when a lovely piece of play provides us with the added bonus of an interval lead. Richie Wellens is at the heart of an intricate move and Dean Shiels bursts into the area to slip the ball past Julian Speroni. That goal totally changes the game as we come out for the second half looking a different, more confident side. Palace are now forced to do most of the back-pedalling with Sully having a much more relaxed time at the other end.

LuaLua limps off to huge applause after the latest of several heavy tackles and Waide Fairhurst takes his place. Both teams enjoy let-offs as Stokes has an effort ruled out for offside for Palace and Spicer, so deadly against Plymouth, spoons an effort over a gaping target. But after 75 minutes we clinch the game – and with a great goal. Wellens feeds Fairhurst, the youngster crosses from the right and James Hayter sends an instant shot beyond Speroni. After struggling to score all season, Hayter's now popped up with three in the last four matches.

The fans can enjoy a comfortable last 15 minutes of Keepmoat action this term as we look much more likely to add to our lead than Palace do to pull a goal back. Martin Woods is particularly unlucky with a blistering free-kick that is superbly saved by Speroni.

I join Sean and the players for a lap around the pitch afterwards to thank the fans for their support, then I give a rousing little speech in the Premier Lounge. I tell some of our most loyal followers that we aim to be looking at the top section of the Championship next season, whilst reminding them how well we've done to finish above so many big clubs this time around.

Elsewhere today, Saints are officially relegated, ten-point penalty or not, and the Blades close in on an automatic promotion place as they win and Birmingham lose to Preston. I'm sure there's a wry smile on Neil Warnock's face as United's last game is at Palace of all places.

Wolverhampton Wanderers 1 Doncaster Rovers 0, Sunday 3 May

FOR months, our final Championship match of the season at Wolves had a dramatic ring about it. Perhaps the title-chasers would need a point or even three to secure automatic promotion, while we could very easily have been looking for a victory to secure our survival. And it would all boil down to Sean O'Driscoll taking our football purists to play a team of which he has been a long-term supporter. The fiction writers couldn't have come up with a better script.

Except, of course, that it didn't work out that way. Instead of having so much to lose, both clubs are guaranteed winners as party time hits Molineux. Wolves have already secured promotion and the title itself, while our survival has been a virtual certainty for weeks.

Everyone loves a party, of course, and few more than I. The match is a complete sell-out with Wolves putting on a big screen in a local park to compensate some of their fans who have missed out on tickets. We go there with a heavily-depleted squad but I'm quietly confident that we can still put on a great showing. The league table can say what it likes but I'd still prefer to watch our lot than Wolves any day of the week.

In any case, we have actually got a fair few more points than Wolves since we met them just before Christmas. In fact I've calculated that since that day we have been the second best team in the Championship – bettered only by our promotion-chasing neighbours Sheffield United.

I'm pleased to see our players give Wolves rightful respect for their fine achievements this season by forming a tunnel of applause as the champions run onto the pitch. But what pleases me much more is to reflect that they are certainly not in awe of Wolves or any other club in this league. Far from it. Instead we have a lot of big game players in our squad, lads who seem able to click into an even higher gear come the most important or high-profile occasions. So I think we can be the party poopers.

Well, it doesn't happen, but as the papers report afterwards we more than make our point. In many ways the game summarises what happened in the first half of the season before we met Wolves at the Keepmoat. We enjoy plenty of good possession, show a huge amount of skill on the ball, create several chances, miss them – and end up kicked in the teeth. Football can be a very frustrating game.

Proof of what I'm saying is that Wolves award their man of the match title to goalkeeper Wayne Hennessey, who performs heroics to deny our in-form striker James Hayter. In the first half he blocks a close-range effort after Hayter gets clear and, in the second, he flicks out a miraculous hand to somehow scoop a header to safety.

In reply, Wolves hit a post, but rarely trouble Sully. Yet there's a sense almost of inevitability about the final outcome. I'm not starting a conspiracy theory but let's say this was the sort of occasion when the referee is always likely to be kind to the home team. It's almost like the cricket benefit match where the local hero is clean bowled but given not out because the crowd has come to watch him bat. Here, the huge crowd has come largely to see Wolves win – and win they do, courtesy of a last-gasp corner that should never have been. Richard Stearman got his head to it and Sully's last piece of action of a fine season is to pick the ball out of his net.

Three points wouldn't have flattered us; in my mind we outplayed them. The real champions were our lads in blue and white hoops. Wolves may have been in all gold, but they didn't really shine out there.

So the curtain came down on our season with Rovers in a highly creditable, if unflattering, 14th spot with 58 points – a full dozen more than Delia Smith's Norwich City who occupy the dreaded third and last relegation spot after losing at Charlton. Frustratingly, just three more points would have lifted us into the top half and given us our highest league finish of all time. That's a record we can put right next season.

Around 30 hours or so later the party is back on again as we celebrate our end of season presentation night at The Racecourse. What a sight for sore eyes – and that's just the wives and girlfriends. Boy, how footballers have changed over the years. Here are our lads suited and booted, focused and well spoken, and with some of the best looking young women imaginable. No wonder they call this the beautiful game.

I'm in full flow with my speech – and that's before sampling most of the champagne. But in all sobriety I mean every word, despite the strange look on Mr O'Driscoll's face. I tell everyone that we can be up there challenging for promotion next term. Why not? The meek shall inherit the earth, as they say, and now is the time for 'little' Donny to make it big. I can sense it.

Main prize of the evening is the club's player of the season award which goes to Matty Mills. Even now, I'm wondering whether that will prove the fitting finale as I personally doubt whether he'll still be here come August. He has played superbly and acted admirably whilst speculation has surrounded his future. This young man is a rising star.

There was however plenty of other candidates. Stockie, the players' player of the season, was a major contender for the main award and I could also make out cases for the likes of Sully, Richie Wellens and Paul Heffernan.

Lynne gets her personal wish – the chance to present a trophy to 'dishy' Sully for the champagne moment, his wonder save at the Keepmoat to earn us an FA Cup replay against Aston Villa.

And a great night – and early morning – is had by all. We arrive home bleary-eyed at about 3am – my head telling me I'm getting a little old for parties, my heart wanting to bring on the next one.

Getting back into the Championship was a great part of my dream and I can honestly say it lived up to all my expectations. A rollercoaster ride it certainly was but the post-Christmas boom meant there were undoubtedly more highs than lows. And, as opposed to my first taste of this level of football as a spectator all those years ago, I can now look forward to another crack at it next time around.

PART FOUR:
I DO IT MY WAY

11

*

THE FANS' CHAIRMAN

SIR ALEX FERGUSON, Manchester United manager: "May I take the opportunity to congratulate you and your club on a marvellous achievement in gaining promotion to the Championship. It has been an amazing journey for you over the last few years and, although there may have been one or two hiccups along the way, your drive and determination has proved a big advantage to your club. I now hope you establish yourself in the Championship and, from there, keep rising. It is not impossible with the ambition shown by your team. I have written personally to Sean O'Driscoll to congratulate him and his players. I am sure he realises that having the backing of a good chairman is equally important when it comes to progressing to the next level of football, and I wish you every success. I will be watching your results."

GARETH THOMAS, chairman of Viking Supporters Co-operative: "Many masquerade as the fans' chairman, most being soon found out and falling short in the light of day. But that title can rightly be applied to John Ryan. We've chatted regularly over the past five years and John is always approachable – he never shies away from the supporters and his answer when people want to talk is always 'yes'. He has always attended our fans' Annual General Meeting and, whenever invited to a function, will either come himself or send a suitable club representative. He knows the fans need contact with the club and he ensures that there is always an opportunity for fans to get their message across. Doncaster Rovers are not supported and run by some nameless millionaire, but by a true fan. John Ryan goes the extra mile. He's banged his drum on the Kop in the past and today he's still banging that drum to put my team on the football map. Long may he keep on drumming."

NEIL WARNOCK, *manager of Crystal Palace: "The relationship between a manager and his chairman is vital. Cloughie used to say he could fit what football chairmen knew about the game on a blank piece of paper – well, John Ryan is very knowledgeable. He's great to work for because he is there to help. He does so many things he often looks more like the club's handyman than the chairman."*

PETER HEPWORTH, *retired stockbroker and Doncaster Rovers director: "John is a Rovers man – cut him open and he'll bleed red and white. That's what separates him from many of today's football owners who have no real allegiance to their clubs. John invited me to join the board in 1999 and I've found him to be very enthusiastic, an ultra-optimist and he has done a magnificent job for Rovers. We've come a long way since we had 538 hardy souls watching us play Leigh RMI. John'll rant and rave with the best of them during the 90 minutes because, like me, he is a fan – but he'll be back to his usual genial self ten minutes afterwards. If ever he left Rovers as an official, he'd want to be there at the next game watching – that's John Ryan."*

MY most important pledge when I took over at Doncaster Rovers had nothing directly to do with on-field success, but was a promise to fellow supporters of how I would go about the job of reviving our club.

The title of Fans' Chairman sums up perfectly how I first

saw my role when I took over at Belle Vue in the Conference and equally well now we are at the Keepmoat Stadium in the Championship. Before I took charge Doncaster Rovers had been taken away from its true VIPs over the years; my main job was to give it back to the people who should always matter most; those who pay their money through the turnstiles.

Someone can have the biggest chequebook on earth and wear the loudest club shirt in the stadium, but it doesn't mean a thing unless the football club they are backing is in their heart. Yet, as Kevin Keegan so rightly pointed out in his introduction to this book, even that love needs to be complemented by good business-like common sense or you could still be en route to disaster.

A true fan is a one-club man or woman. Players and managers come and go, but a fan doesn't desert to the team down the road when things aren't going well. I share 100 per cent the agonies and ecstasies of a Saturday afternoon because being a fan comes first. There will come a day when I am no longer the chairman of Doncaster Rovers. But, as far as supporting this club is concerned, it's literally a case of Rovers till I die. Even that won't stop me if I can negotiate a decent view up above.

That's not to say that I expect all Rovers fans to agree with everything we do. If there was one all-important lesson I learnt from my spell as a director at Belle Vue it was that I could never hope to please all my fellow fans all of the time. There are as many opinions on this weird and wonderful sport of ours as there are supporters, as anyone who listens to radio phone-ins or logs into internet forums will soon understand. My job is to act in the best interests of the fans and the club as a whole. Not easy.

I never expected to be welcomed overnight as the answer to Rovers' prayers. Remember again what had happened before I became chairman. Years of disappointment, punctuated by the odd hint of light under the leadership of good, honest men, had been followed by Ken Richardson making hollow promises. Ian Jones, a successful Rovers chairman, was a solicitor, Frank Wilson, whom I met when I went out with his daughter, ran a tyre business and Tony Phillips was in the building trade. Then there was Peter Wetzel, my business partner when I took over. All were good faithful folk whom the club should always be grateful to. But none were what you would term big-hitters. Why should I be any different? Yes, the supporters were delighted their football club was still in business, but they were rightly cautious.

My cause wasn't helped by an unfortunate coincidence that misled some fans. As the initial buyers Westferry were also Isle of Man-based, I was instantly and innocently bracketed with the very old devil I had always opposed. So I accepted that only through time could I build up trust and, in the meantime, pledged to be as truthful and up-front as Richardson had been deceitful in keeping his real cards behind his back.

My way can be described as a benevolent dictatorship. The idea of a perfect democracy is an attractive one in theory, but I can't see how it can possibly work in practice in football. Don't get me wrong, I have a lot of sympathy and time for the so-called fans' clubs such as FC United and AFC Wimbledon set up by supporters feeling they have no say at all in the running of their clubs. Blue Square Premier club Ebbsfleet United threatened to go the whole hog, actually promising that the supporters would be able to pick the team. Hardly surprisingly, they soon back-tracked on that policy once they realised the implications. Consulting and taking stock of people's opinions is one thing but the buck has to stop somewhere. There needs to be clear demarcation zones throughout any organisation if it is going to succeed. Picking football teams is the task of the manager and his assistant. The chairman and the board are there to provide direction and manage the club as a whole.

Summarise Ryan's way like this: elect a committee if you want a good discussion, but to get something done you need a good leader. Particularly in those very fragile early days at Belle Vue, quick decisions needed to be made to get us up and running and, as the man with the chequebook, it was my role to either make them or rubber stamp them. I liken my position now to that of the directly-elected Mayor of Doncaster. Martin Winter and now Peter Davies have the power, within reason, to knock heads together and get things done. You and I may still disagree with many council policies since the new position was created but, at least, everything happens quicker. The important point is that neither I nor the Mayor should stick his head in the sand, remain aloof and believe he is infallible. That's the way of self-delusion. I make no secret of the fact that I am always willing to take on board other people's ideas, as long as I genuinely believe they would benefit the football club.

Today we have three 'Mayors' at Donny Rovers. Dick Watson and Terry Bramall have come on board as joint-major shareholders, so they have an equal say on where we are going. I may still be the public face of Doncaster Rovers but there are three 'musketeers', not just one. That, as I've explained elsewhere, is something which should give fans more reassurance that our future is secure.

Let me address one particular hot potato - whether football clubs can be run as businesses. The first thing to say, as a successful businessman, is that 'investing' in football with a view to getting your hard-earned cash back whilst remaining in office is a complete nonsense. I think many well-intentioned folk realise to their cost that this doesn't happen. The worry is that some new owners buy into clubs with the sole intention of either asset stripping a sinking ship or making a profit when they sell up. You don't need me to tell you that this is part and parcel of the modern game. In my view a good chairman must accept that he or she will always give a lot more than they take and be in football for love not money.

Beware also the inflated ego. No one person can ever be bigger than the football club itself and that remains the case, even though I have been fortunate enough to gain more than my fair share of plaudits from fellow fans over the years. The truth is that Donny Rovers were here before John Ryan came into this world and will be here, God willing, long after I've gone. The three of us therefore are merely the main guardians of the club during this particularly exciting part of our history and are responsible as to whom we pass that privilege on to. There could well come a time when I sell my share in Doncaster Rovers but I would have to be fully satisfied that potential future owners had the best interests of this club at heart. It won't be so much a case of showing me the colour of their money, but whether Rovers would be safe in their hands.

Without banging on too much about money, I put £1m into the club in the first 12 months after I took over and £4m by the time we regained our place in the Football League. That much has been well documented. Naturally each step up the football ladder since then has meant a greater demand for finance. It wouldn't be fair to put a figure on my total investment so far and I don't think you'd expect me to. What I can reveal is that I put my money in as share capital and not as a loan. This means that, although I could sell my shares at some point, there is no question of ever putting the future of the club in danger by suddenly demanding my money back. Too many clubs, however, exist on just such a knife-edge than is healthy for the good of the game.

The way we run things is like this. The three of us agree on a budget at the beginning of each season and try our level best to stick with it. Sounds simple, doesn't it? But there are endless variables that occur during a long football season and the best-laid plans must include room for flexibility. Proceeds from cup runs and live TV, transfers in and out and a thousand and one other things will play a part in the final analysis.

Going into the Championship has been fantastic for the club, but inevitably it has had major implications for our finances. Last season we went in with a playing budget of £4.9m, expecting to lose about £2m. In the end that figure was nearer £3m despite attendances at the Keepmoat rising to an average of just over 12,000. Then it was up to the three of us – and anyone else who wished to contribute – to make up the deficit. That way Doncaster Rovers remained as close as you'd get these days to a debt-free football club. The 2009/10 season saw us kick off with £6m in the playing kitty and our likely losses reduced by the £3m or so brought in over the summer through the reluctant sales of Matt Mills and Richie Wellens. At least that was the theory...

The playing side is handed over lock, stock and barrel to Sean O'Driscoll. He manages the budget himself and is present at all our board meetings, therefore being kept up-to-date with how the club is progressing financially. Sean is in many ways one of the very few genuine football managers still left in the game. Rather than constantly seeking instant and risky solutions by signing endless players, he takes it on board that he bears some of the responsibility, along with the rest of the coaching staff, to improve what we have and utilise our resources wisely.

The result is the team is a close-knit unit, very much like a family. We have a ceiling on wages and, hopefully, that improves team spirit. There was no chance, for example, that we were going to employ striker Lee Hughes, from Oldham Athletic last term, when he was asking for around twice the cash of any of our other players. What would that have done for morale at the Keepmoat? Much the same applied to our thinking when Mills and Wellens, two of our 'Gallacticos', moved on to Reading and Leicester City respectively. Breaking our wage structure for the sake of one or two individuals would have been very counter-productive.

Despite that, I remain fiercely ambitious. Sean was quoted as saying last season that he worked for a chairman who wanted to win the Champions League. Show me a chairman who doesn't want to win trophies and I'll show you someone who shouldn't be in a job. We may have achieved all the promises I set out when I first took over the club but that doesn't mean my work is complete. Life moves on and the one option none of us has in life is to stand still.

As a fan, I want the lot. I want to enjoy my matchday experience, see good, entertaining football and, of course, to win. It gives me a great deal of joy and satisfaction that we have established such a strong reputation for the quality of our football and long may that continue. Contrary to what a lot of modern day football officials seem to think, we are in the entertainment industry and it is important that we give something positive to the fans. I can't think of any occasion during my tenure at Donny that we have gone out seeking to merely draw a football match – we always want to get hold of the ball, go forward and outscore and outplay the opposition, whether on our pitch or theirs. Okay, there are times when we will be forced to defend for our lives and we have to make ourselves difficult to beat. We can't promise to get the fans off their seats every minute of every game, particularly as we now come up against better and very well organised opponents week after week. But there's no harm in trying.

I want fellow fans to be able to look back in a few years time and remember more rip-roaring occasions such as when we destroyed Aston Villa 3-0 in the Carling Cup, took Southend United to the cleaners 5-1 in a play-off semi-final and humbled mighty Leeds United at Wembley. We'll be talking about Sean Thornton's long-range bullet, James Coppinger's stunning hat-trick on a five-star Friday night and James Hayter's winning goal against Leeds for a long time to come, I'm sure, because those were all occasions when the football lived up to the hype.

It is also important to me that we are a well-disciplined team. This is another sometimes under-rated feature of our game that has been transformed over the last decade. As Cloughie preached, there is no sense in arguing on the pitch with officials who have already made up their minds and yellow and red cards can become a major handicap, particularly if you don't have the largest of squads. I'd like to believe that Donny Rovers are one of the easiest clubs for referees to handle and that is indeed the feedback I often get from them. Credit here also needs to go to Sean and Richard for they set the tone and the standards both on the training ground and on the touchline on match days. Fans like to see passion and, believe me, they are as passionate as anyone, but we'll leave the ranting and raving to others.

Communication comes with the territory, as far as I'm concerned. People sometimes seem surprised when they see me chatting away with fans at motorway service stations or in the ground or at public meetings. But why on earth, shouldn't I? There are few things as pleasurable as talking about my football club and, particularly, in the company of fellow enthusiasts. I always enjoy attending supporters club events and like to think that I, along with other officials of Doncaster Rovers, are respected because we are open and honest with the public. I may watch from the directors' box and socialise with officials of other football clubs but I'm exactly the same as any fan. I shout, have a go at the referee a bit too much, offer my share of advice on how we should be playing and generally lose myself in the occasion in much the same way as when I started watching my football at Belle Vue. Just as other fans like nothing more than voicing their opinions, whether it is to their mates in the pub or over the airwaves, I could easily talk about Doncaster Rovers 24 hours a day. Honestly. Having said all that, it is the more spontaneous chats that I probably enjoy most. I listen to Radio Sheffield's football phone-in as often as I can and am certainly not averse to going on fans' forums. In fact I get some of my best ideas from them.

I'll back my football knowledge and memory against most of you – with the exception of our wonderful club statistician Tony Bluff, of course. How many of today's billionaire owners would be able to tell you very much about the history of their club? If any of them want to challenge me to a game of Doncaster Rovers Mastermind, I'm here and waiting. But I don't fancy your chances.

The hot topic of the ownership in our game has become even more heated while writing my story. The takeover saga at Portsmouth meant that, according to my calculations, more than half of our Premiership clubs are now in foreign control. Nothing wrong with that *per se*, of course, but I can understand fans being very concerned about the way things are going – and I share many of those worries.

Naturally I have more than a passing interest in Manchester City, a club just down the road from where I live and one that I nearly became involved in. But how different will the City of the future be from the club that my good mate Mike Summerbee recommended to me? With the dust now just beginning to settle, I get the distinct impression that there are mixed feelings among true City fans over where the club is heading after being taken over by the mega-rich Abu Dhabi United Group. On the one hand, they are excited at the prospect of their £200m team competing at last on more than equal terms with the biggest clubs in our land. But once clubs sell out to the highest bidder – irrespective of whom they are – they risk losing some of their identity and tradition which is what makes them great and worthy of support in the first place. I would certainly give a penny for the thoughts now of former City chairman John Wardle who told me just a short time ago that the age of the multi-millionaire owners of Premiership clubs was now at an end - kicked out and replaced by the elite few in billionaires row.

One important factor to look out for is where the money is coming from. Providing it is from share capital, the signs are good. But, if as in the Manchester United takeover by the Glazer family, it is actually financed by loans, alarm bells need to ring. It might be alleged that the world's richest club became the world's poorest overnight – a scenario that, one day, may give some United folk sleepless nights.

Generally, though, I'd say give people the benefit of the doubt. Initial misgivings may not always be right. Nobody knew quite what to expect when Roman Abramovich took over the reigns at Chelsea a few years back but enough time has now passed for people to see that he is into his football and has more than just a short-term interest. Good job when you consider that Chelsea were reported to have a playing budget of £172m in the 2007/8 season.

I may not agree with UEFA president Michel Platini on some things – in fact, most things when I come to think of it – but his latest muse that clubs should be precluded from European competitions if they continue to carry huge debts does make sense. After all, clubs who pay no attention to their balance sheets can be assumed to have an unfair advantage.

Pictured: Rovers directors and our WAGS! A proud moment as our directors line up at Wembley – Dave Morris, Stuart Highfield, Dick Watson, John Ryan, Paul May, Peter Hepworth and Richard Hirst. In the alternative boardroom are directors' wives Marian Watson, Liz Bramall, Renee Milton, Judy Hirst, Diana Highfield and Lynne.

Above: The one and only Kevin Keegan - twice European footballer of the year and very nearly the best player to come from Doncaster.

Above: Stand by my man - quietly-spoken Sean O'Driscoll was an acquired taste for Rovers fans, but the manager has taken our football to a new level.

Above: Hitting a boundary during the annual cricket match between Rovers and Doncaster Town.

Above: A photograph of the Doncaster Rovers squad, taken before our memorable and historic Championship season of 2008/09.

Left: I was such a proud father on my daughter Claire's wedding day.

Above: My lovely wife Lynne.

Below: The Ryan clan - two brothers and a sister. Philip and John with Janet.

Right: Simply the Best - George was a legend and I have my personal memories of the great man.

Left: I'm a keen fan of the system of directly-elected Mayors. Here I am with the new Mayor of Doncaster, Peter Davies.

Right: With referee Mark Halsey, whom I rate as the best of today's whistle-blowers.

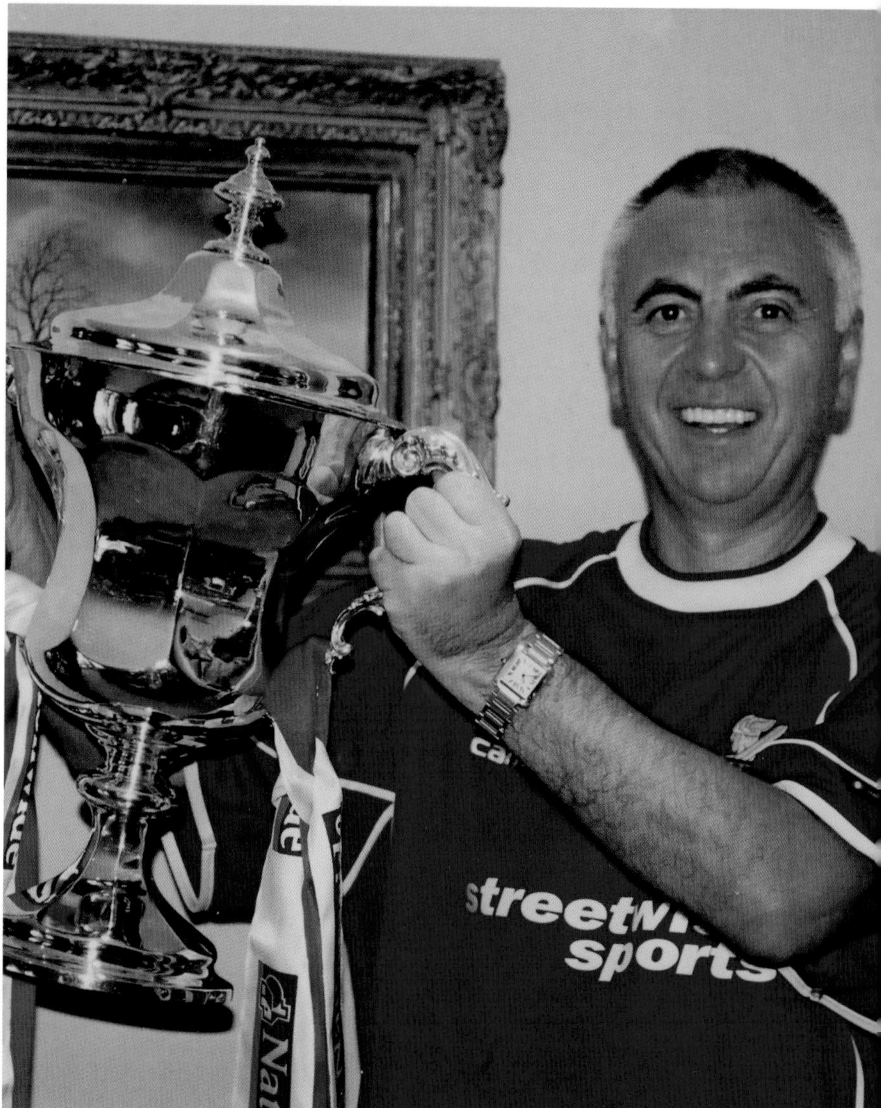

Above: We are the champions! Yours truly holding the League Three trophy. The message is clear - Donny Rovers are going places. Regrets, I have a few – but then again, too few to mention...

An example of a club that has been in financial turmoil in recent times is Newcastle United, where chairman Mike Ashley sported the shirt, raised the beer mug but convinced few people that he was right for the club. But it must be remembered that he did put his money where his mouth is. Cloughie raised a few eyebrows and a lot of knowing laughs when he said that what an average football chairman knows about the game could be written on a blank sheet of paper. Maybe his sharp mind was thinking ahead to the sad events in Geordieland, when Ashley appointed Dennis Wise as his Director of Football shortly after Kevin Keegan made his second coming as manager on Tyneside. KK backed out of the door and very possibly out of football for good and the result was inevitable - a power struggle without any winners as Newcastle slumped back down into the Championship.

The chairman, just like any other official, needs to know his or her place. That is to hire the best manager possible and then let him get on with the job. Don't get me wrong, no chairman is more openly opinionated on the game than me. I will always say what I think but trust that the manager knows me well enough to appreciate that I do so with the best interests of everyone at heart. And, yes, there's plenty of scope for people to disagree with me.

There has, in my view, to be a clear division of responsibilities with the manager having the final say on players coming into the club as well as team selection. Any other way of running things is bound to cause untold complications. Naturally, I hear the same stories about chairmen bringing in players of their own accord – and they can't all be false. But that doesn't happen at Doncaster Rovers and that's even though we have our own Director of Football. The difference here is that Mickey Walker, formerly Dave Penney's assistant and one of the club's great characters over the last decade, is another guy who bats for Donny Rovers rather than for himself. He does a great deal of travelling throughout the week looking at possible players, but he does so knowing that the manager of the football club will always have the final word.

I have always striven to give Doncaster folk a club to be proud of – in touch with the community and providing our fans with entertainment, enjoyment and a host of happy memories. There is in the modern game far too great a gap between the 'stars' and those who effectively help to pay their wages. So, at Doncaster Rovers, we make it clear to all our players when they sign for us that they are part of the community and we expect them to represent us in ways other than purely playing football. To be fair, I think our lads have always taken this on board particularly well.

As our managing director Stuart Highfield will tell you, you could write off Doncaster Rovers as a part of the community in the Richardson era. To be frank, that regime couldn't care less about anyone except themselves. So what I and the other officials at Doncaster Rovers set out to do – and are still doing today – is turn ourselves back into a friendly, family club. One asset we had was our Football In the Community programme. This has since been established as one of the most successful schemes in the country – we call it our 'ears to the ground'. Led by Eric Randerson, the staff visit schools and take part in numerous community activities including breakfast clubs, after-school clubs and even birthday parties. We usually put 200 matchday tickets at their disposal. Here we are looking to host deserving folk, young or otherwise, and treat them to an afternoon or evening of football at the Keepmoat. Clearly there are mutual benefits. We are giving out to the community and they, hopefully, will enjoy their visit here and want to come again.

By being out and about in Doncaster we get to hear things we otherwise wouldn't know about. As I was writing this, I was made aware of a former Doncaster Rovers player, now in his later years, who had fallen upon hard times. We have been trying to get help for him through the Football Association's Benevolent Fund, with Stuart looking at his housing needs as he is in the lettings business. Obviously, we wouldn't want to embarrass the player concerned, nor would we have publicised this at all, except to make a point. If there is anything we can do for someone connected with Doncaster Rovers, whether former player, official or fan, we will help if we possibly can.

A couple of years ago I gained a personal experience that taught me a salutary lesson and encouraged me to support those less fortunate than ourselves. Thanks to my liking for champagne I have been behind a few bars over the years, but this was definitely something different. Welcome to Doncatraz! Yes, Stuart and I got ourselves locked up for a day to raise money for a charity supporting prisoners as they tried to resettle after being let out of the nick. We'd already made a contribution from our pre-season match against Fergie's Manchester United at the Keepmoat and were delighted to join a group of folk for a charity lock-in. Among the others who waited that morning at The Regent public house to get their marching orders were Junior Witter, the outstanding local boxer and Rovers' fan into the bargain, and Christa Ackroyd, of BBC's *Look North*. You volunteer sometimes for these things not really knowing what to expect and my eyes were certainly opened to the real world outside of football that day. Even though part of you knows it's not for real, it shakes you up inside when you are handcuffed and frog-marched inside a prison van. It is both a humiliating and a humbling experience, I can tell you. Then when I saw the gates of Doncaster Prison and watched them close behind me, there was a distinct sinking feeling in my stomach. Many freedoms that we take for granted seemed a mile away because there didn't seem any way past those gates.

The really interesting part, however, was talking with the prisoners. We've all got our image of criminals and if yours is of evil monsters, you could be sadly disappointed. Most of the blokes I spoke with were inside for drug-related offences and, in all honesty, came across as reasonably nice people. It quickly made me realise that there is some truth in that old phrase 'There but for the grace of God go I'. Often we set out upon similar paths in life. As I've already said, I was brought up without money or fuss on a Doncaster council estate and who knows what could have happened to me? Much depends, it seems, on the people you mix with and who influence you, for better or worse. Drugs weren't around in my day in anything like the way they are now. It wasn't a case of us rejecting them, they weren't really an option. Today things are completely different and I'm sure there are many people who dip their toes in the water and then get themselves hooked with all the awful side-effects that brings into their life.

The question that came into my mind was how to get people out of that cycle. Naturally, they deserve their punishment and must serve their time and I fully respect those who have suffered as victims – or relatives of victims – who believe those sentences can be too lenient. But, also, society needs to do more than purely contain them in a cell, let them out again, and be surprised when they fall back into a life of crime over and over again. Some of the blokes I spoke to were more content in prison than in the outside world. They become institutionalised but at least they are getting their meals, their accommodation and they don't have to worry about everyday issues such as paying bills.

Changing that is difficult, but this is where the charity comes in. Housing is clearly an extremely important issue as a large percentage lose their homes, for whatever reason, when they are sent inside. It's very hard to start getting back on track without having a reliable roof over your head. Our fund-raising role that day was to phone our friends for 'ransom' money – or, in my case, to ensure I stayed out of trouble a bit longer perhaps. Altogether the club raised over £25,000 from the United game and the lock-in and I hope that cash helps to give some people new hope.

Another way in which we regularly help charities at Donny is through the Community Shield match at Wembley. Each club takes £5,000 from the game which is the traditional curtain-raiser for the football season. Last year, for example, we split the money three ways. After hearing about a young boy with a heart defect we gave a donation to the Sheffield Children's Hospital.

A further amount went to the Harry Priestley House for autistic children at Thorne, near Doncaster, and Stuart kindly shook a few hands to provide help for the NSPCC, who have a local branch in White Rose Way. The local Freemasons agreed to match the cash that we put in to present £3,000 towards a Peace Room there. And, as already described, at the end of last season we illustrated our continuing support for this wonderful cause by playing in green against Crystal Palace.

I have always recognised that the fortunes of the town and the club should go hand in hand. A successful football club adds greatly to the economy and spirit of an area and the town, naturally, is the focal point of our support. Alongside our rise over the last decade, there have been highly significant improvements in Doncaster itself that are fast challenging the traditional view of it being a 'flat cap town'. Just consider the magnificent work at the racecourse, improvements to shopping and retail, the futuristic buildings on the Lakeside and, not least, the opening of the strangely-named Robin Hood Airport. I must say I never quite saw the sense in that particular name, nor in its other title of Doncaster-Sheffield Airport as, quite simply, it is nowhere near Sheffield. But what is good to see, as someone who travels particularly frequently, is that many airports throughout the globe now refer to it solely as 'Doncaster' – just another way in which the town is being put on the world map.

I would like to see Doncaster continue to flourish and hopefully obtain city status in the not-too-distant future. Anything is possible when you have people with hope and vision at the helm and certainly the progress already made has surprised a good many outsiders. In any case, Doncaster must be at the top of the list as it is the biggest town in the land with a population in the borough of around 275,000.

Our early problems apart we have always had a flourishing relationship with the council, helped in no small measure by the presence of Martin Winter, the town's now former directly-elected Mayor. A rugby league man by nature, the Mayor, who was replaced in June 2009, bought into our vision of being part of a successful and flourishing community and supported us at every turn. Bless him, he even promised to stay away from the Conference play-off final at Stoke City because he didn't have the best of records when seeing us in the flesh. Thankfully that hoodoo has since been overcome and we were delighted he was there to support us at Wembley for our victory against Leeds United.

My personal role as chairman is ever changing and should never, in my mind, be cast in stone. Certainly the job I began more than ten years ago was rather different to the one I have now. The common denominator, I would say, is that I have always been the main driver of the football club, although my direct involvement in day-to-day affairs varies depending on whom I am working with. A good example is publicity, an area that comes quite naturally to me.

As I've already said, Doncaster Rovers had become a laughing stock through the Ken Richardson regime. But the real danger was that once the laughter had died down, we would encounter something even worse – being forgotten about altogether. That was one reason why I quickly established good links with the media. Doncaster Rovers became a 'story' again when Ian and Glynn Snodin, Neville Southall, Steve Nicol and other well-known faces came in to help our seemingly dead club take our first tentative steps towards recovery. I enjoyed speaking with the local and national media to tell them the good news.

Three or four years down the road, however, and we were not quite such a novelty as we were still toiling away in the Conference. It was during this time that I added a bit of calculated madness to my methods. Certainly I don't think I have ever seen journalists so excited as when I told them that the chairman was going to make an appearance in a Conference match and create a record into the bargain. Mind you, it would be stretching it a bit to say that our manager Dave Penney was quite so excited. I think he would have happily dished out a valium if it had put me off the seemingly crazy idea.

Rarely can a few minutes of inaction from a non-player 30 years past his best have resulted in so many column inches. An afternoon that would otherwise have scarcely merited a couple of lines – the result was irrelevant to the destiny of both sides – instead brought a media throng to Hereford, who weren't complaining themselves at the thought of an extra 1,000 on the gate. In addition, I did 50 interviews in the days after the game, appearing with such football legends as Jeremy Clarkson and Edwina Currie.

When nothing much is going on you have to kick-start

something and see where the rollercoaster will take you. Fortunately for us, we got promotion a couple of weeks later via the Conference play-offs back into the Football League and Doncaster Rovers were a big national story once again.

Generally, talking to the media is an area of the game you either like or you don't. I don't regard talking about my beloved Doncaster Rovers to anyone who cares to listen as much of a hardship. As my friends will tell you, I'm a straightforward, plain-talking sort of guy and I've adopted the same approach with the media. If someone asks me a question, I'll give them an honest answer, but not necessarily the one they expect.

Some folk treat the written press as if they are handling snakes, but I don't go with that at all. Reporters, like everyone else, are doing a job and there are good ones and not-so-good ones. I've been misquoted a fair few times but start by giving folk the benefit of the doubt and more often than not haven't been let down. Over the years I've enjoyed great links with several media folk. Radio Sheffield's Paul Walker, Andy Giddings and Seth Bennett always gave us a fair crack when we were at the bottom of the pile and have taken great pleasure in our subsequent success story. I've done a few stints as an 'expert' with their commentators and been interviewed on many occasions. As I've already said, one way I keep in touch with fellow fans is through the station's excellent *Football Heaven* phone-in programme. I listen to the one-hour show live when I can or replay it on the internet, switching off when Sheffield Wednesday fans come on. Only joking, of course, as the show reminds me always just what a soccer hotbed we have in South Yorkshire. For the same radio station covers both Sheffield clubs, Barnsley, Rotherham, Chesterfield and ourselves – six full-time clubs within a fairly narrow radius.

Peter Catt, of the *Doncaster Free Press*, is another good

mate. Blimey, he's probably the only person still around who has been a Rovers fan longer than I have. Again, it's great that someone who has been around long enough to know the whole story, warts and all, can now sit in our superb stadium and enjoy the type of football we are serving up. Well done, Mr A, and I'm not letting on why you have that nickname, wide boy! The *Sheffield Star* have also done us proud over the years and again they have a Donny reporter in Steve Hossack who did the Conference trail with us and so knows most of what there is to know about Doncaster Rovers. The coverage we have had locally has been enthusiastic, informative and comprehensive and we couldn't have asked for any more.

It's always been more difficult to deal with reporters from the tabloids, but generally we've fared well. They have always associated me with my cosmetic surgery business and I don't suppose I can complain too much about being continually bracketed with Melinda Messenger. Tabloid hacks can be a law unto themselves, however, such as one reporter who said he wanted my view on a controversial topic – and if I didn't provide him with a quote, he'd make one up! I can't remember what the subject was, but fortunately I was able to give him plenty of my own words.

You get back what you give out to a great extent in this world and generally the press have revelled in what has been a true fairytale success story. In turn, I'm delighted we have undergone a press revolution at Doncaster Rovers to complement our transformation on the pitch. Visitors to Belle Vue will recall that the facilities there were among the sparsest for the media, even if they were assured of a warm, friendly welcome. Poor souls, there was hardly space for them to balance a cup of tea – if they were lucky enough to get one. Yet now we have facilities at the Keepmoat that are the envy of almost all of our fellow clubs in the

Championship. In fact only Derby and Birmingham, both Premier League clubs the season before, matched us in officially providing for every media need last term. Even they'd be struggling to find anything to compare with our Toppings pies, made in Doncaster and apparently as good as you'll taste anywhere. I must treat myself one day...

The degree of my involvement with the media varies, naturally, on the manager of the club. It will surprise no one when I say that Dave Penney was a good deal happier to deal with the media than our current boss Sean O'Driscoll – and I'm not implying any criticism of the latter. So I am often the club's main spokesperson these days because the role comes more naturally to me.

I'm not called upon on a daily basis exactly, but will normally field several enquiries a week. Naturally, as we have moved up the leagues, the TV has taken more of an interest in us and I've even been able to test out my penalty-taking skills on my pitch at home against reporters from Sky Sports News. Typically, they waited for me to miss one and broadcast that. Just shows the media always prefers the bad news. Seriously, though, I am personally delighted that Donny Rovers are big news these days – long may it continue.

One of my abiding principles as chairman is to try to create stability – and as far as managers are concerned that means you don't want to have too many of them. We all know clubs where managers appear to be coming and going every few months. Show me such a club and I'll bet they are not very successful. Contrast this with the leading clubs in the land and the long tenures of the likes of Sir Alex Ferguson at Manchester United and Arsene Wenger at Arsenal and my point is obvious.

It makes no sense to have constant change at the top. I read recently that the average time a current Championship manager spends in any one post is between 12 and 13 months. Such short-term thinking has many adverse implications. A manager on borrowed time will inevitably concentrate on trying to achieve instant success through the transfer market, rather than trying to develop the players he already has and paying attention to the club's youngsters. Early this season I noted that the Forest manager Billy Davies, admittedly one of the biggest moaners in the modern game, claimed that only if he was given a long-term contract could he be expected to look to the future and work with the club's academy. On this occasion, I agree with him.

As I have already described, my first managerial appointment was Ian Snodin, who came back to the club with his brother Glynn as his assistant, before subsequently being succeeded by Steve Wignall, Dave Penney and most latterly Sean O'Driscoll. The hardest change of all was clearly the departure of Dave Penney, who led us for five mostly glorious years, again as already outlined. The fact that Dave is no longer here shouldn't detract from what he achieved.

It's helpful, however, to look at the distinct role of a manager and realise that usually it is more time-limited than that, say, of an administrator. Under Dave Penney, we achieved our first and most important aim of getting back into the Football League and then simply swept most of our opponents aside in claiming the League Three title 12 months later. Dave was a devout believer in a high-tempo game based on a 4-4-2 formation and some of the football we produced in his time here was breathtaking to watch.

We won countless admirers not only for our giantkilling ability but also for the sheer quality of our play during the run to the Carling Cup quarter-final in 2005/6. If there was a disappointment, however, it was how we fared in League One after being knocked out of the cup in that epic tie against

Arsenal a few days before Christmas. I certainly felt that we had the quality in the squad to at least make the play-offs, yet it didn't really happen for us. We finished in a creditable enough ninth spot but the pressure was then on to take the next step forward. There had been strong rumours linking Dave Penney with a move towards the end of the season.

I have always insisted I would not stand in the way of the ambition of either a player or a member of my staff and that was the case with the manager. Nottingham Forest were without a manager at the time after the resignation of Gary Megson and they were one of the clubs reported to be interested. I apparently surprised a few folk when I told Radio Nottingham that if they wanted Dave they'd better come and get him. It wasn't that I wanted Dave to leave at that point – I didn't. But I couldn't realistically have stood in his way if a club of Forest's stature had made an official approach. But neither Forest, nor anyone else for that matter, asked for permission to speak to him.

We stepped up the budget for the following season, brought a couple of players in and began the 2006/7 season bursting with optimism. There was a definite feeling, almost an expectation, that this time we would conquer League One and win a coveted place in the Championship. Early results, however, were a disappointment. We struggled for goals and points and looked in a bit of a rut. The end came quite quickly and wasn't universally well received. Ironically, in retrospect, Dave's last game was a 1-1 draw at Belle Vue against a side who always seemed to do well against us – Sean O'Driscoll's Bournemouth.

We often hear the phrase 'mutual agreement' when a manager leaves a football club – it's usually a piece of spin to hide the fact that the boss was actually sacked. Well, in Dave's case, I'll make no secret that the responsibility for what happened was mine. As the chairman, I was the one who decided that a parting of the ways would benefit both Dave and Rovers. I'm not saying that Dave was happy at first, but he didn't particularly disagree with what I thought. Over time the message and the tactics can become a bit familiar and I could see us becoming an average League One side, falling short of my promise of Championship soccer. We gave Dave a £100,000 pay-off, which I consider he thoroughly deserved after all he did for Rovers over eight years as a player and then manager. I was also delighted that he walked into a good job at Darlington although I admit I was more than a little surprised he wasn't courted by League One clubs or above. Dave got a great reception when he brought Darlington here for a Johnstone's Paint Trophy match shortly after the opening of the new stadium and we still talk from time to time. I was delighted to give Dave a very positive recommendation for the job at League One Oldham Athletic and I fully expect him to do well there.

In short, without Dave Penney this dream could never have happened but someone has to make tough decisions and that someone was me. The only way to judge such a decision is to give it time and see what happens. I took a lot of criticism from unhappy fans but all I can say is that both Dave Penney and Doncaster Rovers have flourished since.

The next few days were a deliberate smokescreen, in which I encouraged the media to talk about Kevin Keegan, knowing my real target could not have been more different. Yet, as I have already said, there was only one name in the frame as far as I was concerned – Sean O'Driscoll, or 'Sean Who?' as he was known at first. I will never forget that trip down to the south coast a year or so previously when we were thrashed 5-0 at Bournemouth – however much I wish I could. We were four goals down within the first 20 minutes or so and beaten out of sight by a seemingly modest home side who passed around us all night.

All in all, it was one of the best performances I had ever seen at League One level and certain factors made it all the more significant. Yes, we lost a few football matches that season but we had clashed swords with Manchester City, Aston Villa and Arsenal and hadn't been outplayed or outclassed by any of them. In fact that Bournemouth game was one of very few occasions during our rise up the leagues when we have been handed a lesson in the fundamentals of the game.

The other factor that caught my imagination was the lack of resources at O'Driscoll's disposal. Sure he had good players such as Brian Stock and James Hayter who have followed him to South Yorkshire and made their mark here – but Bournemouth were then a shoestring club whose financial problems since have taken few by surprise. The man had been working miracles for years there, without really getting noticed.

Many chairmen might want a big name to instantly please the fans - I was looking a bit deeper than that. My thinking was that if Sean O'Driscoll and his faithful and likeable assistant Richard O'Kelly could produce such excellent football and keep the Cherries in League One with only a few pennies to scrape together, what could they do for a better resourced club such as Doncaster Rovers?

Naturally I discussed my feelings with my fellow directors and then made my move. It wasn't totally straightforward. O'Driscoll had spent 26 years as a player and official at Bournemouth and it was a wrench for him to leave a place where he was greatly appreciated. Yet the novelty of the approach appealed to him. He liked the idea that he was wanted. Bournemouth's form in League One may have won him plenty of admirers, but he had rarely been mentioned when vacancies came up. Also he bought into my vision. He immediately understood my ambition and the fact that I was backing my words up with actions. Here was a club that would support the way he wanted to play the game and, crucially, had the resources to go further than he could have hoped to achieve on the south coast.

The looks on some of the faces at the press conference told me the public would need a fair deal of convincing. They'd seen a great Rovers favourite in Penney depart and in his place came a man most had barely heard of. We produced a reasonable first performance to draw 0-0 in a league game at Huddersfield on the night following Sean's appointment but the next few weeks and months were anything but easy. We didn't score many goals or win many games and the murmuring of the fans turned quickly to heated criticism. I was soon under very heavy pressure to go back on my gut instinct and get rid of the mild-mannered manager.

Quite apart from the moderate form, O'Driscoll was always going to be an acquired taste for the media and the fans. The public like tubthumping managers who make their presence felt on the touchline and come out with interesting comments in the press – but this man was neither. In fact the bloke is quiet, not good at projecting himself and far more at home with a cup of tea than a bottle of champagne. Getting a word out of Sean is quite difficult on occasions and he doesn't enjoy the press side at all. He just doesn't feel comfortable with it. But there's more to football than public image and certainly far more to this deep thinker than meets the eye. I could see he was enthusiastic in getting his tactics and methods through to the players and that they, in turn, enjoyed working with him.

O'Driscoll carefully changed the shape of the side, ensuring we still played the good football we'd become known for under Penney whilst adding more variation and guile going forward. The game is littered with examples of managers who could so easily have been sacked by their clubs if the supporters had their way – Sir Alex Ferguson, Brian Clough and Martin O'Neill among them – but who have gone on to become very successful. I stood by my man and gave him what all new managers need and so rarely get – time.

Things began to turn for O'Driscoll with our run to the Millennium Stadium and eventual glory in the Johnstone's Paint Trophy and, so far, we haven't looked back. I've got the highest regard for him and genuinely hope he is our manager for many years to come – how many chairmen would dare put that statement into print? I labelled him as the Arsene Wenger of League One and now we're in the Championship have seen no reason to change my opinion. Wenger's qualities are tactical and he gets the last ounce out of the talent at his disposal at Arsenal. His eyesight may not always be the best but his persona on the touchline is usually that of a man who has got his message across and expects his players to do the job. It's much the same with Sean. Tactically he is up there with the best and he has no reason to rant or rave. He tells me that the players go out there knowing what they need to do and that's fair enough.

In many ways he comes across as a stoical figure like the former England and Manchester City boss Sven-Göran Eriksson – but that doesn't mean his heart doesn't beat just as fast as the rest of us. Personally, I have never known a more hard-working boss. I phone him two or three times a week at the very least and, often, he is on his way to a match many miles from home checking on this or that player. The relationship between us – very different characters it has to be said – works extremely well. I knew that if we were going to make it to the Championship we would need a manager confident in his ability to punch above his weight – that is Sean to a tee. He doesn't look at Newcastle, Middlesbrough or Derby County and wonder how a small club like Donny can compete with them. He simplifies the game down to its basics – eleven against eleven, his tactics and know-how against another human being and their ideas – and just gets on with the job. You won't hear Sean going over the top when we've won, or getting too down in the dumps when the result has gone the other way. He always looks behind the scoreline to the quality of our performance and helps to keep everyone's feet on the ground.

Clubs get the management they deserve these days by continually putting them in a position where they feel they are only three or four defeats away from the axe. The result is a manic merry-go-round of the same folk being hounded out of a job one day and being welcomed as the Messiah in another part of the country the next. One particularly self-defeating trend in our game is what I call caretaker or new manager syndrome. Anyone who has been involved in football at any level has experienced it, I'm sure. The manager goes out of the revolving door and in his place comes a temporary or full-time appointment. The problems of the previous few weeks and months are then instantly blotted out by two or three victories, usually helped by a couple of previously disaffected players coming back into the side with a point to prove. The almost inevitable result is that the caretaker's role is made permanent or the new manager is further welcomed as the answer to all the club's problems. But surely what has occurred is more often than not just the result of human nature and a bit of psychology. It's the easiest thing in the world to come into a job and make a peace offering to players who have fallen out of favour. In turn, some players who had previously resigned themselves to being out of the team or even looking for a move elsewhere are given an instant lift by the idea that the past has been forgotten and they can start again with a clean slate. In many ways it is a case of a change, almost any change, being as good as a rest. Staff in any office are usually keen to impress a new boss and I'm sure this happens when a new broom sweeps into a football club.

So far, so good, you may well say, but how long does this last? It doesn't matter how well your new man has started, there will inevitably be a time when things even out and the grumbles begin. All of a sudden the chairman finds himself in exactly the same situation – with the exception that he has had to pay off the deposed manager and his coaching staff and employ new ones with the bait of cash being available for new additions. I could expand on this scenario much further but I trust you get my point. I'd rather advocate the Doncaster Rovers way of building gradually, taking into account the longer term as well as last Saturday's result. The re-establishment of the youth side here has been a very important part of the progress we have made. I urge Sean O'Driscoll and Richard O'Kelly to bring young players through as a way of ensuring this club continues to thrive in the future. I'd like to think that Sean can do just that, knowing he is a part of our longer-term plans himself.

It gives me huge pleasure to walk around Doncaster these days and notice the way the football landscape has changed in the last few years. There was a time – and it wasn't very long ago – when you'd scarcely spot a Rovers shirt among those wearing the colours of Leeds United, Sheffield Wednesday and Manchester United in particular. Today Doncaster is packed with proud Rovers fans and it would take a brave man indeed to sport Leeds's colours. It's such a shame when you visit places and you barely know where you are. Young fans easily get on the bandwagon of the elite clubs of the land and their local bread and butter clubs are left in the background. That's not something that's ultimately sustainable for our game, nor a climate that a fans' chairman should leave unchallenged.

However far we rise in football – and I don't think we've

finished yet – we will never forget the grass roots and 'real football'. I met fantastic people and visited great clubs in the Conference and they will always be in my mind as I set about my job in the future. The Premier League and its associated TV coverage has done a great deal for the game. It has taken English football and put it on a truly global stage where it is loved and appreciated all over the world. But we must not allow the wealth and often greed of a few to destroy the rest of our game. The way the financial rewards are distributed these days is little more than a disgrace. Each and every step you make up the pyramid brings the same dilemma – the need for more cash and the very real possibility of debt. Then there's this one and only step into the magical world of the Premier League where the money is suddenly thrown at you. Naturally one of the main issues is spiralling wages and again the problems come from the top downwards. Each time a major Premiership star agrees a £100,000-a-week deal, it creates potential difficulties for us down the line. For inevitably we have to measure ourselves against that high benchmark and players and agents quickly want more cash.

To put things into perspective, we don't have any superstars at Doncaster Rovers. Typical of the way things are is our goalkeeper Neil Sullivan, who has perhaps the most glamourous background of any of our players having been with Spurs and Leeds United. Neil is a gentle giant who happily puts a fair deal of his time into a local charity based at Sheffield Children's Hospital along with two other patrons, our Director of Football Mickey Walker and Kevin Keegan. Goalkeepers, like heavyweight boxers, seem to go on forever these days and Sully is a fantastic role model for the younger players.

Compared with other Championship clubs, neither the players nor Sean and his assistant Richard O'Kelly are on huge bucks by any means, but all get good bonuses for results. They got a healthy reward for keeping us in the Championship in 2008/09 and have an even bigger incentive to steer us into the Premier League.

There's a lot to be said for job satisfaction, even in this mercenary day and age. And one of the reasons we have always had a fair amount of continuity at Rovers is that the players tend to be happy. They get on well with each other, are in a friendly, supportive environment and the style of football we play here is attractive. They also enjoy playing for Sean. Ask an average player whether he'd prefer to play in a passing team or one where the ball spends most of its time flying above their heads and the answer is obvious. We play to a pattern where the ball is kept on the ground and moved quickly in the manner, you might say, of a Brian Clough team. Which means that our midfield is given the opportunity to play; an ideal platform for the talents of Richie Wellens, Brian Stock, James Coppinger and Paul Green in recent years.

I would wager that most fans could have named the side for much of last season and not gone too far wrong. Continuity is a key factor of our club at all levels. We've had continuity in the boardroom, continuity of management and, as far as possible, a settled squad. Several lads from the Conference days stayed with us a good while – I'm talking about Andy Warrington, Simon Marples, Ricky Ravenhill, Steve Foster and, of course, Greenie himself. There have to be changes as players go through their careers and a club is on an upward curve such as ourselves, but I don't see us as being a club that will suddenly bring in a dozen players in a transfer window. I'm not sure I've got a chequebook big enough and in any case it goes very much against the team ethic that we are at pains to promote here.

Although I spend a fair amount of time abroad, I attend

the vast majority of Rovers matches home and away and when absent listen avidly to every kick, if I possibly can. After all, I wouldn't want to miss the best bit after all the work that goes into getting a side on the pitch. Like every other fan, the most exciting thing of all, even after all these years, is the next game. That will never change.

12

*

PRAISE AND GRUMBLE

ONE of my favourite listens is a post-match phone-in show on Radio Sheffield going by the name of *Praise or Grumble*. As you can imagine this gives football supporters the chance to let off a little steam whether they have been delighted or disgusted by what they have seen on a Saturday afternoon.

Unfortunately, I don't get a chance to ring in myself, but please allow me the opportunity to indulge myself a little here. This is my personal 'Praise and Grumble' about some of the clubs, characters and issues in our modern game. As my glass is half-full, they are mostly of the 'praise' variety but, let's face it, life wouldn't be the same without a good old grumble in the right place.

So let's start by turning to one subject that occupies a fair amount of my attention – the whistle-blowers! Anyone who has sat near me at a Rovers match will recognise that I invariably give the referee the benefit of my views during the 90 minutes. So perhaps it is time to set the record straight.

Being a referee, or officiating on the line for that matter, is a very difficult job. Some whistle-blowers at Donny over the years would have finished second to Ken Richardson in a popularity contest – and that's saying something. If a referee has got things wrong in my opinion, I will tell them so. But I am not so blinkered as certain other people in the game who seem to think every official is conspiring against their team. I am among the first people to say 'well done' to a referee if, in my view, he (or she) has had a particularly good game. And they don't get too much stick from our manager Sean O'Driscoll, who is usually as quiet as a mouse on the touchline.

In fact, from the moment they arrive at the ground until the final whistle, we will generally give the officials breathing space to do their jobs to the best of their ability – and get on with our own. There are clubs and managers where this has not been the case and the most obvious example was my good mate Neil Warnock, particularly when he was at Bramall Lane. He seemed to be continually running the gauntlet of the officials as he menacingly patrolled the touchline – but did he get more decisions in favour of his team as a result? There is a school of thought in the game that it can even go the opposite way on occasions.

Overall, after nearly 50 years watching football matches, I'd say that refs are much maligned without due cause. They generally do a far better job than they are given credit for and the task they have is far more testing than the average fan imagines. Test supporters on the rules of the game and you'll discover that we don't always know as much as we think. Even last season I was taken aback over something as seemingly simple as the pass-back law. There I was roaring for an indirect free-kick to be given to Rovers when a Cardiff City defender controlled the ball with his thigh in the 1-1 draw at the Keepmoat and diverted the ball back to his goalkeeper. It took that wise old owl Peter Ridsdale, the

Bluebirds chairman and former chairman of Leeds United, to tell me that the referee was right because that doesn't count as a pass-back. So, even at my age, this game sometimes causes us to live and learn.

It is true, I would suggest, that the quality improves greatly the higher you climb up the football ladder. No disrespect to the officials in the Conference, but they don't compare with the standard we have since witnessed in League One and now The Championship. The art of refereeing is threefold in my eyes.

The first skill is to apply the laws of the game and in this respect most officials score very highly. The areas that are far more challenging are those of common sense and man-management. It is these that divide the top refs from the not-so-good. We've all seen matches that are halted every few seconds for a so-called infringement and others, just as fiercely contested, that appear to flow with the referee scarcely being noticed. No prizes for guessing which approach is conducive to an afternoon's entertainment. Man-management in any form of life is a very difficult art and, quite frankly, some officials have it and others haven't. None of us advocate a softly, softly approach where even bad or dangerous challenges go unpunished yet, at the same time, if a referee is dishing out noticeably more yellow and red cards than his fellow officials it is likely to be a negative sign. Good man-managers command the instant respect of people they are working with. They don't have to force the issue.

One official I have long admired is Mark Halsey, who is a very good advertisement for referees having played the game themselves. As we all know, this is something of a rarity as the retiring age of top-class referees has meant it is difficult to go through the ranks and make it as an official unless you start quite early. Mark, however, was a player at Conference level and it shows in the way he manages players. One vivid example which comes to mind was a true blood and thunder FA Cup-tie involving Rovers at Southend United which finished in a 1-0 away win. This was the sort of clash where a lesser official could easily have lost control, but Mark performed magnificently. Afterwards I told him that, in my opinion, he'd been the 'best player on the pitch' and I was sure he'd make it all the way to the Premiership. That has of course happened, with Mark also officiating in the Carling Cup final in 2008 when Tottenham Hotspur defeated Chelsea 2-1 at Wembley.

As I've stated already, I was dismayed when I felt that Mark was hung out to dry by his colleagues after making what I considered to be the correct decision in sending off the England captain John Terry during Chelsea's 3-1 Premiership victory at Manchester City. I, for one, was on the phone giving Mark support – this was another occasion in which being a referee became a very lonely place. But even that was put into stark perspective at the start of the current season when, just a couple of weeks after kindly agreeing to officiate at Mickey Walker's testimonial along with Howard Webb and Uriah Rennie, Mark was taken ill after the opening day of the Premiership season. My very best wishes go to Mark for his full recovery from cancer but, in the meantime, the game is all the poorer without him.

In the same week as the Terry fiasco, I wrote an urgent plea on behalf of officials in the Rovers programme for the match against Charlton Athletic. In my experience referees, like goalkeepers, can mature and improve dramatically with age and I think it was self-defeating to force them to retire as early as 47. In my notes I argued that, providing they are still able to pass what has over the years become a vigorous fitness test, they should be considered young enough until the more realistic age of 55.

The issue of age had been on my lips since the League

One play-off semi-final when Paul Taylor refereed our first leg against Southend United at Roots Hall. Again, some chairmen may have been less inclined to praise Paul after he sent off Paul Heffernan towards the end of an entertaining goalless draw – particularly as it meant that Heffs, one of our top marksmen, was automatically out of the remaining games of the season. But to be honest I thought that Taylor had a very accomplished game and was both surprised and disappointed when he told me afterwards that this could well have been his last game as he was past his 47th birthday. I felt so strongly about the situation that I spoke to Messrs Allison and Hackett and made my views known. I was delighted when, later in the summer, Paul sent me an email thanking and informing me that he'd been granted an extra year. It was also a positive move in my opinion when Peter Walton and Uriah Rennie, who are also both excellent officials, were given the same extension. We need more of that kind of action because we don't have such a limitless supply of top officials to discard their experience and ability lightly.

We all know the game is played at a fairly frantic pace these days. This calls for the referee to have both a cool head and excellent man-management skills and these are often developed through experience. Another top referee who exemplifies what I'm saying here is Nigel Miller. When I first saw him referee, I have to admit I was far from impressed. If anything, he tended to mess things up more than most. But the last time I saw him take charge in a pulsating 2-2 draw with Huddersfield Town was a completely different story. Despite the fact that he sent off Matty Mills – quite rightly, I might add – I thought he had a magnificent game and wasn't shy in telling him so afterwards. Also it's great to see Andrew Marriner in action. He was the referee for our famous Conference play-off final against Dagenham and

Redbridge and has proved the point that cream really does rise to the top by making it into the Premiership. I'm pleased to say also that with folk like David Allison and Keith Hackett in top posts, there is a common sense approach to a lot of refereeing issues these days. Allison is one of the game's unsung heroes - looking after Football League referees - and I've always found him to be fair and objective. The best talent generally is coming through into the Football League and the Premiership, and both Allison and Hackett have been instrumental in giving some flexibility to the age law I touched upon earlier.

It is true that when you look at who is refereeing your match on a Saturday or perhaps in midweek, your heart can either skip an extra beat or sink a little. Obviously, I'm not going to drop my foot in it by telling you the referees I would rather not see at the Keepmoat in future, as I don't particularly want to end up before the FA on a disrepute charge. But every now and again we, like any other club, make our point that an official may not be the best choice for a particular game, perhaps because of previous history. All clubs probably think there are refs who don't tend to handle their games particularly well and that's fair enough. But what I would emphasise here is that I genuinely believe they make honest mistakes. You'll always get conspiracy theories and there have been much-publicised stories of how referees have been lavishly entertained before games, particularly abroad. But the truth is that it would not make any sense for officials to show any deliberate bias and I don't think that happens. You've got to remember that referees have assessors on their backs and, should they be shown to have made an important error, are probably more likely to be dropped for the next match than any of the players.

It would be extremely helpful for fans and club officials, however, if referees were encouraged to give interviews after a match to explain key incidents. I have often thought that a particular decision was ridiculous until I have spoken with an official afterwards and he has explained what he saw and why he took the action he did. Let me tell you of some contrasting incidents. We all looked on in disbelief back in 2004 when Pedro Mendes, then of Tottenham Hotspur, was denied what we could all see on TV was a blatant goal in a match against Manchester United at Old Trafford. Mendes, more recently of Portsmouth, launched a fantastic bolt out of the blue from just inside his own half that looped over the goalkeeper, hit the crossbar and bounced a good couple of feet over the United line. The game was scoreless at the time and a goal would probably have given Spurs a rare and notable victory over their illustrious rivals. But instead the United goalkeeper, Roy Carroll, desperately scooped the ball back into play and the 'goal' was not given. The incident will certainly strike a chord with fans of our neighbours Chesterfield, who were denied what might well have been an FA Cup-final appearance by a controversial decision in their semi-final tie against Premiership Middlesbrough in 1997. The underdogs were leading 2-1 when a shot from Jonathan Howard hit the bar and again was shown by TV cameras to have gone over the line. Last season it was our turn to be 'robbed' when Forest's Lee Camp scooped a ball back into play from well over the line at the Keepmoat in a game that finished 0-0.

The point I am making is this – the decisions in all these instances were clearly wrong, yet that does not mean you can attribute blame to the officials. They can only give decisions on what they actually see and, from where they were standing in the United game for example, it was clearly impossible to know for sure that the ball had crossed the line. X-ray vision is a quality given only, it seems, to a certain Russian linesman who was just about the only person on the planet to be sure that Geoff Hurst's second goal for England against West Germany was over the line in the 1966 World Cup final. Bless him. Forty odd years later, he's long gone and we're still debating it.

Perhaps, however, he was employing the same errant logic as the referee at our Conference game against Southport, who decided that a long-range blockbuster from one of their players had indeed crossed the line after striking the underside of the bar. There was no way I could be sure from where I was sitting, so I went over afterwards to the spot where the referee was standing and was even less convinced. He told me that it had been his 'gut instinct' that the ball had gone in. This was all very well and good, but a Southport official and referee who was standing in just the right spot confirmed it hadn't even been close. You probably realise by now where all this is leading…

Goal-line technology should surely come into play. This is the one aspect of the game in which resorting to cameras to clear up disputes surely makes sound sense. Such judgements can be the difference between a team achieving great glory or failing and can even cost managers their livelihoods, so let's take advantage of the technology at our disposal to increase our chances of getting the right verdict. On rare occasions there will still be doubt, as in the Hurst goal but, more often than not, technology will confirm whether or not a ball has gone over the line. Last season we had the phantom goal when Reading were credited with a score at Watford when the ball had clearly gone out for a goal-kick, and this term kicked off with Neil Warnock in a justifiable rage at Bristol City where Crystal Palace were not awarded a goal even though the ball actually hit the stanchion at the back of the goal and rebounded back into play. Mistakes are indeed part and parcel of an imperfect sport, but when we can give officials the technology to ensure embarrassing episodes such as these don't happen again, surely that makes good sense.

We could also help Football League referees by taking a leaf out of the book of the Premiership by introducing microphone links between the officials. A classic example occurred in our opening fixture of last season at Derby County. Early in the game Rams striker Rob Hulse clearly used his arm to bundle the ball against our post from close range. You could tell from the half-hearted reaction of our goalkeeper Neil Sullivan that he thought a free-kick was a virtual formality. But, when you look back at the tape, you see that neither the referee, nor his assistant on the relevant side of the field, were able to see it. If Hulse's effort had gone into the net, the goal would have stood and there would have been a highly unnecessary controversy. Yet the fourth official would have had no difficulty using a monitor to track the offence and in the Premiership would have relayed the information to the referee.

Perhaps the most public example of the necessary intervention of the fourth official reportedly came in extra-time of the 2006 World Cup final between France and Italy. The referee didn't see Zinedine Zidane's infamous poleaxing of Italian defender Marco Materazzi, but imagine the furore afterwards if such an incident had gone unpunished. Putting to one side the provocation that may well have occurred, Zidane had to be sent off and was apparently ejected because the fourth official, who was in a better position to view the incident, told the referee what had happened. This surely is not asking too much. Often the fourth official's role seems to be limited largely to policing the technical areas, which is a waste.

As for other instant decisions such as penalty calls when the ball remains in play, it is more difficult to see how technology could play a useful part. I really don't think the game would benefit anyway. Half the after-match debates are about debatable decisions and to take that away would often leave us with little to remember a game for. Human frailty is a big part of life and football.

I haven't got any statistics at my fingertips but I'm sure that you could make a case for the idea that the 'homer' referee does actually exist. Let's put it this way – there have been times when an away side hasn't had a 50-50 verdict in front of Liverpool's Kop and Manchester United went four years without conceding a penalty at Old Trafford. Such discrepancies are more down to psychological factors than intentional bias, in my opinion. We must remember that all officials are human beings and that, when 50,000 fans demand a decision, it is more likely to be given than if an incident is greeted with complete silence at the other end of the park. It's all part and parcel of playing away from home and goes a long way to explaining why most teams win more often on their own patch.

The job of officials has been shown to be incredibly hard, quite apart from the influence of the fans. A survey at Leicester University shed more light on a vexed topic that has been discussed for ages – the offside law. It showed that it is almost impossible on occasions for assistant referees to decide whether a player is onside when the ball is played. The action literally can happen so quickly that it is too fast for the human eye to take in reliably. Considering that, we should marvel at just how often they are shown to be correct when TV has dissected the incident.

Offside, however, is one part of the game that needs further thought. We would all surely be much better off if the law reverted to what it was a few years ago. This whole question of whether a player is interfering with play or when - if at all - he becomes active is open to too much interpretation. One official will see it one way, the following week you may get a referee who takes the opposite view. Ask the players and the thing that irks them most of all is inconsistency. They need to know where they stand and if an opposition striker is standing in yards of space behind your defence, you should be able to presume he is offside. But the current offside law is causing a lot of head-scratching and that can't be right.

There are times, naturally, when referees drop pretty unforgivable clangers that, once you are over the initial shock, leave you with a good story to dine out on. One poor Telford United player couldn't believe it when he smashed a long-range shot into the back of our net at Belle Vue only for the referee to remain motionless and for play to go on. What virtually everyone else in the ground saw – me included – was the ball hitting against the stanchion at the back of the goal and rebounding into play. But the referee must have thought it had come back off the post. The Telford lad was celebrating with a few of his mates when our team were the first to realise that the goal had not actually been given. So then we went up the other end of the pitch – aided by several Telford players still being in a huddle – and should have scored ourselves. Fortunately, we didn't because that would really have added insult to injury.

Last, but certainly not least on the subject of referees, I'd like to give a thumbs up to female officials. Up to going to press, we haven't actually been refereed by a member of the fairer sex, although there have been a few running the line. As someone who has made his living with the help of lovely ladies, you might expect me to be on their side. The first piece of discrimination we had to tackle when my partner Peter Wetzel and I took over at Doncaster was the ban on females going into the boardroom. This wasn't anything unique to Belle Vue, it was the case at many Football League clubs. Times have, of course, changed and there have since been several high-profile women in football management, notably Karren Brady at Birmingham City and Delia Smith, at Norwich. Banishing officials from the boardroom because they were female was ridiculous and there was also no reason why partners shouldn't be allowed hospitality. My wife, Lynne, often goes with me to matches and I wouldn't think much of a club that didn't allow her to accompany me into the boardroom. The same principle applies to female officials. The former Luton Town manager Mike Newell got himself into some particularly hot water for his comments on a referee's assistant. I certainly wouldn't want to immerse myself in that debate, but where I stand is pretty clear. Providing they can do the job, there simply isn't a problem. If Melinda Messenger herself should walk out at the Keepmoat you won't find me complaining – so long as she didn't give me a red card. More seriously, people will say that it is more difficult for a woman to control 22 males on a football pitch and there is some sense in that argument. But, for me, if a woman can work her way up from the lower leagues, taking in her stride all the flak she will inevitably get, then she is well-qualified for any problems she will encounter in the big-time game.

TURNING to broader issues, it might surprise a few folk to know how strong an affinity I have with both the Manchester giants. Living as I do in Cheshire, United and City are almost on my doorstep and at different times in my life I could have had my pick of either club.

With United, I nearly pulled off the business sale of the century - buying 20 per cent of arguably the world's greatest club for just £1m. No, this wasn't a knock-down figure caused by the world financial crisis, but cold sober reality back in 1986. This was when Michael Knighton - who later acquired a fair amount of notoriety through his spell at

Carlisle United - was attempting to buy the club. My interest was through my company Transform, which I was heading at the time with a business partner Paul Cartwright who, unfortunately as it turned out, had no interest in football at all. Our company was cash rich, so there was no financial reason why we shouldn't have snapped their hands off.

I did my utmost to persuade Paul that we wouldn't so much be buying into a football club as an institution and this was a gamble we really couldn't lose. But Paul wasn't for budging and, without his backing, our hands were tied. You can imagine I'm sure what a 20 per cent share in United would be worth nowadays – more like £200m; not a bad return on a £1m investment. All good anglers will know what I mean – United was the business fish that got away.

Notwithstanding that disappointment, I will always have time for United. There is something in their very name that conjures up an image of the beautiful game at its very best. It touched my football soul in a very deep way that our two clubs, so different in stature, were able to come together at the beginning of the 2007/8 season to mark what I saw as a time of closure. For not only were we embarking on a season that was to end our 50-year exile from the second-flight of English football, we were also massively mindful that 2008 was the 50th anniversary of one of the most tragic days in football – the Munich Air Disaster in which eight of Manchester United's finest lost their lives. And, of course, United produced their own perfect ending by winning both the Premier League and the Champions League.

The occasion was a pre-season friendly, arranged as a fulfilment of Sir Alex Ferguson's promise to officially celebrate the opening of the Keepmoat Stadium. Bridging the half-century between the United of yesterday and the United of today was the great Sir Bobby Charlton, who got a fantastic ovation from the fans as he walked out onto our pitch that Friday evening. Bobby was a survivor of that awful night in Germany before going on to become one of England's all-time heroes in the 1966 World Cup-winning side. Bobby has always been part of the fabric at Old Trafford yet reminded me that, as an Ashington lad, he always had a great affinity with Doncaster - not least because he was great mates with David Pegg, the Donny-born United player, who was one of the victims. Bobby discovered much in common between our two then-mining communities and it was poignant indeed that David Pegg's sister, who still lives in Doncaster, was able to put up a plaque at the Keepmoat in memory of the Busby Babes.

It was also another opportunity to chat with one of the most successful managers of all time, Sir Alex himself. I have had the pleasure of being in his company on numerous occasions, getting an insight into the man and his club. His image is that of the brusque, unyielding Scot but, personally, I have always found him to be a charming person, who certainly impresses me with the breadth of his football knowledge. During one get-together at The Edge Hotel a few years back, the great man took delight in reproving me for my incorrect pronunciation of Michael McIndoe, and he left me in no doubt that he knew all about the talents of the winger and certain other Rovers players. It's that sort of attention to detail that marks him out among his peers. It meant a great deal to me when Fergie took the time to write and congratulate us on getting back into the Championship. I'm not his only South Yorkshire football buddy, of course. It is a part of football folklore that Fergie could have got the boot from Old Trafford but for a certain Mark Robins popping up with the only goal in an FA Cup third-round tie at Nottingham Forest in 1990. Fergie had been searching for his first elusive piece of silverware for four years and they were already out of the title race before going to Brian

Clough's men as underdogs. We will never know whether United would have achieved all they have in the last couple of decades, but for that priceless 1-0 victory. Perhaps this is a salutary lesson to trigger-happy chairmen who bow to the demands of angry fans and give their managers the boot almost before their feet are under the table. Success never came quickly for Fergie, nor did it for Cloughie who spent two-and-a-half seasons in the old Second Division before even getting Forest promoted. Today, I'm pretty confident that neither would have been given that long to prove their worth. As it happened, success in the final after a replay against Crystal Palace both jet-propelled United into their current successful era and also won Fergie the breathing space he needed.

United's gain has been football's gain, too, as I found when I was banned from Belle Vue by Mr Richardson. I bought six executive tickets at Manchester United and feasted on the football served up by the likes of Eric Cantona, David Beckham, Ryan Giggs and the many superstars of that time. I particularly enjoyed it as, playing in red, United were the next best thing to watching Doncaster. Through my company, I also helped to sponsor a number of events including one that was very close to my heart. It was a play about the Busby era which naturally takes our minds back to the tragedy of Munich. One of the heroes on that awful night was Harry Gregg, the former Rovers goalkeeper. He had become a big name at Belle Vue by December 1957, with Rovers having already turned down a substantial bid for his services from Sheffield Wednesday. But when Manchester United came calling with a world record £23,000 fee for a goalkeeper, there was only going to be one answer. Harry was en route to Old Trafford.

Harry was responsible for dragging several people to safety from that blazing aircraft, including a small baby. A few months later, he played a leading role for Northern Ireland when they reached the quarter-finals of the World Cup in Sweden – the best achievement in their history. The Irish were managed by one Peter Doherty, who had recently been sacked as manager of Doncaster Rovers. Fate allowed Gregg to fulfil his potential at Old Trafford, although he was on the receiving end in the FA Cup Final of 1958 when shoulder-charged into the net by famous England forward Nat Lofthouse of Bolton Wanderers. These days, there wouldn't even be an argument as the free-kick would be awarded in favour of the goalkeeper – but, back then, the goal stood and Bolton won 2-0.

I can't leave the subject of United without referring to the legend that was George Best. Sadly, I can't remember seeing him play, apart from one testimonial match in which he featured for a United side at Belle Vue to raise money for the family of our centre-half John Nicholson, who'd been killed in a car crash. I mostly knew him during his later years and regarded him as a friend. One occasion I particularly remember was a speaking engagement in Doncaster with his friend and former business partner Mike Summerbee. Together they were called the 'Manchester Whingers', being fed a series of questions by the BBC's Tony Gubba, another good friend of mine. George stayed overnight in a hotel in Doncaster. Next morning I greeted him at breakfast and asked him what he would like – thinking perhaps that a full English might be in order. "A Chardonnay would be nice," replied George. That said it all.

I was known as Mr Champagne Man for a time but, for most of us, alcohol doesn't get the upper hand. I saw from the times I was with George how people would always be offering to buy the great man drinks. Sadly, the temptation and opportunity made things all the harder for him. George's mum died from the effects of alcohol and, as we know, he passed away a few years ago after having undergone a liver transplant. It's not up to us to pass judgement on his lifestyle but I'll gladly do so on his football – George was fantastic. He had a God-given ability and elegance that few could ever match. It is just so sad that his career peaked so soon and that we never got the opportunity to view him in the finals of the World Cup. Personally, I will always treasure a photograph I have of George making a presentation to me after I'd made my celebrated appearance at Hereford in 2003. It read: 'From the world's greatest player to the oldest'. To be bracketed in the same sentence as George, even in jest, was quite a compliment.

If Manchester United was the club that got away, City was the one that I voluntarily let out of my grasp. Again my experience of City mostly came during my time away from Belle Vue. One of the friends I made at City was former winger Summerbee, or 'Buzzer' as he is known in the game, who still works at the club. He encouraged me to become a shareholder at Maine Road, albeit on a fairly limited scale, and I held these shares until selling out late in 2007 to the controversial owner Thaksin Shinawatra, the former Thai Prime Minister. Mike, who is City through and through, came with me to Belle Vue for the proud occasion when Alick Jeffrey was made Rovers president and shared some of his memories of the great man's playing days. Then he and former City chairman and playing legend Francis Lee approached me with an offer most people couldn't refuse. It was during the 2003/4 season and the ownership of the club was again in the balance. The duo said that if I made a bid for Mike Bowler's shares, they would back me to become City chairman. It was an unbelievable thought and honour – but an offer I had no choice but to refuse. To become involved with City would have compromised any future involvement with my true love, Doncaster Rovers, and that is the sole reason why I turned this golden opportunity down. Again if I had taken City on, subsequent events would have made me a far richer man. But you can't buy the joy I have had at Rovers and the decision I made was the right one for me.

Manchester City and John Ryan was destined never to be, but one link I will always have in my mind with them was a certain winger with a sweet left foot – I'm referring, of course, to Tony Coleman. Tony was an extremely popular player at Belle Vue in the late 1960s, although things didn't always go to plan. Having played a major part in our challenge for the Fourth Division title in 1965 Coleman fluffed his lines more than a bit when the finishing line was in sight at home to Notts County. We kicked off that match needing just a single point to clinch top place, but ended up frustrated as we lost the game 1-0. But that was only the beginning of Coleman's troubles. He got so mad that he actually thumped the referee and was understandably instantly sent off by the stunned official, a Mr Pickles. You may be surprised to learn that he only received a 28-day ban for an incident that was serious by anyone's standards. Luckily for Coleman, the Rovers and Notts players both testified that the referee had provoked him by calling him a dirty so-and-so!

Coleman fitted happily into Maine Road and was part of City's Championship-winning side in 1968, alongside both Summerbee and Lee. Yet there again he apparently had his moments. Sydney Rose, who also became a close friend and was a City director, told me that he once had an irate father come to the club complaining that Coleman was responsible for his daughter becoming pregnant. How that issue was finally resolved, I guess I'll never know, but I'd prefer to remember Tony's qualities as a player and that wonderful left foot of his. What became of him? Last I heard he was a lorry driver in Australia and, as such, had slipped completely off the radar.

I've got another surprise for City fans; I brought a trophy to your club. It happened during the managerial reign of a certain Donny lad called Kevin Keegan. I contacted Keegan to say I'd love to show him just what his hometown club had achieved by winning the Third Division title. Kevin, being Kevin, took it in the right spirit. Off he went around the pitch with the trophy wearing a Donny shirt and a wig, restoring him to the familiar frizzy-haired Keegan image of his pomp. It was a lovely moment and the only time I've managed to get him to sport Rovers colours. My wife Lynne and I then had lunch with Keegan and the City players at which he showed them the trophy and said: "This is what the game should be all about lads – silverware. How about us going out and trying to win some?" He then asked the assembled squad what they thought I was famous for.

For once the answer didn't include Melinda Messenger and her boobs, but former England striker Robbie Fowler said: "He is the oldest professional footballer in Britain." How my fame had spread! We've had a couple of other chances to view Keegan, the manager, in action – although not, as some mistakenly thought, as our boss. The first was a pre-season friendly at Belle Vue in which Joey Barton made the mistake of taking his anger out on someone not quite his size - Leo Fortune-West, our formidable centre-forward. After young Barton had come off considerably the worse for wear, Keegan mused: "The stupid lad. You would have thought he'd have learned not to have a go at someone 6'4" tall and built like a brick s---house." Typically, Keegan stood by Barton, both through his jail sentence and suspension. Should the young man ever become the good role model he aspires to be, Keegan is one person he really should thank.

I was thrilled to welcome Kevin to the Keepmoat when

his Newcastle United side came here for a prestigious friendly before the start of the 2008/09 season. Kevin was extremely complimentary about the place – quite a culture shock no doubt after what he'd experienced at Belle Vue – and spent ages signing each and every autograph request. That, however, is probably the closest we'll get to luring Keegan to Doncaster as a manager. Someone even more famous than me once said 'never say never', so we can't rule out totally the idea that Keegan will ever manage here – but, in all honesty, it is highly unlikely.

One of my greatest and more realistic regrets is that we never got Keegan playing for Rovers. As you probably know, the Donny-born lad signed instead for Scunthorpe United, from whom he made his move into the limelight to Liverpool in 1971. Naturally, he had huge talent but he would never have been European Player of the Year twice, won numerous honours with Liverpool or captained his country on ability alone. He was the best example I have ever found of someone who maximised every ounce of their God-given talent through sheer hard work and a fantastic attitude. He also happens to be one of the nicest, friendliest human beings you could hope to meet.

King Kev only played once at Belle Vue – with Liverpool in 1973 – and I remember it as if it was yesterday. The story began with what looked to everyone in the country like a straightforward FA Cup third-round victory for Bill Shankly's mighty side, top of the First Division, against a Rovers team propping up the entire Football League. To make the tie even more of a formality, the original match was at Anfield where the Merseysiders enjoyed an aura of invincibility for years. Teams far, far better than us would take one look at that famous 'This is Anfield' sign as they walked out onto the pitch and prepare to retreat with their tails firmly between their legs. Needless to say, they were unbeaten at home going into the match and anyone giving Rovers half a chance would have been looked at twice.

The afternoon started predictably enough with Keegan opening the scoring after just six minutes. I was standing behind the goal, surrounded by Liverpool fans, and remember one turning round to me with a wry smile and saying: "Don't worry, mate, we'll ease up once we've got six!" To be honest, it was difficult to argue with him. But what happened next silenced the Kop and stunned the rest of the football world. Big Brendan O'Callaghan hauled us level just before half-time and Peter Kitchen, a great mate of mine who went on to score bucket loads of goals for Orient, actually nosed us in front. The interval score of Liverpool 1, Doncaster Rovers 2 was probably the most unlikely statistic seen at the ground until dear old Havant & Waterlooville rode into town.

Liverpool, of course, simply had to throw the Red Sea at us, but it took them until the 70th minute for Keegan – who else? – to net their equaliser. Still we refused to buckle and, giving almost as good as we got, kept the scoreline to 2-2 until the very last minute, when there came an incident that will live with me for the rest of my days. Kitchen was sent through the middle and lobbed the ball carefully over the Liverpool and England goalkeeper Ray Clemence. Time stood still, as the ball seemed bound, according to my bird's eye view, for the back of the net. Yet instead it hit the bar and rebounded back into play where Emlyn 'Crazy Horse' Hughes, another former England captain, somehow won the chase to get to the ball and headed it perilously away. Again the ball clipped the Liverpool bar before going out for a corner. If only, Kitchen's shot had been a few inches lower or Hughes' clearance had gone into his own net, as it so easily could have done, we would have been celebrating one of the greatest of FA Cup stories. As so often, however, the replay showed that often the underdogs only get one real bite of the cherry. The game drew an amazing crowd of 25,000 to Belle Vue; all the more so as it was played on a Tuesday afternoon because we were in the midst of power cuts at the time and couldn't use the floodlights. Liverpool inevitably ran out comfortable 2-0 winners – and there was to be another team who may have been mourning our misfortune a few months later. Shankly's crew brushed aside Newcastle United 3-0 to win the FA Cup in style – Keegan scoring twice, with Steve Heighway getting the other. So perhaps the Geordies would have been grateful, too, had Kitchen's shot only been a couple of inches lower.

Through being at the bottom of the football ladder as we have – and so nearly having fallen off it altogether – you find out who your friends really are. Having met a whole host of football folk from both Non-League level and the Football League, I can honestly say that the vast majority are a credit to the game. And they include some who would literally give you the shirt off their backs, if you needed it. That is how I discovered a side to Neil Warnock not always portrayed in the media.

I've known Neil for years and the image is accurate to a certain extent – he is extremely passionate about football and life. Like me, he has mostly experienced football at the lower end of the scale, managing at the likes of Scarborough and Bury before becoming better known at Sheffield United and now Crystal Palace. Neil was one of the first people in the game I turned to when I took over as chairman at Belle Vue and the place was in a state of complete uproar. We were struggling even for playing kit – and he was only too happy to supply us with one. I can't remember to be honest if we actually wore those United shirts the following Saturday at Dover but, as they say, it's the thought that counts. From then on, there was always an empathy between Rovers and

Sheffield United. You need folk you can turn to in this world and Neil has always been prepared to do us a favour if he possibly could. Perhaps the best example was loaning us his talented, yet unpredictable, forward Jonathan Forte, who did well for us in two separate spells. It gave me a lot of satisfaction, having been a regular visitor to Bramall Lane when it also used to house a cricket ground, when Neil achieved his long-term ambition by taking Sheffield United into the Premiership a few seasons ago. It was a magnificent achievement and I honestly believe they would still be there but for a set of circumstances that really set my blood boiling.

I'm referring, of course, to the Carlos Tevez affair. How West Ham United got off so lightly for basically fielding a player who wasn't theirs, I have no idea. But I'm not being cynical when I say that if the eggs had been in the opposite baskets – West Ham United had been relegated and the Blades were in the dock – the punishment from the Football Association would have been different.

Believe me, there are many chairmen and directors who are still very annoyed about the Tevez incident. They, like me, believe that the only possible penalty at the time should have been a points deduction that would have reprieved the Blades from the drop back down to the Championship. I've always had a lot of respect for West Ham as the club who brought us Martin Peters, Geoff Hurst and the incomparable Bobby Moore, thereby forming the backbone of England's World Cup-winning team of 1966. They have also been renowned for the entertaining nature of their football. But what happened during that time must surely have disturbed the Upton Park legends. A lot of people should hang their heads in shame.

Personally, I'm a great believer in 'what goes around, comes around' and one day West Ham's great escape will catch up with them. Not even the West Ham-biased media will be able to spare them from that judgement. I was naturally delighted when an independent tribunal chaired by Lord Griffiths ruled that Sheffield United should be entitled to financial compensation and that a figure was subsequently agreed between the two clubs. I trust that, in time, both the Blades players and Neil Warnock, who paid a very heavy personal price for the FA's leniency with the Hammers, will also be compensated adequately.

Warnock left a club that his heart will always belong to after the Blades lost their final match 2-1 to Wigan at Bramall Lane. He was a broken man and basically forced out of the club, not least by the antics of a 'superstar' who should have known better. The unscripted performance of Hollywood movie actor Sean Bean, who at the time was on the board of directors at Bramall Lane, was extremely distasteful. Neil alleged in his autobiography that Bean burst into his office, hurling abuse at him in full view of his family. How anyone could have done that to a manager who had done so much for his football club and at such a devastating time, I'll never know. Perhaps he really should stick to films in future.

Now the manager of Crystal Palace, I respect Neil as a shrewd judge of the game and that was reflected by some comments he made to me on the eve of our first season in the Championship. He commended us for our organisation and predicted that we'd fare okay, but warned us that, as one of the smaller clubs, we would be fighting a difficult battle with officials. You were certainly spot on, on both counts Neil.

Warnock's days at Bramall Lane may have gone but we thoroughly enjoyed the experience of being able to welcome Sheffield United to the Keepmoat for the very first time. Kevin McCabe, the Blades' chairman, sent me a lovely letter after we clinched promotion with our victory over Leeds United and that, for me, is a measure of the man and his club. Sheffield United have built intelligently off the field by developing their business portfolio and I honestly hope they make it back to the Premiership, where they belong, very soon.

Another club I have a fair amount of time for dates back to my university days. For it was a very short walk from my flat in George Road, West Bridgford, to the City Ground and a Forest team in the late-1960s of many talents. Those were heady days indeed on Trentside watching the likes of winger supreme Ian Storey-Moore, super smooth Welsh defender Terry Hennessey and midfield dynamo Henry Newton. In 1967 they managed to finish second only to Manchester United in Division One and reach the semi-finals of the FA Cup. The Forest story in subsequent years has been one of the most topsy-turvy in the history of the game. Under the great Brian Clough, they rose from the old Second Division to win both the Football League and the European Cup twice – an incredible achievement for a club of their comparatively modest size and means.

I'm a firm believer in the 'beautiful game' being played the right way and, in that philosophy, I share much with this man whom I consider to have been one of the greatest managers ever to grace football. Among Cloughie's legendary oft-quoted comments was: "If God had meant us to play football in the sky, he'd not have given us grass". And Doncaster Rovers are one of the modern-day clubs who are committed to keeping the ball on the deck and trying to entertain our fans. I was more than interested to see the film *The Damned United,* in which that versatile actor Michael Sheen starred as a youthful Clough during his 44 ill-fated days as manager of the then-champions Leeds United. There was also a powerful documentary on ITV1 featuring his widow Barbara, sons Nigel and Simon, and heroes from his subsequent 18 years in charge at Nottingham Forest.

My personal experiences of the man were all positive. I first came across him in the late 1980s when we were both on holiday in Majorca during the summer. We were in the same hotel and I got the opportunity to chat with the great man for a couple of hours or so. There were tell-tale signs then of his physical deterioration; Clough was so sharp and full of life during his halcyon days. But I found him friendly and interesting. It was reassuring that, despite having made it right to the top of English and European football as he did with Derby County and then Forest, he maintained an interest and appreciation for the game nearer its grass roots. This, of course, befitted another of his favourite sayings that he learnt his trade at lowly Hartlepool before taking on the challenges which made his name. In later years, he probably spent more time watching his son Nigel's side at Burton Albion than the so-called big boys. It was really encouraging when he spoke with me after we had enjoyed the better of an entertaining 1-1 draw at Burton in our Conference days and remarked that we were the best passing side he had seen there for a long time. He was also present at Stoke for the play-off final against Dagenham and Redbridge – the game that was the springboard for our current success – and again he was particularly generous in his comments.

What singles Cloughie out from other great managers such as Sir Matt Busby and Sir Alex Ferguson at Manchester United, Bill Shankly and Bob Paisley at Liverpool and now Arsene Wenger at Arsenal, were the clubs at which he had his success. Neither Derby nor Forest, despite their loyal fan bases, have been the biggest or most successful of clubs at any other stage of their histories other than when Cloughie and his assistant Peter Taylor were in charge. He had that difficult to define ability of being able to bring out the very best in players who wouldn't have regarded themselves as superstars. That is something I believe we have started to replicate here at Doncaster Rovers. Getting to the top of the tree either in this country or in Europe without massive financial backing is now virtually impossible and it is difficult to believe that we will see the likes of Forest or Ipswich Town winning the top division again. But that doesn't mean that we can't take many of the same principles on board and enjoy our dream. In one of the most fascinating clips in the Cloughie documentary, he tackled Don Revie on the issue of wanting to win the league 'better' and I, for one, can understand what he meant. His sides were based on excellent discipline, particularly toward the officials, and were known as one of the most pleasurable sides to referee. That has been said on many occasions by officials after Doncaster games and is a compliment that I take particular pleasure from. Generally speaking, you don't see Donny players getting involved with referees - instead they are taught to get on with the game. After all, it is very rare that officials change their minds and silly bookings and sendings-off can only blight clubs like us.

I wonder what Cloughie would have made of our Boxing Day visit to the City Ground when we demolished Forest 4-2 with a display of football that would surely have been up his street. The second goal, scored delightfully by Martin Woods, came after a passage of play in which we'd strung about 21 passes together and was put forward as one of the best of the season. Afterwards, I spoke with the Forest chief executive Mark Arthur and said: "Today we played more like the Forest of old - and Forest were more like Doncaster Rovers!" And it was difficult for Arthur, a fair-minded and likeable bloke, to disagree. A few days later came another interesting landmark in the season when Nigel Clough took the leap from Burton Albion to occupy his father's former managerial seat at Derby County. Naturally it will be almost impossible for Nigel ever to live up to the successes of his father, but I don't think that will worry him unduly. I've met him on several occasions and he is a very level-headed sort of guy who showed amazing and rare loyalty to Albion, where he stayed for ten years. Like Brian, Nigel has learnt his trade in the right sort of place and, given time, could become a very good manager. I'm sure many people in the game will join with me in wishing him the very best of good fortune.

Nottingham was the buzz football city recently thanks to Sven-Göran Eriksson's revolution at nearby Meadow Lane. It was one of the most unlikely stories of the decade when the former England and Mexico manager suddenly signed a five-year deal at the oldest Football League club, shortly after they had announced a Middle Eastern takeover. Sven is another big name whom I got the opportunity to meet when he was manager of Manchester City. His very first game in charge was a pre-season friendly at the Keepmoat Stadium against Rovers. The man is quietly spoken and very charming, as the fairer sex can testify. I genuinely hope that he can help to bring success to Notts County, who have lingered in the bottom division for too long and flirted with relegation from the Football League in recent seasons. It said a lot for their ambition and financial resources when they signed Lee Hughes, whom we looked at last season, and then Sol Campbell, the former England defender, who infamously lasted for just one match despite also signing a five-year contract. Stories have been coming out of Meadow Lane so thick and fast with their new owners departing as quickly and strangely as they came. There are few worse things in football than falsely raising good folk's expectations.

So, on to Leeds United. They claim to be the biggest club in Yorkshire; a fact the two Sheffield sides would no doubt dispute. But, to be fair, I have some very good memories of them. Rovers and Leeds share a common bond thanks to the late Billy Bremner. One of the main stalwarts of Don Revie's greatest ever Leeds side that probably missed out on more than it won in the late 1960s and early 1970s, he was also a fabulous and passionate skipper of Scotland. When I first became a director at Rovers, I gladly put some money forward to bring Billy back to Belle Vue for a second spell as manager after he'd achieved a fair amount of success first time around. During that time I got to know Billy fairly well and developed a real liking for the wee man. Laying a wreath at the side of Billy's statue at Elland Road was one highlight of our trip there for an eagerly-awaited League One clash in 2007/8.

Not so long ago, let's recall, Leeds United were symbolic of what was going wrong in Doncaster. Wherever you looked around our proud town, you would see the white scarves of Leeds and little of the red of Rovers. The new generation of supporters had apparently been lost to our big neighbours down the road. Football-wise, we were light years apart of course, with big-spending Leeds reaching the semi-finals of the Champions League under David O'Leary while we were at the bottom of the pile. The clashes between our two clubs two seasons ago were therefore not just about points – and ultimate glory – but highlighted just how far we had come and how far the once-mighty Leeds had fallen.

That most outspoken of sports pundits Mike Parry put it in his usual subtle way in the build-up to the play-off final when he said that little old Donny had no right to even be on the same pitch as Leeds. As already described, I was on the phone to put him right and remind him of our recent success story, as well as repeating my widely publicised prediction that we would be victorious. But even Parry's approach was positively friendly compared with the club he was sticking up for. Leeds, you may remember, were docked 15 points at the start of the 2007/8 season The reason stated was that they had failed to exit administration with an agreed Company Voluntary Agreement (CVA) in place. The Football League claimed Leeds had failed to adhere to their insolvency policy and the punishment was upheld on appeal with the support of the majority of the other 71 clubs. It was the talk of the football world at the time, but apparently bypassed the attention of the Leeds programme editor when we went to Elland Road for our League One fixture. For the programme proudly printed the club's own alternative league table, with Leeds having their 15 points back! Not surprisingly in view of the fact that they had made an excellent start to the season, this rogue table saw Leeds well clear at the top, with Swansea City, Forest, Carlisle and ourselves in what they thought were our rightful places.

Mind you, don't ever expect too warm a welcome when you go to Leeds. Even the normal cordial greeting on the lines of 'welcome to our friends from Doncaster' was conspicuous by its absence in the same publication. The reason for the bogus table, of course, was that by this time chairman Ken Bates had announced that Leeds were appealing against the points deduction. That alone was a cause for great annoyance, not only for us, but other clubs in that season's promotion race. So had I got any sympathy with the cause Bates and Leeds were fighting? Not at all. In fact, they were lucky to get off so lightly.

When we flash back to the summer in question, Leeds's very future in the Football League was in grave doubt after they went into administration at the end of their relegation year in the Championship, once they realised their cause was lost. The aim was cynical and crystal clear. They wanted to serve their sentence – normally a ten-point penalty – and start out in League One on a level playing field. What happened next was very complex and it would not be a great idea for me to delve too deeply into such muddy waters. Suffice to say this: the package that saved Leeds was at the expense of a lot of other businesses, who either went short of properly earned cash or went out of existence altogether.

Personally, I think Leeds did well to wipe off an estimated £30m worth of debt for the expense of 15 points and more lost friends in the game. They could so easily have been moved down another division. It just made things worse, therefore, when the club went back on its promise not to appeal against the decision and potentially threw the whole of League One into chaos by demanding another hearing. Had that been successful – God forbid – we would probably still be fighting out the outcome to the 2007/8 season in the courts to this day. Nottingham Forest and Rovers would have launched legal action immediately and there could easily have been others.

Rubbing shoulders with the Earl and Countess of Harewood and Mr Bates that day was an interesting experience. It proved to be a grey day for most of the 33,000 fans as a stunning free-kick from Brian Stock gave us a fully deserved 1-0 victory. Only our 3,000 fans felt like singing and Bates, unsurprisingly, was in a grumpy mood. After berating our directors for making too much noise during the game, he wanted our Director of Football and former assistant manager Mickey Walker thrown out of the boardroom afterwards. It wouldn't have been so bad, but Mickey used to work at Elland Road and had nipped in to see a mate. Never mind, we were all due to meet again a couple of months later and, again, it wasn't just the South Yorkshire weather that was frosty. It was a bitterly cold night in Yorkshire and the pitch at the Keepmoat was frozen ahead of what was scheduled to be a high noon showdown on the Saturday. Almost all the rest of the afternoon programme went ahead and Leeds went on the rampage letting it be known that we were a tin-pot club who could not even get the game on. Yet there was nothing to be gained from our point of view from a postponement that would have been avoided had the game been played at the usual 3pm kick-off. And why did we have to kick off so early? Because of the reputation of Leeds United supporters. To be honest, I think the weather actually did Bates and Leeds a favour. They were going through a bad spell at the time and we fancied ourselves very strongly to get another three points. When the match was re-scheduled, Gary McAllister was starting to pull Leeds around and, despite soaking up Rovers pressure for much of the night, got their revenge with a 1-0 success.

The one thing I will say for Bates is that when we were celebrating our famous victory at Wembley, he came up to me and admitted that the better team won. I couldn't fault him for that. I also enjoyed some good light-hearted banter with some United fans during the following summer when they spotted me at an airport. Don't get me wrong. I'm not someone to hold grudges and I have no desire to keep berating Leeds in future. For all the problems between us, I respect the fact that Leeds should be a Premiership club and it is just a matter of time before they start rising again.

My last 'grumble' is a very major one – and is about the running of our game in general in this country. For at a time when, if you don't look too closely, football appears to be thriving, I feel that we are on the very verge of a major wake-up call and that the Football Association, or Sweet FA, as I prefer to call them, are living in cloud cuckoo's land, totally unprepared for when football suffers a huge hangover from the years of non-stop partying at the very top.

It shouldn't take a Prince Hamlet to recognise that there is something sick in the state of our national treasure. For amid the unprecedented hype is growing disillusionment which even I, with my childlike passion, simply can't ignore. Just consider this analogy for a moment. Should the Premiership's elite of Manchester United, Chelsea, Liverpool and Arsenal play all their matches downhill on Yeovil's famous old slope, there would be a national outcry. But that is exactly what is happening in our sport, not just in the Premiership but across the board and certainly into our grass roots. There is no level playing field in football anymore and the authorities complicitly rest on their laurels while the very soul is being ripped out of our national sport.

As chairman of a Football League club, I would have loved the opportunity to do something about it. That's why I put myself forward in a poll to become the regional representative on the Football Association. Yet I knew full well that I wouldn't be universally welcome at the party. For from what I have seen over the years, the very organisation that should be standing up for the average club in the street is merely maintaining the lop-sided status quo.

The first thing I would have done is campaign for a wage cap in the Championship. I accept, albeit reluctantly, that such prudent common sense will never find favour among the Premiership fat cats – they will remain in a luxurious, inflated world of their own. But for how long can we continue to ignore the warning signs? Last season's Championship became almost as much a battle for financial survival as success on the field. The most celebrated case, of course, was Southampton. Rumours of their impending demise circulated freely throughout the season until they finally collapsed into administration, leaving far more than their Championship future at stake. Thankfully, the Saints have since found new owners and begun life afresh in League One, with just a ten-point penalty to remind them of just how close they came to extinction. I speak for many chairmen, I'm sure, in wishing the south coast club well.

But they weren't the only ones; far from it. There were also much-publicised problems at Charlton Athletic, who like the Saints were relegated to League One, and Watford, who lived to fight another Championship season. Already in 2009/10 the Hornets have been rescued from the very brink of administration and there has been considerable concern over the future of Crystal Palace with their ongoing financial worries. Rumours were also rife during the summer that Derby County's American owners had pulled the plug on future spending and this may explain some of the Rams' problems in the first half of the 2009/10 campaign.

Indeed as I write, Portsmouth are on the very brink after a series of takeovers seemingly failed to plug the leek in their finances. And this was a club that was celebrating FA Cup glory just a couple of seasons ago. Surely it is time for folk with the good of the game at heart to get together and tackle the financial madness before communities lose their clubs.

The way money is distributed through the leagues is a total disgrace. The Premiership guards extravagant riches; the Championship picks off almost all of the Football League proceeds; and League One and Two is basically left to rot. That is the very opposite of what football in this country should be all about.

Partly as a result of the bitter pill of experience that we have swallowed, I have far more than the usual token sympathy for our brothers in distress – the clubs that may well not see it through the present difficult economic times. It now seems unthinkable that Doncaster folk could ever go without their football team, yet that is the prospect facing other communities fairly and squarely in the face.

I would call upon the football authorities now to have a radical re-think on the way we are heading. Elite clubs can't afford long-term to just watch others falling by the wayside.

In the end the losers will be football fans nationwide. Let's have legislation to ensure the proceeds from television money and other sponsorship are more equally shared. Let's have guarantees that money which is meant to go into youth and grass roots football reaches them as intended. Perhaps you can appreciate now why people such as I are not invited to feast at the table? Certainly my attempt during the summer of 2009 to be elected onto the FA and speak up for our less well-off clubs has led me to that unmistakeable conclusion. For the ballot – or rather two ballots – that I contested had all the transparency of an Iranian general election.

The story was that I stood in opposition to the long-serving representative Barry Taylor of Barnsley. All together, the poll was open to 20 Football League and Non-League clubs who were each supposed to be sent ballot papers and return their vote. I spoke to as many clubs as I could and was very confident of claiming eleven votes and therefore being elected. But, when the result was announced, it was 9-8 in favour of Taylor.

Naturally I have no problem bowing the knee to democracy, but I had good reason to doubt this was in fact the case. My main complaint was that Taylor sent out official FA ballot papers to some of the clubs, therefore creating the false impression that his candidacy was being backed by the FA. Also, one of the 20 clubs contacted me afterwards to say that they had not received a ballot paper at all. Interestingly, neither Rotherham United nor Leeds United were allowed to vote because of their recent financial problems – a situation I don't really understand but which would have made little difference as their vote was very likely to be split between us.

Despite being patronised in some of the national media, my appeal against the result was successful and an unprecedented second poll was held in August. Once again I find it very hard to believe that the result came out 9-7 in favour of Taylor who, therefore, is now entitled to be on the FA for life.

Some folk will inevitably see this as a personal issue between me and the Barnsley director. But that is completely besides the point. I was not standing to win a private battle, but because I genuinely believe that the FA needs shaking up. When Lord Triesman was appointed chairman, I naively felt that reform was in the air but remain far from convinced up to this point.

We are living, let's recall, in days when there is a wide public call for transparency in the way our authorities are run. I, like thousands of others, have been sickened by the revelations of how MPs have used and abused the system of expenses and now was as good a time as any to begin clearing the murky waters of football. There has, after all, been a number of very damaging financial allegations made about key figures in the game in recent years that, while never proven, have nevertheless widened the gulf between the game and a large proportion of its supporters.

Football has to be about more than money if it is to continue to capture the imagination of the paying public for decades to come. We are in extreme danger of pricing ordinary folk out of the game and that, too, needs to be urgently addressed. Even before the credit crunch began to bite, there were increasing fears that the prices charged for watching football are just too high. Football can't expect the fans to continue to dig deeper and deeper into their pockets while the clubs they idolise spend cash they simply don't have and run up huge debts. The prospect of half-empty stadia, even in the Premiership, faces those who currently exploit the loyalty of their followers.

All will remain ship-shape on the surface while football is the darling of TV. Yet the media-led gravy train will grind to a halt one day. The excitement of watching the best players day after day has already been reduced greatly by over-familiarity. Even prawn sandwiches can become mundane and boring when eaten with every meal. The unpalatable truth is that much of what is being served up nowadays is both boring and predictable.

How many times do you genuinely get off your seat during an average 90 minutes? I honestly fear that football clubs have become too obsessed with being 'a results business' to recognise that we are also in the entertainment industry. Only the truly partisan will stomach one without the other for long.

No doubt my voice will remain one in the wilderness. It is all-too-easy for the FA to ignore the bleatings of the chairman of Doncaster Rovers. But I believe that genuine football supporters will recognise and appreciate where I am coming from.

13

*

'KING' ALICK JEFFREY

IDOLATRY should carry a psychological health warning. All too often the best place to leave the object of your worship, be it a soccer or other celebrity 'god', is on the pedestal you have created. That way there's no chance of his or her image being tarnished. More dangerous, by far, to actually meet and discover fallible flesh and blood like the rest of us. They may not be in the best of moods when you see them or even share your passion for the subject that made them famous – or in the case of Sean Bean, your idol could be Sharpe by name, but blunt and ignorant by nature.

My idol, 'King' Alick Jeffrey, had further than most to fall, so high was my opinion of him, but he proved to be every inch the man I admired as a legend on the field. Put simply; football is my passion, Doncaster Rovers my club and Alick the greatest player ever to pull on the famous Rovers shirt. More than that, he was also the best footballer I ever set eyes on – and that was merely in his 'second coming' after a broken leg had robbed him of his rightful place in the game.

One of the greatest privileges I enjoyed after taking over Donny Rovers was inviting King Alick back to his home at Belle Vue as the club's first president. To accompany my treasured memories of Alick Jeffrey, the footballer, I gained a buddy, a comrade in arms, as he became a part of Rovers' revival. To some the friendship between a multi-millionaire and a publican may have seemed strange – yet our love of football and Rovers, in particular, ensured we always shared common ground. Our similarly extrovert natures also strengthened our bond.

The remarkable truth about Alick was that he was both as humble as they come and completely free of the bitterness and regret you might expect from a man who could have become the Wayne Rooney of his era but for outrageous bad fortune. Sat to the left of the bus driver on our way to 'glamourous' locations such as Scarborough, Forest Green Rovers or Morecambe – and I'm not demeaning those clubs in any way – he could have been any other soccer official. He'd keep away from the card schools that filled the time of the young men who were playing that day, but instantly become the life and soul of the party whenever there was banter and high-spirited chat. An entertainer on the field, he was a natural entertainer off it too. It wouldn't take too much of an excuse for Alick to pick up the microphone and give us the benefit of his singing talents. In the style of Frank Sinatra, whose autobiography became his near constant companion on his travels, Alick did it his way.

The genial publican who, along with his wife Sheila, became popular hosts at the Black Bull for 20 happy years, was totally proud of being part and parcel once again of the club he loved so much. My abiding sadness was that he never lived to see the joy of Rovers winning back our place in the Football League and the glories that followed. He passed away on 22 November 2000, just four days after suddenly being taken ill during a holiday in Benidorm with Sheila. He was just 61 years of age.

Interest in Alick was so great that a public service was held at his beloved Belle Vue, attended by some 750 people. It was an honour for me to give the eulogy and share something of the nature of the man with my fellow mourners. Funerals are inevitably emotional occasions, but here there was a great outpouring of love and affection for a man who certainly lives on in our minds and hearts. I spoke from my heart of the humility and pride of a truly wonderful man.

Very appropriately, the road outside the new Keepmoat Stadium was named Alick Jeffrey Way to give his memory pride of place whenever we play at our new stadium. Nobody could have deserved the honour more.

Occasionally I'll hear a story of a Doncaster man going to some far-off country, striking up a conversation with someone who remembers 'that great footballer who came from Doncaster'. Outsiders might be forgiven for thinking they were talking about Kevin Keegan, but King Kev himself has no such misapprehension. "I know," he'll tell me with a twinkle in his eye and that look of humble sincerity on his face, "I wasn't the greatest footballer to come from Doncaster – that was Alick." I'm sure there's a jovial man in the sky looking down on us and sharing still in our achievements and disappointments. Alongside him, perhaps, as so often in life, will be the great Charlie Williams – his mate, fellow footballer and performer who achieved so much in his own right.

Prior to becoming a household name as a comedian and entertainer, Charlie combined with Alick to form a very popular duo, performing cabaret together in the local pubs and clubs. Charlie used to tell all who cared to listen that if it hadn't been for his prowess on the field, Alick could easily have made a living as an entertainer. Instead it was our joy to enjoy his natural talent, combined with a spontaneity that is particularly rare.

When Alick was seeing out his professional days at Lincoln City, team-mate Phil Hubbard recalled going to a social club one night after a home match and finding the great man none too impressed with the hired act. "I can do better than that," said Alick and he proved it too, by grabbing the microphone and treating the astonished customers to an impromptu turn of his own. That was Alick Jeffrey, ever the individual, the semi-eccentric, a man for all seasons.

So was a man who could so easily have been an all-time football great any the less for the atrocious luck that ruined his dream? No, he wasn't. A man who had mixed with the stars of his day was never too big for the humble surroundings of rundown Doncaster Rovers in the Vauxhall Conference. Actually, he counted it as a privilege. So just how good was Alick Jeffrey and why should I devote a whole chapter of my life story to him rather than mention him along the way, as I have with so many more of my football friends?

Of course, we can all romanticise. I admit that I wear red and white glasses, at least some of the time. And, of course, I never actually saw the REAL Alick Jeffrey kick a ball. So let me instead hand over to some of the people who definitely know what they are talking about – Alick's contemporaries in the game. I can't quote all of them, not only because it would take up so much space, but as it would take away, in part, from journalist Peter Whittell's charming book, *Alick Jeffrey - The Original Boy Wonder*.

The late Sir Stanley Matthews, the former England and Blackpool wing wizard, said: "I predict that he can become one of the greatest inside-forwards in the game. His play bears the stamp of genius." Listen to England World Cup winner Nobby Stiles: "Although he was young, he was already idolised by many. He was certainly on the brink of signing for Manchester United and becoming a Busby Babe." And Jackie Milburn, the former Newcastle and England forward, put it this way: "The boy has everything. He is by far the best youngster I have ever seen." They were talking, let's remember, about a mere 17-year-old, barely a man in football terms but someone who already had the world at his feet. There was more than a passing resemblance with the modern day phenomena that is Manchester United and England's Rooney.

Like Wayne, Alick had a strong and big build that provided him with body strength well beyond his tender years. Explosive pace saw him leave defenders in his wake and his ability to strike a ball was such that his colleagues in training would marvel. In the air, he was more Cristiano Ronaldo than Rooney, as he was able to spring remarkably high and head with great power and accuracy. Yet in manner, he was neither. You would never have caught Alick gesticulating wildly at officials or exhibiting any of the other behaviour typical of modern superstars. His football talent alone did the talking and, boy, was that eloquent.

Hailing from the fairly anonymous village of Rawmarsh, near Rotherham, the lad was a childhood prodigy. From school teams, to Rotherham Boys, to Yorkshire Boys and then England – Alick always looked three steps ahead of the rest of the field. His national debut came in March 1954 when England celebrated the Golden Jubilee of the English Schools FA with a 2-1 victory over Wales in the Victory Shield. Fittingly, Alick was the first to get his name on the scoresheet in front of a 20,000 crowd at Watford.

Amazingly, there were 90,000 in the ground when Alick made his Wembley debut against Scotland in the Victory Shield, although apparently the young man found it more daunting to stand up in front of the whole of his school at assembly when presented with a travel bag as a 'mark of appreciation' for the honour he had brought to them. One significant face in the crowd at Maine Road for a later 0-0 Jubilee international with Wales was none other than Sir Matt Busby, the Manchester United manager. Alick then notched twice in a 4-0 win over Scotland, prompting statistically-minded journalist George Fellows to say that although it was normally 28/1 against an England schoolboy going on to play full international football, he wouldn't wager a farthing against that happening to our Alick.

As you can well imagine it wasn't just Doncaster Rovers who had been monitoring Alick's progress with great interest, no fewer than 19 out of the 22 First Division clubs offered the young prodigy a place on their groundstaff. Yet, happily for us, his local roots counted for much in his decision to sign for Rovers, as did the chance to develop under the guidance of another noted inside-forward, Peter Doherty, the manager at Belle Vue.

One of the main reasons why Alick remained the life and soul of the party after his broken leg was his very philosophical approach. But for that fateful night in Bristol, it is highly probable that he would have been with the Manchester United squad on that awful evening in Munich in 1958 and, perhaps, another tragic victim of the crash that shocked the world. The United link was undoubtedly very strong and it was almost inevitable that young Alick would have signed for Sir Matt Busby. Doherty had already been issuing the traditional 'hands off' warning to other clubs, United included, from the start of the 1955/6 season. Sir Matt was quoted as saying of the young starlet: "I will come and get you in time" and realistically, just like today, what United wanted they would have got. No one at Belle Vue would have stood in his way.

In early February 1956, just eleven days after Alick's 17th birthday, he signed professional forms at Belle Vue to the great delight - and relief no doubt - of Doherty who acclaimed Alick as the 'greatest signing I have ever made.' We live now in a football world in which local roots don't mean anything like as much as they did then, with the game being the poorer for it in my opinion. But, although he was United-bound before his sad injury, there was a real bond between him and Doncaster Rovers which nothing could break. Don't underestimate the fact that he made sacrifices to sign up in the first place. He had already played for the England amateur team by that point and there was the prospect - a very attractive one at that time - of taking part in the Olympic Games in Australia. Turning professional ended that particular dream.

We must also remember that cash, holidays, TV sets and cars would even then have been offered to the most promising lads, turning their heads and tempting them to join the big boys. But listen carefully to Alick's words. "Doncaster Rovers aren't big or famous YET - but I chose them for two reasons. Doncaster is near my home and I would be staying with my mum and dad. And as an inside-forward I want to learn my job under the guidance of the man nearly everyone says was the greatest inside-forward of his day." He also appreciated the fact that Rovers treated him so well after making him the youngest Football League player since the war when he made his first-team debut as a 15-year-old on 15 September 1954. Alick apparently did all that was asked of him that day, although he was unable to get his name on the scoresheet despite Rovers overturning a 5-2 defeat at Craven Cottage only the previous weekend with an impressive 4-0 victory.

Doherty ensured the young lad wasn't over-played too soon and it was six appearances and four months later - to the day in fact - when Alick notched his first goal in Donny colours in the 3-2 win over Plymouth Argyle. Also in the team that day was Charlie Williams, who made his first-team and League debuts in 1949/50. The two got on famously and, along with Harry Gregg, our talented goalkeeper who went on to play for Manchester United, became three of a kind. Although young in years, Alick was immediately up there with the most senior when it came to playing practical jokes and tricks on his colleagues and that effervescent personality was to characterise him both on and off the field for the rest of his life.

Nobby Stiles, the Manchester United and England World Cup winning hero who will always be remembered for that joyful Wembley jig after our triumph in 1966, spoke fondly to me of his admiration for the young Jeffrey. Nobby, whose son John later played for Rovers, told me personally he was in no doubt that the young man was Old Trafford-bound and remembered going to Maine Road later that season to view the prodigy in action in the epic FA Cup fourth-round marathon with Aston Villa. Those were the days when Cup football, like Wimbledon tennis matches, was a battle to the finish. There was no such thing as a penalty shoot-out in those days and this tie went to an astonishing four replays. The two teams had already drawn 0-0 at Belle Vue in front of 28,000, and shared four goals at Villa Park in front of an enthralled 36,000 spectators in the first replay, when they lined up at Maine Road just five days later. Nobby was there to see Alick score our goal in a 1-1 draw before the drama went on to Hillsborough where, once again, the two sides couldn't manage a goal between them. The fifth and final match was at West Bromwich Albion's Hawthorns ground and, fittingly, it was young Alick who brought the epic saga to a happy ending with two goals in our 3-1 victory.

That was the end of the West Midlanders' dream of a classic Birmingham versus Aston Villa tie to relish but, more significantly, confirmation that a true star has been born. But football was a bit different in those days. Not only was the fifth-round tie at Birmingham City held just four days later, Alick wasn't able to play as he had been chosen to represent England Youth instead, against Wales. The young maestro helped himself to a hat-trick as England won the match 7-2, but Rovers fans will forever be left wondering whether his killer touch could have enabled us to go one stage better than going down 2-1, after a commendable performance.

Alick's start to the 1956/7 season was truly the stuff of dreams, yet it was to end all-too-soon in an absolute nightmare. By this time the young lad had developed into a finely-built and tuned athlete. I would venture to say that, save for his awful injury, Jeffrey would have been the lad we were looking for to help bring the World Cup home from Sweden in 1958 - and who knows how good he could still have been when we finally did taste glory on our own patch in 1966.

Alick had already impressed on his debut for England Under 23s against Denmark in Copenhagen in September 1956, when he earned rave reviews after having a hand in two of the goals in a comfortable 3-0 win. The future was set fair for the prodigal son who had actually taken the place of the injured Johnny Haynes. The following month's international against France in front of more than 26,000 fans at Ashton Gate seemed the ideal stage for our boy to further impress. The key incident occurred just nine minutes into the game when Alick clashed with French defender Richard Tylinski. It wasn't a vicious tackle, or even a foul – more the type of harmless-looking collision that occurs routinely in any football match. The bad luck was that Alick was in the act of half-turning and the Frenchman inadvertently caught him at an awkward angle. There was a sickening crack with everyone immediately fearing for young Alick's welfare.

Players made frantic signals for a stretcher and he was taken to Bristol Royal Infirmary where it was quickly confirmed the starlet had broken his leg in two places.

These were the days, of course, when there was nothing like the saturation football coverage of today. Alick's girlfriend and wife-to-be Sheila was watching on TV at a relative's house and ran all the way home to tell her father the shock news. Typically, immediately after his dreadful injury, Alick announced that no-one was at fault for what happened and that, fingers crossed, he should be playing again after Christmas. He continued to be endlessly optimistic when allowed home and revealed his gratitude to the supporters for the fan mail that had nearly swamped him in hospital and the personal support of Rovers manager Doherty.

Contrary to public rumour, I'm no surgeon, but I can only take an educated guess that, perhaps with today's medical expertise, Alick could have returned much sooner. But, suffice to say, several different specialists and plaster casts couldn't produce the expected improvement, with Sheila revealing afterwards how no explanation was ever offered by the medical authorities over why the break failed to heal.

Whenever asked about what was happening, Alick would say: "It's just one of those things." It is difficult to believe one of today's superstars would be as philosophical as fame and fortune literally walked out on him. I can't imagine, either, that they would have passed the time by entertaining their colleagues with a few songs at after-match get-togethers to keep their mates' spirits high. But that's exactly what Alick did, although he was in pretty good company. For singing with him and throwing in the odd gag was none other than Charlie Williams. Together they started working in the South Yorkshire clubs.

There were two more shocks in store before love-struck Alick was able to tie the knot with his beloved Sheila. Rovers suffered another body blow when Doherty walked out - apparently over a clash of personalities with certain directors, although no official explanation was ever given – then came the immeasurably more tragic Munich Air Disaster. A total of 23 people died that awful night, including eight stars of Manchester United present and future. Doncaster folk will forever recall the bravery of Harry Gregg who, ignoring the very real threat of fire, went back into the aircraft twice to haul out a 20-month-old baby and then the eternally grateful mother, Mrs Vera Lukic, wife of the Yugoslavian air attaché in London.

The Jeffrey wedding held in Rawmarsh on 29 March 1959 wasn't quite the celebrity affair it would have been today. There was no sign of *Hello!* magazine or Max Clifford. But the scrum of everyday folk delighting in the happiness of a local hero was such that the official photographer was the one who couldn't get near enough to take any pictures. Instead of the soccer mansion, the couple lived with Alick's grandmother in Pottery Street and there was no time even for a honeymoon as the stricken star didn't want to interrupt his rigorous training programme. His best man, Roy Brown, a fringe player at Rovers, saw more than most of Alick during that time and said his friend never doubted that he would make it back onto the field.

Amazingly, Doherty, by this time manager of Bristol City, made a £15,000 offer - quite a fee in those days - to take Alick, still a long way from fitness, to Ashton Gate. But as the second anniversary of his injury approached, the bombshell finally dropped. Medical experts from the club, the Football Association and their insurers announced that Alick would never play top-class football again. Rovers were given £15,000 in compensation, with Alick himself receiving £4,000 from the insurers and £500 from the players' union. There was more than a hint from Alick's reaction that he wasn't happy with the way the issue was resolved. He felt that, given more time, he could have yet proven his fitness. Just listen to his lament: "I'm on the scrapheap, left with a scrapbook and £4,000 compensation. Laugh, if you like, and say what am I grumbling about? Four thousand pounds is big money; I know that's what people are saying. Well, it is a lot of cash. But I didn't break a leg only on that black night against Young France two years ago, I broke my heart."

There was the soul of a true football man. The money, although deeply appreciated, meant absolutely nothing to him compared with the loss of his dream. He would have paid it back a thousand times over just to be able to turn the clock back. Alick, first and foremost, loved the game rather than its rewards. Typical of the young man was an innocent misadventure one day in February 1959 when he went to watch some of his mates playing for Parkgate Youth Club Old Boys against Mexborough High Terrace. Parkgate were a man short and Alick volunteered to play in goal! His appearance was a favour for some friends and no doubt provided an afternoon nobody who witnessed it was likely to forget, as Alick kept his goal intact in a 6-0 Parkgate victory. But it also inevitably alerted local press attention and, in turn, brought the wrath of the Sheffield and Hallamshire FA on young Alick. Happily, with the help of national press opinion in his favour, common sense prevailed and Alick was let off with just a reprimand.

But where there's a will, there's a way, and Alick did then get an unlikely chance to resurrect his career - in the bracing atmosphere of Skegness, then in the Midland League. Agents would probably hold their hands up in horror, but it took a good round figure to persuade Alick out of his involuntary retirement - absolutely nothing. A masterplan hatched by Skeggy boss George Raynor - yes, the same George Raynor who had taken Sweden to the World Cup final in 1958 - got around the tricky matter of Alick's insurance pay-out and went right to the heart of his love for the game. Raynor promised Alick six months of hard labour on the coast in a last-gasp bid to get him fit enough to take to the field again. Truly, too good an offer to turn down.

In a just world, I'd be recalling Alick's smooth return to action – yet it was anything but. Incredibly, Alick broke his other leg playing in a public trial against Skeggy's first team. That after he had scored a hat-trick inside the opening 15 minutes. Fortunately, this break proved less stubborn and Alick was soon back on the field and heading for more emotional heartbreak. A bid to bring him back into league football with his beloved Rovers hit the rocks as player and club alike admitted they just couldn't afford to return their full respective insurance pay-outs. "I could have wept," said Alick. These weren't the crocodile tears of a mercenary but the genuine reaction of someone who just wanted to play.

Instead Alick stayed at Skegness where his double-act with Charlie Williams was re-joined, both on and off the field. Jeffrey heartily recommended his mate - then 32 years of age and with his days numbered at Belle Vue - and the two became local legends, both as players and for swapping the clubs of South Yorkshire for coastal Lincolnshire. By now Alick and Sheila were entertaining a duo of their own; as their second child was born another unexpected opportunity opened up Down Under. Prague FC of Sydney were a multi-national side made up of Austrians, Dutch, Argentinian and English players - as well as a handful of Aussies. But, more poignantly, the Aussie FA did not come under the jurisdiction of FIFA, so Alick could actually get paid for enjoying himself. Sheila described their three years in the sun as being 'like a holiday' and there could have been few better ways of strengthening Alick's bones. But, if you think he'd left behind all thoughts of chilly Doncaster, you obviously never knew our Alick.

Exactly how things fell into place for Alick to return to Rovers in December 1963 remain something of a mystery. Somehow, the rule the insurance pay-out needed to be returned in full should Alick play full-time football was overturned, otherwise it is very unlikely that Rovers could have afforded him. I'm just glad that, whether someone in the FA pulled strings or otherwise, Alick Jeffrey did return, both for the good of football as a whole and, of course, Donny Rovers.

It also gave a still young John Ryan the welcome opportunity to see the great man in action. What followed, albeit from Jeffrey mark II, changed my football life forever. Seeing this one great player developed my love affair with football and Rovers to a far deeper level. Even today, I surprise Lynne every now and again by leaping into the air like a salmon, neck muscles bulging, to power in a header in a re-enactment of one of Alick's great goals against Darlington. Or I'll skip across my polished floor and produce an imaginary back heel to celebrate another golden moment. Call me crazy or childlike, if you wish, but this is my passion.

The Alick Jeffrey who went on to score 93 more goals for Rovers during the next six seasons was a player who nearly had it all – pace, strength, skill, heading ability and a deadly short back-swing that would send the ball towards its inevitable target a precious split-second before the goalkeeper was expecting it. Yet I knew – and Alick knew – he forever carried the scars of the injury back in 1956.

In his first full season back at Belle Vue, Alick netted an amazing 36 goals causing our new player-manager Bill

Leivers, the former Manchester City defender, to reflect that only his label as a Fourth Division player was standing between him and a place in England manager Sir Alf Ramsey's thoughts. A certain Don Revie, who was beginning to turn Leeds United into a real force, also considered bringing Alick back into the big-time yet concluded apparently that he didn't have the necessary application to make the step up. True, he'd worked hard to get down to his target weight of 13 stones, but his love of the good life had spread far beyond the borders of Doncaster. Alick, bless him, was no respecter of early nights and not averse to the odd drink too many. Co-striker Alfie Hale, who became Alick's chauffeur when he lost his driving licence, recalls days when he'd arrive to pick the great man up only to find him still in bed. Alick apparently would tell his friend not to worry by saying: "They can't start without me!" The term loveable rogue was always associated with him.

Alick netted 22 goals during our Fourth Division title-winning season in 1965/66, forming a fantastic partnership with Laurie Sheffield, who actually outscored him with 28. Nicknamed 'the comeback kid', life was pretty good for Alick and his young family – he now had three children – but tragedy struck again when he was injured in the car accident that claimed the life of Rovers colleague John Nicholson. Alick, who broke several ribs and was also badly cut and bruised, was in hospital for 16 days. He later confided that the accident, plus an air-pocket in his head that added to his worries, caused him to consider giving up the game for good.

We went back down just 12 months later and remarkably Alick found himself in a Rovers team managed by none other than George Raynor. After previously always wearing the number eight, nine and ten shirts, Alick found himself on the wing from where he scored half of his 12 goals during a reasonably successful season, He began 1968/69 in fine fettle too but, despite an early run of five successive victories, Raynor lost his job and Alick, in effect, saw the door close on him too.

He didn't get on as famously with new Rovers boss Lawrie McMenemy and, although playing in front of 48,330 in an FA Cup tie at Liverpool provided one final highlight, his last game for Rovers came in a 0-0 draw against Halifax Town in front of a more modest 8,656 spectators. A few days short of his 30th birthday, Alick had made 262 league appearances for Rovers, scoring 127 goals – the second-highest in our history.

A short spell at Lincoln City followed before he and Sheila slipped seamlessly into the pub trade, learning from the school of hard knocks at The Fox in Stainforth, before becoming the much-loved hosts of the Black Bull in Doncaster. This was another very important part of Alick's life and one that should not be under-estimated. Goodness knows how many folk he entertained over the years with his football stories. These days you're more likely to go to the pub and see footballers on Sky Sports. Back then, they were often larger-than-life characters such as Alick behind the bar. He was in his element chatting with the market traders and all the other regulars and his sing-a-longs and late nights became almost as legendary as his goals. His 50th birthday party went into folklore and not just because his great friend Charlie Williams helped provide the entertainment.

He even managed one last and memorable appearance on the hallowed turf of Belle Vue for a testimonial match for young Geordie goalkeeper Paul Malcolm, who had seen his Rovers career ended with a broken leg. Alick was pushed onto the pitch in a wheelchair by a certain Paul Gascoigne, then a fast-rising Newcastle starlet. Gazza even stuffed a football up his shirt to mimic Alick's ample midriff.

What Alick didn't find so funny, however, was Rovers' fast-fading fortunes. A succession of big-name managers such as Stan Anderson, Billy Bremner (second time around), Dave Mackay and Joe Kinnear couldn't stem the tide before things got worse – so much worse – under the Richardson regime.

It was five months after Alick and Sheila left the Black Bull, calling time on their 23-year pub career, that Rovers lost their Football League place. It left Alick, along with all true Rovers supporters, both shocked and angry.

I'm thrilled I was able to give Alick a more positive experience of Rovers again before his untimely death. I think the fact that he viewed me as someone who had helped to save his football club was another good reason for our close friendship. I helped to scatter Alick's ashes over the Belle Vue pitch but, although he never made it to see us play at the Keepmoat, he remains a strong presence in my heart. I have a thousand real-life memories of the man who became my idol.

Rest in peace, King Alick, and God bless you.

14

*

PLAYING AT HOME

PREMIERSHIP referee Mark Halsey: "I refereed the charity game on John's own football pitch – and, yes, he did tackle Brian Robson! More seriously, John's a caring guy away from football. Since I have been sidelined with cancer, he has phoned me on many occasions to wish me and my wife Michelle, who is also suffering, well. I've had a lot of support from football folk and that's a side of the game people sometimes don't see."

NEIL WARNOCK, Crystal Palace manager: "I've got a lot of time for John and his lovely wife Lynne; they are a fabulous couple. Long may they – and Doncaster Rovers – continue to thrive. The Keepmoat Stadium is a tribute to John Ryan and Doncaster Rovers. We used to come out of Belle Vue praying our cars hadn't disappeared into the pot holes and now they have this magnificent ground. It is a remarkable transformation."

HOME is where the heart is, as they say, and a very important part of my personal dream. So many people are successful in one area of their life, but find this is at the expense of another. As I have explained elsewhere, I have suffered my fair share of emotional pain. Nobody comes through the trauma of a divorce totally unscathed – even if it was I who initiated it – and then there was the tragically early death of my ex-wife and mother of our two children, Denise. So I, of all people, certainly do not take domestic bliss for granted and am thrilled that in later years this aspect of my life now complements the rest of the John Ryan story.

This has been due in no small measure to a lovely woman called Lynne, whom I'm now proud to call my wife. Love is the strangest thing – you can spend your whole life looking and never truly find it, or it can pop up out of the blue in the most unlikely of circumstances. I have to tread carefully here because when I first met Lynne Cartwright I was still married – and so for that matter was she. It was in 1980, two years after I had got wed to Denise. In fact Denise and I, and Lynne and her then-husband Paul, used to go out together as a foursome. Paul was a fellow shareholder in Transform. The first time my eyes set on Lynne was in a French restaurant. As she walked into the room, I thought she looked like Britt Ekland – and I still do. I couldn't believe it. There I was dining with two women; one the image of Elizabeth Taylor and the other a true Britt. Call it my psychic side if you wish, but I knew from that first meeting that she was someone special in my life. I didn't set out to make things happen, but I knew that one day things would be different.

We would all meet occasionally, and Paul and I also used to play tennis together. The path of true love still didn't run very predictably. I divorced Denise in 1992 and lived for several years afterwards with a lovely lady called Sandra. It was during this time that I hit the headlines for the wrong reasons by being featured in an ITV programme called

Neighbours at War. I must admit neither of us saw what was around the corner when we took up residence at a lovely house in the small, leafy Cheshire village of Great Budworth. It was always going to be a temporary stop as I wanted to come back 'home' to Knutsford. But our stay was ultimately made memorable by the antics of a couple of busybody villagers who did their absolute best to make our life hell. The duo never spoke directly to me about their complaints, but did their utmost to turn the local Vale Royal Council against us, claiming that one rich man was bullying the village. So what, you might ask, were the main reasons for their anger? A hedge, a few lamp posts with 25 watt bulbs, security gates and a barbecue, would you believe.

It wasn't that I totally changed the character of the house and its surrounds as they were already much to my liking. I must admit it never even crossed my mind that the additions we made would need planning permission. All the antagonism was caused by the two men and we had no problem with anyone else in what was a friendly village. They managed to get the TV interested in their cause but the programme, which was among the 100 most-watched in that particular year, backfired on them quite spectacularly. Sandra and I defended our cause strongly with me calling the duo 'mini-Hitlers' and expressing my opinion that their stance was founded mostly on jealousy – goodness knows what they would have thought of me had they known I was just a lad from a Doncaster council estate. The national papers, including the *Sun* and *Daily Mail*, enthusiastically covered the story.

Afterwards I was contacted by the council, explained my situation to them and gained retrospective planning permission for the improvements. Meanwhile, the two complainants certainly didn't gain in popularity and subsequently left the village. To be honest, I regarded the whole episode as a good laugh. I certainly didn't set out to annoy my neighbours but you have to try and keep things like this in perspective. I only stayed in the village for about three years but, as I said previously, I was only passing through in the first place.

My life instead went in a different direction. Meanwhile, Lynne and Paul had gone their separate ways and, after a few more years, we got together. It was one of the happiest days of my life when we got married in July 2004 – the ceremony being held at our local and historic Over Peover Church. Interestingly, the church was where General George Patton worshipped during World War Two, as the famous American was billeted to the village. The reception was at our house with around 200 guests, complete with singing waiters and a very special piece of silverware. I'd told the Rovers manager Dave Penney that I wanted him to win the League Three title, so could he bring the trophy to my wedding – and he and the boys obliged in style. Joining Rovers players and officials were the likes of that amazing crackerjack of a sports commentator Stuart Hall and Farokh Engineer, the great former Lancashire and India wicketkeeper. Other highlights included an Elvis Presley impersonator – at least I think he was an impersonator.

In every way it was the special day we had long envisaged. Both our first weddings had been at register offices, so this was something very different. Lynne is exactly the same age as me, but it's just my luck that she looks 20 years younger. Like me, Lynne wasn't born with a silver spoon in her mouth. She was brought up in Swinton and lived in a two-up and two-down for many years. But, like yours truly, she was always ambitious and wanted to progress in her life.

She always had nature on her side, winning the illustrious titles of Miss Trelawne in Cornwall and Miss

Salford rugby league, even cheering on the Reds at Wembley on one famous occasion. She was always sports-minded but rugby league was principally her favourite until I started to convert her to the beautiful game. Young Lynne left school at 15 and originally went into the Post Office only to decide that it wasn't for her. Her father William was all in favour of Lynne 'getting a proper job', but instead she followed her heart and opened a beauty clinic in Manchester.

One of the first venues to offer sunbeds in the north of England, the clinic was extremely successful and gave her a handsome return when she finally sold up. It was after this that she got married to Paul and brought up her family. Lynne and I have now known each other for nearly three decades and I've got no hesitation in saying we are happily married and a good match for each other. I would describe the foundation of our relationship as the friendship we developed over the years and its nature as that of soulmates. It's great for me that I can have Lynne by my side when watching Rovers – she has become a very passionate fan herself – and that we have the same goals in life generally. My life is, as you can imagine, very hectic as I balance the twin roles as chairman of Doncaster Rovers and my work with MYA. And it's true that I get involved in a thousand different things all at the same time. But we do try to spend as much time as humanly possible together too. We both love travelling and enjoy having breaks at our homes in both Majorca and Cape Town. I am fortunate that, just as with my football dream, my personal dream has also come true.

Between us we now have five children of whom we are very proud. My oldest daughter Claire was born in the hot summer of 1976 only a few days apart from my good friend and business partner Aaron Rea, and is now the mother of my sole grandchild (to date), William. She is currently carving out a career for herself with our company MYA.

Gemma, who is eight years Claire's junior, achieved a top degree at Loughborough University and is now working for Laura Ashley in the field of interior design. She has recently moved into a lovely cottage in Cheshire with her boyfriend David. I also have good relationships with Lynne's three children Zoe, Amelia and Joe. Zoe is profoundly deaf, beautiful like her mother and very talented. She made us both very proud when she won first prize at the BAFTA awards for a film she made for Channel Four, and she has also performed a lot of stunt work for the popular *Jonathan Creek* programme. She is the under-water woman. Amelia is based in Madrid with her partner Nacho and is a keen football fan. Her best friend Alison is the partner of Darren Fletcher, the Manchester United and Scotland star, who was so unluckily suspended from the Champions League final in May 2009 against Barcelona. Darren has visited our house on several occasions and is one of those footballers who remains very down-to-earth despite his lofty achievements. Joe is a very keen Rovers fan who is currently at university. I'm pleased he's so keen because, generally, you won't find a more laid-back person. His motto in life seems to be: 'aim low and you won't be disappointed'. But he is a great lad nevertheless.

Lynne and I live together at a house I had built eleven years ago within shouting distance of Jodrell Bank. This is in a beautiful part of Cheshire known to some as 'Millionaires Row', recently the subject of a Channel Four documentary. The house, set in three acres of land and which I named Centuryan House to mark both the time it was built and its owners, is also my work base. Naturally, I'm pretty busy with Doncaster Rovers, MYA and Bowden Properties competing for my attention, but I do not consider myself to be a workaholic. I'm now in the happy position of being able to work when I choose to. The day-to-day running of the cosmetic surgery business Make Yourself Amazing is in the hands of my business partner Aaron Rea, and I am able nowadays to take an active but more back-seat role. Donny Rovers takes up the greater part of my time, yet I would hesitate to call it work. It is more my pleasure, hobby and passion all rolled into one, as anyone who has seen the Rovers memorabilia in my office and sports room will soon realise.

I do have another passion that has stood the test of time and is a big part of my home life today. It is my love of model railways. I'll always remember one special Christmas when I was just five years old and was bought a Hornby Dublo 3 Rail Duchess of Montrose and became well and truly hooked. I was very conveniently placed living in Donny, of course, as my hometown has a traditional railway heritage that is on a different track to anywhere in the world – both the record breaking Mallard and Flying Scotsman were built there. So I suppose the golden age of steam was always going to be extra special for me. I have a lot to thank two of my uncles for; who both worked at the Plant Works in Doncaster, where the wonderful, sleek A4s were built for fostering what has become a life-long interest. As a true Doncastrian, I developed a fascination for the East Coast Main Line in the 1950s.

As you can imagine I was too busy during the majority of my working life to devote as much time as I would have liked to model railways yet the dream lived on. And it was after I sold Transform that I finally got the time and space in my busy life to fully realise my own Over Peover layout, named after the village in which we live. Today, I have a wonderful hand-built and vast layout inside and running outside in a large shed at the bottom of my garden that recreates those halcyon days in my own home.

I am incredibly grateful for the fantastic work of railway modeller Norman Solomon for his efforts in doing the majority of the layout. But, as the ultra-attentive chairman that I am, I didn't want everything to be done by a third party, so I played my part in creating the more scenic aspects. I also have a great interest in weathering locos and stock, so have directed my own efforts into those disciplines as I believe in things looking realistic.

What better or more relaxing way can there be to spend a spare afternoon than tinkering with the tracks and trucks and lingering over the locos and lines. To me it's still pure olde worlde magic. And it was a great compliment in 2009 when my creation was extensively featured in a glossy 16-page supplement called *British Railway Modelling,* which is railway modelling's version of *The Bible*. There is also a DVD entitled *The Right Track to Over Peover,* explaining exactly how the track was put together.

This *was* going to be my final project but - you've guessed it - there is more to come. I am summoning myself for one more supreme effort to build an even bigger creation that will necessitate the shed itself being extended. When I gaze upon those working signals and listen to the inimitable clickety-click of locos hurtling down the track puffing steam through painstakingly created countryside, it is truly breathtaking and I think to myself what a shame it is that in this day and age young children don't seem to grasp the fascination of model railways anymore.

I pay more attention these days to my personal health, doing my best to pursue a reasonably healthy diet and time for exercise. I may have officially retired now as the world's oldest professional footballer – Sean O'Driscoll and Richard O'Kelly need have no sleepless nights about team selection – but I do have my own five-a-side football pitch at home and occasionally make an appearance in a charity match. There was a particularly memorable game here a few years back between teams of former Rovers and Manchester

United stars, supplemented by the likes of champion boxer Ricky Hatton. The Rovers team included Dave Penney, Mickey Walker and me, while the United line-up boasted Norman Whiteside, Clayton Blackmore, Viv Anderson and a certain former England captain by the name of Bryan Robson. I still remember the moment when J Ryan tackled B Robson and came away with the ball as clean as a whistle. In fact I mention it to him every time I see him, funnily enough. Robbo did get the small consolation of netting the winning goal.

Other sports I enjoy from home include tennis and table tennis, usually against my affable young gardener Matty. There have been occasions when I have been forced to wear the 'I am the chump' T-shirt, although not as often as the age gap between us would suggest. Away from home, I also enjoy taking part in the annual Doncaster Rovers versus Doncaster Town cricket match, alongside such seasoned professionals as Mickey Walker who claims to be a mixture of Sir Don Bradman and Shane Warne.

Helping to keep me on the straight and narrow at home are my loyal personal assistant Sue Matthews, whom I first met when we were next-door neighbours, and Pam Boyle, our housekeeper. Along with our other houses in Majorca and Cape Town, I also have an apartment in Dubai. Lynne is always urging me to take as many holidays as possible and it's fair to say that I haven't got too many objections. So one way or another, my work-life balance is far better now than it has ever been.

A little further from home, I regard the Rovers staff as part of my extended family and none more so than my dear brother Philip. He has not had the easiest or luckiest of times in life, being very badly-injured as a pedestrian on a zebra crossing at the age of 26. He was sent scuttling through the windscreen and was in hospital for several weeks. In some ways, he was fortunate to escape with his life. In the last few years Philip has been an unpaid freelance photographer at Donny Rovers, using his developing skills to produce many superb photos and becoming well-liked by the players. A great deal of credit should go here to our media manager Steve Uttley who has combined his own invaluable work by taking Philip under his wing. This year we celebrated a very special occasion when Philip turned 50. This coincided with our weekend trip to St Mary's to face Southampton and was good reason for a birthday party attended by our sister Janet, Dick and Marion Watson, Sean O'Driscoll and Richard O'Kelly. Brian Stock presented a grateful Philip with a Rovers shirt and I gave him £1,000 worth of shares in the club. So I'm not the only Ryan with a stake in Rovers. Needless to say it made the weekend just perfect when we went on to win the following day's match 2-1.

Nowadays two of my closest allies are Terry Bramall, one of the most successful people ever to come from Doncaster, and his former Keepmoat colleague Dick Watson, who are equal major shareholders. This came about after I was introduced to Terry about three years ago at a time when I was beginning to realise that if the club was going to go any further, I needed to spread the load. Terry keeps a lower profile but is a major presence behind the scenes, whilst Dick has taken on the role as my vice-chairman. We have all become very good mates. Practically, Dick and Terry have done a huge amount to make Rovers a more professional organisation off the field. Long gone now are our happy but hazardous ways, replaced by business plans, proper strategy meetings and regular board meetings.

Many of the Rovers team have been with me from the very start or near the beginning of this remarkable journey. Stuart Highfield, Peter May, Peter Hepworth and our president Trevor Milton have been stalwarts of what has become a very strong board. All are local men with a genuine affinity with the club.

I'd like also to give a mention here to our chief executive Dave Morris, and not just because he was nominated recently in the press as being the member of staff most in need of a spot of cosmetic surgery. Fortunately, his wife Chris took the joke in good heart. I still recall the dingy cabin that was Dave's office at Belle Vue and it's fair to say that he has grown with us. Now he has a plush office at the Keepmoat and is a very efficient and dependable chief executive.

Rovers is often described as a friendly, family football club and I think I've been a positive part of that. It made me chuckle a little during the summer when Premiership referee Uriah Rennie wrote that visiting Donny Rovers was rather like going around to his auntie's for tea. This was because he could always guarantee being treated with old-fashioned reverence and good manners whenever he was here. I like that. I'd like to think that the club is a part of old England in the best sense of that phrase.

The Premiership giants who played at Belle Vue during our Carling Cup run in 2005 may be wondering what I am talking about, as at that time our facilities were admittedly Spartan. But, in all honesty, our philosophy hasn't really changed that much. Even at Belle Vue our motto was 'what we have, we share' – it just happens that we have a lot more to share at the modern Keepmoat Stadium.

The visiting changing room is a credit to all concerned and there are separate and excellent rooms for male and female match officials. We always ensure that they feel at home and are offered refreshments when they come here – not to influence them in any way, but merely to show them the respect they deserve. The directors' lounge remains open for officials afterwards whatever has happened in the match

The Ryan family at Christmas: John and Lynne Ryan with (from left) her children Joe, Zoe and Amelia; his daughter Gemma and her partner David

and I think they appreciate that. Similarly, the opposition players are offered food after the game, which is something of a rarity at Football League level.

All this may run contrary to the very modern phrase of 'making our ground like a fortress' in which you sometimes hear all kinds of horror stories of how the home team tries to make the opposition's stay as uncomfortable as possible. While I am here, the Donny Rovers way will always be hospitable and generous – the only thing I want our guests to be upset by is the quality of the football.

15

*

SIMPLY THE BREAST

NAZAR KAZZAZI, Fellow of the Royal College of Surgeons, breast surgery specialist and MYA medical director: "I'd heard a great deal about John Ryan before I got the chance to meet him. I was told of his successful policies when running Transform but what really attracted my attention was more personal. Everyone I spoke with who had worked with John remembered him, praised him and said he cared for his patients and all his employees. It didn't matter whether they'd been at the top or bottom of his business ladder, they respected him for his humanitarian approach.

"That's why when I was told John was in the process of setting up MYA, I let him know I would be more than interested. From our very first meeting I realised that working with him would be a good match because we both share the same high professional standards.

"The first few years of MYA have totally confirmed that initial view of John that he is a very clever and successful businessman. I advised John that the credit crunch wouldn't affect us. If clients had the money, the real issue was providing value for that money

and that is what we do at MYA. And that will continue to be the case even if patient numbers ever go down.

"I've been involved with cosmetic surgery since 2001 and the technologies are still developing – and will continue to do so. Breast augmentation is by far the most popular treatment and has improved significantly in the last few years. These days we use textured implants that are less likely to cause any complications and there have been big developments in the profiles and shapes of implants that have broadened the possibilities for women whatever their size and shape. In addition, we no longer rely on eyeball judgements but on precise measurements and analysis.

"Breast surgery is providing greater satisfaction than ever with fewer and fewer problems. Personally, I believe that MYA is unique in always striving to produce a high-quality service and keeping bang up-to-date with developments in our industry. Another key to our success is having the most skilled and experienced surgeons in the business. Hiring the best surgeons and closely observing that we maintain our practice is an important part of my role with MYA - and what the public has come to expect from a John Ryan-run organisation."

BIG BROTHER 8 *contestant Amy Alexandra-Ward was so delighted with her cosmetic surgery that she has now joined MYA as a patient co-ordinator based at our Leeds clinic. She says: "I had a witch's nose – and I hated it. The problem went back to when I was 12 and broke my nose during a school swimming lesson. At first, it didn't bother me too much but, as I got a bit older, that all changed, especially when I went into modelling. I would never dare leave the house without being smothered in make-up.*

"It didn't stop me from jumping at the chance to go into the Big Brother *house and I wasn't too self-conscious during my two-and-a-half weeks or so there. Nobody said anything to my face, but when I got out into the real world again and read some magazines and forums I found plenty of horrible comments about my nose.*

"My friend, Naomi Millbank-Smith, from Channel 4's Shipwrecked *raved about MYA, so that's how I found out about the company. As I was based in Kent at the time, I was directed to the London clinic. The whole experience was positive. I saw a patient co-ordinator and then the surgeon and was able to explain everything that I didn't like about my nose. He reassured me that the bump was rectifiable and told me exactly what he could do. I left there really excited but had eight weeks in panto at Tamworth before I had the chance to have the operation at Highgate Hospital, London, in January 2008.*

"I think everyone is a bit worried about undergoing surgery, but the staff there did everything to put me at ease. I had my op at about noon and I was told it lasted about an hour. I remember coming round and thinking it couldn't really be all over because it had all happened so quickly. I was warned that I might feel groggy afterwards because of the anaesthetic, but there was none of that at all. Within 20 minutes, I was talking to my mum on the phone and feeling well. The splint came off after a week and it was then that I got my first real look at my new nose. It was great – my nose was softer, more refined. The bone that had formed the bump had been removed. It had caused me to have a harsh look, but now I looked fine.

"I really enjoyed living in London and the hectic social life but, after a while, I decided I needed to start to think about my future. The thought just came to me that I'd love to work for MYA. I had a successful interview and now here I am. I've not been here long, but I love it already. Our main target audience is young women between 18 and 25 years old and I feel that, because of my own experience, I am in a good position to help. I know just how apprehensive they feel when they come to see me and I am able to encourage them that all will really be well. Some of my other friends have now had surgery with MYA and again they are very happy with what has happened to them.

"I'm really happy to be working for John Ryan, whom I heard

had been in the cosmetic surgery business when it was more of a taboo subject. And, yes, if I feel the need for more cosmetic surgery myself in the future, I will do so."

I HAD intended saying goodbye to the cosmetic surgery business by the age of 50 – instead I'm going stronger than ever as I approach my swinging sixties! That says a lot for the persuasive powers of a certain young man called Aaron Rea and the compulsive nature of what I'm convinced is one of the businesses not only of the noughties, but for many years to come.

By the time I eventually sold Transform I was 52 years young and had bought myself a model football club in Doncaster Rovers. It never crossed my mind for a moment that I'd ever go back, even though I'd thoroughly enjoyed the experience. After all, I'd sold up to make my fortune and with the express intention of enjoying my leisure time to the full while I still had the benefits of good health.

The story of MYA or Make Yourself Amazing lives up to the name. If I'd known when we set up that within a year we'd come head-to-head with the worst economic recession since the 1920s, I would never have started up again – even if Melinda Messenger herself had tried to persuade me.

In the event I was incredibly impressed with the enthusiasm and vision of Aaron, a young buck who is almost half my age. He was obviously prepared to devote all his energy and ability into starting a successful new business and he wanted me, the old buck if you like, to work with him. Take Aaron who is vibrant and young and John Ryan, who is just vibrant, and you could have a winning team, I thought.

It was not quite the case of going back to my old job when I was the pioneer, the man in control of the day-to-day running of a fast-moving business. This time I'm opening doors, providing advice and generally overseeing all that is going on. Things had moved on in the cosmetic surgery business in the four years that I was away but, with due respect, some of the established names in the industry hadn't necessarily moved with them. A number of them have saddled themselves with a great deal of debt and have therefore stalled in the face of the current extremely difficult economic climate.

The bare facts are these – we started out in June 2007 with four clinics in London, Manchester, Newcastle and Leeds. Inside two years we expanded to ten clinics with room for yet more to come, and achieved a turnover in 2008/9 of some £10m without the burden of any debt. As with relationships, and football clubs for that matter, it can be easier second time around. When I was a youngster at the cutting edge of a business and ploughing new territory, I made my share of mistakes. Now, with the experience of what went right and what went decidedly pear-shaped behind me, I'm in a good position to avoid those mistakes.

One of my main priorities, as with the football club, has been to put the right building blocks in place. In the field of cosmetic surgery there is simply no substitute for quality. I was in the happy position of knowing a good proportion of the very best surgeons in the country and persuaded them to become part of my new venture. They are fully backed up by very professional, talented and enthusiastic staff who make clients at home from the moment they make an enquiry onwards. I would like to say a personal thank you to the likes of Simon MacMillan, Laura McCrindle and Anne Harrison but, in all honesty, there are too many great folk to mention.

The pre-enlightenment days of the 1970s when cosmetic surgery was regarded as being strictly off-limits save for women with huge bank accounts, egos and prepared to take leave of the senses were, of course, well behind us by the time MYA came into being. These days it has far greater and wider public credibility. Techniques have been refined and improved and the ever-expanding number of treatments have come within the financial compass of ordinary folk and not just the privileged few.

For someone forever associated with Melinda and her wonderful enhanced assets, it comes as a delight that some things do actually stay the same. Breasts are still best in the cosmetic surgery business. In fact, breast augmentation, or boob jobs as they are more commonly known, dominate our business more than ever. At the last count they accounted for around 80 per cent of our surgical procedures.

Whereas the public may still relate to the page three models, WAGs and other beautiful celebrities, my excitement is that everyday women are having their looks and their outlooks transformed. It is, if you forgive the pun, a very uplifting experience – comparable to seeing the smiles on thousands of faces at Donny Rovers.

The business remains a largely female domain, but 'new men' are slowly coming out of the woodwork. In the summer of 2009 I went under my own surgeon's knife in Manchester to have some work done on my eyes. Having been in cosmetic surgery since the mid-1970s, I suppose it was overdue that I underwent some treatment myself. Throughout my career I had always remained a little shame-faced when answering quite honestly that I had never had any cosmetic surgery myself. Yet I didn't do so to prove a point to anyone else, I went because I wanted to undo a little of the ageing process.

The operation was called a blepharoplasty, which removes excessive skin over the upper eyelids. To you and me that means getting rid of some excess 'baggage'.

Knowledge is important when it comes to facing medical issues and I arrived at the hospital at 7.30am on a Monday morning feeling reasonably relaxed as I, more than anyone else, was aware how safe the procedure was and that the hands I was putting myself into were genuinely expert. Yet, being human, I was a little nervous as you don't go into hospital every day.

On such occasions, a kind and friendly face is worth a great deal and it was very reassuring when the receptionist was bright and cheery as she gave me the form to fill in my basic details. I then had a few minutes to see whether Donny Rovers were featured in the morning newspaper before being shown to my room. The first face I saw there was from the kitchen, asking me what food I'd like later in the day. Now this was my kind of place. It got a little more medical as a very pleasant nurse came to take my blood pressure. She told me that the reading suggested I was very relaxed – good job no one takes my blood pressure during a Rovers match.

I was in a privileged position, of course, in that I knew both the anaesthetist and the surgeon, Mr Mahdi, very well after having worked with them both for many years. Mind you, that didn't prevent the same lovely nurse from bringing me down to earth with a bump by handing me a gown and some exceedingly silly-looking paper knickers. That softened the blow a fair bit when the anaesthetist came in to give me an injection in the back of my hand to put me out for the count. I'd usually have welcomed a chat, but not in those knickers.

Mr Mahdi then arrived and marked up around my eyes in preparation for the treatment. He asked me whether I was looking forward to it and, you know, in a strange way I actually was. I was then taken down to the operating room and the next thing I knew I was waking up back in my hospital room being welcomed with the news that I'd just gained two black eyes. I also had some swelling to contend with for a few days, as promised. But, other than that, I honestly didn't feel too bad – in fact, pretty good for a 59-year-old who looked as if he'd just gone a couple of rounds with Frank Bruno. Sue, my PA, came to collect and drive me home and, for once, I was a good boy and took it easy for the rest of the day and slept normally. I couldn't believe how little pain there was even if I decided to keep away from mirrors. Next day I woke to find the swelling had increased, although I was in no discomfort at all.

Let's face it, no one wants to get it wrong when the boss is in the hot seat. I was up and about and attending a meeting with my fellow directors Terry and Dick the following evening and have had no problems since. Just a week afterwards the swelling was barely noticeable at all and nothing untoward happened thereafter. I can say, hand on heart, that I would have no hesitation in having some more work done in the future if I considered it necessary, after all, there's no point in growing old gracefully.

You may say, with some justification, that it was not surprising that 'the boss' was given good treatment. After all, few members of staff in their right mind would want to come up short when their employer is in town. We certainly don't think that new clients, in particular, will consider their operation to be a breeze. Quite the opposite. Everyone is an individual and deals with things in different ways, but I'd expect most clients to be both excited and very apprehensive in the weeks before a procedure. What we strive to do is to provide clients with as much information and access to others on the same path as possible.

People come to us with a lot of questions and very often unsure about exactly what they want. As I've said breast augmentation is by far the most popular procedure but there's more to consider than merely putting yourself down for a boob job.

Everyone who gets in contact with MYA with a view to a procedure will firstly be introduced to their patient co-ordinator at a local clinic. This is not necessarily a medically-trained member of staff but an important point of contact able to discuss freely with you what you are hoping to achieve. All patients must be over the age of 18 by law, but there is no upper age limit. This is not a hard sales pitch because that ultimately could be the wrong route for both parties. It is an opportunity to ask some of the many questions that will be on a potential patient's mind and for us to introduce them to what may be possible. There will be times when, very tactfully of course, a person is told that in our view his or her expectations are unlikely to be met and therefore we would not advise them to pursue a surgical procedure.

The next stage – usually within a week but certainly in the next month – is to be introduced to a surgeon. It is very important for each client to meet the person who will actually be performing the operation and you will always have the choice to opt for a different surgeon if you feel more comfortable with someone else. You will be shown exactly what the operation entails and the difference it is going to make to your appearance. You can also chat to someone who has already undergone a similar operation, if you so wish.

Patients often come to us by word of mouth, having been recommended by friends who have been pleased with their results. But it is still very comforting and useful for them to be able to converse freely with others and this is one of the purposes of our very popular forum on the MYA internet site. A largely anything-goes discussion takes place daily and this is often the right opportunity for folk to bring up issues as they actually arise, whether they are speaking before or after their operation. The forum is very supportive and encouraging in its tone, as you find that people are more than willing to share what they are discovering.

Just tune in to the emotions and joy of this woman who posted on our forum in October 2009 and you will get a far better idea of just how helpful this can be:

> 'The surgery is a big deal, I am four weeks post op now and know what you're feeling, I felt too. I was terrified! Started wondering if I really needed them, were my old ones really that bad, what if something went wrong....etc. But you know what.........I was worrying about nothing! My new boobs look amazing, I couldn't have asked for a better result. I was expecting a 32D but have ended up a 32E/F! I have no pain now and they have finally both dropped (my left dropped first so I was a little lop-sided for a couple of weeks ha ha).The surgeon and anaesthetist will be with you every step of the way, monitoring your stats and making sure it all goes well. I cried when they were taking me into theatre (yes I am a big wuss, I know!) they had to tell me to calm down because I was sending my blood pressure through the roof! When I came round I felt so silly as I'd made such a fuss over what now seemed like nothing! Don't let the fear take over is my advice, I did and I let it ruin the experience for me, I should have been excited but I was so frightened! You have nothing to worry about and you will love your new boobs! The surgeons are amazing. And MYA as a whole is a brilliant company. I had a lovely patient co-ordinator who really put me at ease and my surgeon and anaesthetist were very comforting too. Good luck with your ops girlies! Xxx'

Once you are happy with this, you are then handed over to a nurse who is another important part of the chain. We need to be aware of your medical history to ensure that you are fit and healthy enough to undergo surgery. Once again, we will always be frank and honest with you rather than treating the outcome as a formality. The same nurse remains in charge of your case from that point onwards. The operation will take place at a private hospital – only non-surgical procedures occur at the clinics themselves – where the atmosphere will be relaxed and professional. You are not ill and therefore will not find yourself alongside patients being treated for medical conditions. Sometimes an overnight stay will be necessary, otherwise you can expect to be back home later the same day. 'Crazy dancing' is not recommended for around six weeks after surgery but you should be able to return to the workplace after about a week, depending of course on your healing process and the physicality of the type of job you do. The satisfaction rate among women who have had breast operations is amazingly high. Frequently they speak of having increased self confidence and, of course, feeling more attractive and sexy.

Breast operations usually cost around £4,000 but the company frequently has offers available that can knock the price down still further and our two most popular loans allow you either 0 per cent finance or to spread your payment over a number of years through low monthly payments.

Don't worry if you are unsure about exactly the size of breast you are looking for. You will be given expert advice based on the size and shape of your breasts now and your body in general. You are never on your own once you contact MYA. At all times you will be able to chat and share your worries and thoughts with others who have either had their procedure already or are waiting to go to clinic. You will soon realise that others are just as excited and, yes, fearful, as you are but have been there, done it and worn the sports bra! But don't listen to me, listen to the clients who come through our doors. Here is just a small selection of true personal stories that make working in cosmetic surgery so rewarding, even for an old-stager such as me.

LAURA DUNN, *above*, is a 25-year-old mum-of-two who is looking forward to her wedding in September 2010 even more after finally sorting out a problem that had haunted her for at least half her young life: "I have always been very conscious of my nose. It was wonky, pointed down slightly to the right, and it protruded quite far out, with a bump and pointed down worse when I smiled. It certainly didn't help when a boy of 12 during my time at Middle School started putting his index finger above his nose and this thumb under to make a witches nose. Even my sister used to call me 'big nose'. Despite my parents trying their best to reassure me that I looked just fine, the problem was only going to get worse in my mind as I got older. I couldn't regard myself as attractive and my confidence took a massive dent as boys I used to fancy made it clear they didn't fancy me. And those knock-backs are a seriously big deal for a young girl.

"I didn't like what I saw in the mirror and used to adopt more and more elaborate tricks to look more photogenic when confronted with a camera, including tilting my head to ensure it could only capture my better side. I missed out on a lot of social life because I was uncomfortable with my appearance. In truth, I had wanted to sort my nose out for ages. My Dad was never keen on the idea because he thought I was doing away with his genes and I needed something to kick-start me into making a decision and that came when I got engaged to my fiancé Martin. It was the thought of those wedding photos that finally did it for me. When you think about it you take two permanent reminders from your big day – the ring and your photos. I couldn't bear the thought of wanting to get rid of my photos because I hated how I looked from some angles.

"One challenge I had was not having much idea of what my nose would look like if I had surgery. As a graphic designer, I went to the trouble of 'Photoshopping' my nose so I knew how I wanted to look. But unlike a breast operation, for example, it wasn't possible to be precise about how it would actually turn out. I would have to take a step of faith if I went under the knife. One thing that comforted me was that three of my ten girlfriends had already had some cosmetic surgery, so it didn't seem such an unusual thing to do.

"I'd been researching the cosmetic surgery industry for a couple of years and chose MYA because it seemed a very personable company. I saw their website and it featured real people rather than just celebrities. It also sold me their aftercare and support offered to clients. Jodie at the Birmingham clinic was my first contact and she was just absolutely fantastic. She made me feel very much at ease and introduced me to my surgeon, Mr Brian Musgrove. I had met a few surgeons and Mr Musgrove was by far the best. Professional and highly-skilled I knew that I wouldn't want anyone else but him to do the procedure so, as soon as I got home, I got the money together and booked the procedure for three weeks later on 8 June at the Manchester Lifestyle Hospital.

"Everything was suddenly moving very quickly after years of thinking about what to do, but I was still very nervous when the time for the operation came around. I cried all night – I knew I had made a big cash commitment and also I didn't want to come out looking like a completely different person. It was very helpful to me that I was first in the following day, so I didn't have any more time to wait and worry. Before I knew it, I was back on the ward. I'd been out for about eleven-and-a-half hours and there was no pain at all, although my eyes looked horrific. I was amazed that I was up and about and enjoying the lovely food at the hospital very quickly after the operation. I had braced myself for the worst despite my MYA nurse, Karen, reassuring me it wasn't a painful procedure. You just hear so many horror stories but I had absolutely nothing to worry about.

"Staff at the hospital were friendly and attentive and I actually enjoyed my stay there. Towards the evening the bruising started to come out around my eyes, I looked in the mirror and laughed...having a sense of humour helps when you look like that! Next day I went home and spent the next few days relaxing and doing nothing. I didn't need to take any of the painkillers they gave me and slept at night with no problems. The best thing that soothed my nose as it was itchy underneath and often runny for the first few days, was gently holding a damp cotton wool pad under my nostrils. I also drank plenty of water, which helped with the swelling believe it or not. Gel eye masks kept in the fridge are great for the black eyes.

"By day five my nose was completely clear. I could breathe through it easily and the bruising had started to fade. After two weeks I couldn't even begin to explain how happy I was with the results. I looked very different and even with the bruising and swelling I was happy with what I saw in the mirror. It was very strange though to see my new nose for the first time. I think I sat in front of the mirror for an hour just smiling and checking it out from all angles. I now have a straight nose that fits my face and doesn't droop down when I smile. The reactions I have had are great, with everyone shocked that having your nose re-shaped could make so much difference and those who thought I didn't need it agreeing that the results are really fantastic. It just goes to show that choosing the right surgeon who will give you the perfect nose for YOU ensures great results. MYA are a great company. I wanted to get the surgery done very quickly because of work and family commitments and they allowed me to choose a date that suited me best. I still can't believe I have a cute nose. If I'd have known that my nose could look this good and make such a difference then I would have done it years ago.

"I'm even more excited about my wedding day now. I'd already bought myself a wedding dress but decided to treat myself to another one to celebrate my new look. I now spend time talking to others about their various operations. I spoke with a 60-year-old who thought she might be too old for surgery, but told her there really aren't any age limits."

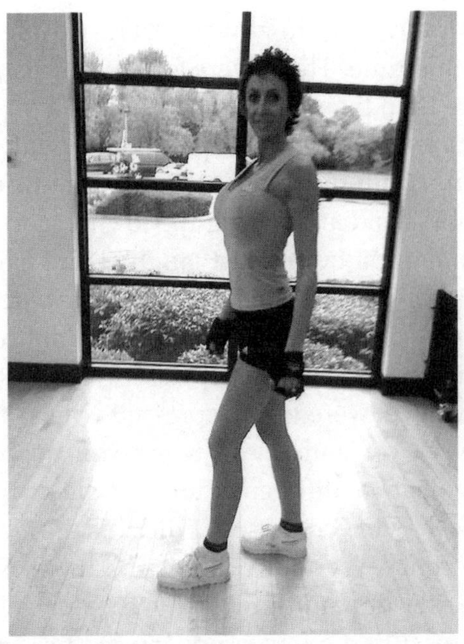

EMMA CHAMPION, *above*, 34, has undergone two breast augmentations – one each in the different eras of cosmetic surgery – and she may not be finished just yet. She is the office manager of a company producing special effects for films and TV.

She says: "I've swapped five sets of chicken fillets for two fabulous boobs and I couldn't be happier about it. Only a woman can really appreciate just how much it means to me. When you're growing up you just hope your boobs are going to get bigger, but once you're 18 the die is cast – and I was left miserable about my flat chest. Coming from a one-parent family having a boob job was way out of my price range and, in any case, such operations were nothing like as popular as they are today. It looked as if I was stuck with my 32A bust.

"It took two years of saving up for me to do something about it. The easy part was choosing Transform, then John

Ryan's company, as they were THE cosmetic surgery business at that time. There were far fewer businesses in the market place than there are now.

"I learnt a lot from my first operation. I vividly remember the surgeon coming round with seven different sized implants in his hand and asking me to choose one. Eagerly I went for the biggest but he just laughed and explained that wouldn't be possible as I had little breast tissue to work with. The most I was allowed was a 340CC implant but, after the operation, I was a 32C and very pleased with what I saw. My friends at the bank were very impressed when I walked back in after a week off with these wonderful boobs. The men seemed to look at me differently too, but the really important thing was how I viewed myself. I did this for me.

"The good news certainly didn't end there. Not only did my boobs settle down without any problem but, over the years, my breast tissue increased. My mother, in particular, thought I was crazy but I thought the time was right again to go for bigger and better boobs. Why not? This time Transform couldn't help me. They weren't in favour of me having a second op, but it was a far different matter when I approached MYA. I was attracted to approach them by the company's sexy and classy image and when I eventually found out that John Ryan was involved that was a further point in their favour.

"It was a very positive thing for me when I was welcomed and advised by young girls who had experienced a bit of Botox themselves. Previously I'd been in the hands of a patient co-ordinator in her 40s, now I was with girls whom I could better relate to and understood how I was thinking. When I saw the surgeon, Mr Singh, he provided me with just the response I was looking for. He said I would be able to have a 615 or 700CC due to my increased breast tissue and I was thrilled. I now realised that even if you begin your journey with a sad 32A, you can have a beautiful large bust if you are prepared to wait a few years between operations.

"The hospital experience in London in June 2009 matched the sleek and modern image. It was so different to what was the norm ten years back. The anaesthetist was such a laugh, Mr Singh is an incredible surgeon and everything happened like clockwork. I was admitted at 9.30am and by 12.30pm was back in my room watching *Loose Women*. Altogether MYA were vibrant, trendy and bang up-to-date with the modern cosmetic world. As for me, I'm now a fabulous 32F and wouldn't have wanted it any other way. I feel even luckier than women born with natural assets. After all, you can have the best of boobs in your youth but they are destined to go south in your thirties. Who knows, I may even go back again in another ten years."

BEING fearful, particularly of the unknown, goes with the territory. Many clients are very nervous prior to their surgery but then again, like 22-year-old JOANNE MORROW, many report afterwards that they just wished they could have relaxed and enjoyed the experience more. It was nothing like as bad as anticipated.

"Being the odd one out in your family is not a good thing – when all the other females are well endowed up-front," says Joanne, *pictured overleaf*. "I was the one who was always told that my breasts would grow as I got older. But it never happened and left me very unhappy with how I looked. To be honest I was almost embarrassed with my appearance.

"I did my research on the internet and was very impressed when I read about this company that had an aftercare policy lasting five years – especially as the others seemed to be offering just six months. I was hugely

impressed with the MYA website which looked great and included some very good before and after photos.

"Anyway I eventually I plucked up enough courage to do something about it and with my partner's support booked a consultation with MYA. I met my surgeon the same day and once I'd spoken with Dr Adamo I had no reason to look elsewhere. It was reassuring also to know that John Ryan, whom I knew used to run Transform, was involved as here was someone with years and years of experience. Some of these companies are quite faceless, but MYA were up-front. A week later I was due for my operation. Only problem was that I was absolutely terrified. I realised that the danger of having cosmetic surgery these days is far reduced as they use a different kind of implant, but having any kind of operation is major.

"I'd never had surgery before and had all those usual worries about not waking up. Apart from that, the most frightening prospect was that of having a cannula put in the back of my hand. I was told that it really hurt – but although it stung a bit, it turned out to be nothing like as painful. Nevertheless I was a complete bag of nerves. I was so terrified, staff had to tell me to calm down. I was crying and just so scared. I remember the moment the cannula was put in my hand and then opening my eyes and asking when I was having my surgery. The answer was that it was all over and done with. You can imagine how thrilled and relieved I was.

"Within one hour of being back I got up out of my bed to go to the toilet, surprising staff with the speed of my recovery, and I was allowed home the same day. I experienced some discomfort afterwards – as I'd been told to expect – but the only bad day was two days after the op when I felt sick and dizzy as the effect of the anaesthetic wore off.

"And so a 32B has been transformed into a 32 E or F and my confidence and my relationship has blossomed. Prior to the surgery I used to look at myself in the mirror and not like what I see and I passed those insecurities onto my boyfriend. We used to argue because I could see bigger breasted women all around me and I accused him of looking at them. Now all that has changed."

16

*

THEY THINK IT'S ALL OVER

PETER HEPWORTH, retired stockbroker and Rovers director: "The fans may not realise it, but things do change off the field the further you go up the football ladder. In John's early days, we lived by the seat of our pants at times, but to run a Championship club you need to have a sound business model and he has realised that too. Bringing in Dick Watson and Terry Bramall as equal major shareholders is a godsend to Doncaster Rovers. We're not one of the bigger clubs in this league but the likes of Burnley and Barnsley have shown that the Premiership dream can happen. We'll need a bit of luck along the way but our success story has shown that anything is indeed possible."

DICK WATSON, formerly of Keepmoat Plc and one of three major shareholders at Doncaster Rovers: "John Ryan introduced himself to me after a game at Belle Vue against Blackpool. Then he approached my business partner, Terry Bramall, who was happy to become involved and asked whether I would join him on the board too. That's how one became three at Doncaster Rovers. One point we insisted on was that, although we are equal shareholders, John Ryan should continue in his role as chairman and driving force behind Rovers. We joined the board about two-and-a-half years ago, about the time of a management buy-out at our company. I view being involved as an opportunity to give something back to an area in which I have been very successful. An important part of my input has been putting together a business strategy which has been all the more necessary now we are in the Championship. Finances are an extremely important part of a football club. We run without debt and with a playing budget with which the manager Sean O'Driscoll is doing an exceptional job."

NEIL WARNOCK, Crystal Palace manager: "To be competing, as Donny are now, with some of the top clubs in the land is a minor miracle – but they're no one-season wonders in the Championship. They are here to stay, in my view."

GIVE John Ryan and Donny Rovers a good pat on the back for making it to the Championship and staying up for a season – but this dream can only go so far. After all, it's inconceivable that a small club like Rovers could ever make it to the Premiership and dine at football's top table. The prospect of mighty Manchester United, Chelsea, Liverpool and Arsenal visiting the Keepmoat Stadium will always be confined to the occasional cup tie or friendly…

If you believe all that, you haven't taken too much notice of my story so far!

Seriously, I can understand the skeptics and, as I've intimated above, it is becoming more and more difficult to defy the football odds these days. Indeed history may well reveal in a couple of decades time that dear old Donny Rovers were the last team able to escape from the Conference and make it to even the second tier of English football.

But to those who think my dream is now over I say this, with due apology to the late Kenneth Wolstenholme for amending his famous words: I haven't even booked the fat lady, let alone is she getting ready to sing.

Former co-owner of Rovers and my colleague of many years Peter Wetzel said during the summer of 2009 that he sees the club at the crossroads. Either we would speculate further and make that step into the Premiership or become a club more dominated by figures of another kind and settle for our current status, he argued. That same period saw us lose one of our most influential midfielders, Richie Wellens, to Leicester City for £900,000 and then, after long and protracted speculation, Matty Mills finally left the Keepmoat for Reading in a £2m deal.

Some fans inevitably regarded this as a lack of ambition and I was rudely rounded upon by one caller to Radio Sheffield who challenged me to either 'bankroll the club or get out'. Again, I trust that if the gentleman has taken the trouble to read this book, he will now have a more accurate perspective.

The real situation was that we would have liked to have kept both players and we were not forced to sell them to balance the books. From the moment Leicester chairman Milan Mandaric phoned me from an aeroplane in May, it was always going to be touch and go whether we could keep Wellens. I've always liked Richie, both as a player and a person, and it was ironic that the situation arose just before Lynne and I were guests at his wedding. Richie has since been very candid in saying that he was made a financial offer that he really couldn't refuse and I also think that we were well compensated for a player whom, at 29, could just have enjoyed his most prolific seasons with us. At least it showed we'd learnt our lesson from the Greenie experience of 12 months ago and ensured that when the admirers came, one of our most valuable assets was on a contract. Richie called in to our home to see us just before he left and I wished him all the very best for the future – and meant it. Who knows, we may even see him again one day.

Matty was a different kettle of fish in that, as a relative youngster, he should surely have his best years in front of him. After being courted unsuccessfully by Birmingham City towards the end of last season, his chief suitors for most of the summer were Nottingham Forest. The truth was that our number one option was to keep the player, whom we'd signed for a club record £300,000 just 12 months previously, but felt that it would be difficult to resist an offer should a Premiership club come knocking. The situation dragged on because Forest consistently failed to come up with the goods and proved to be a very confusing club to attempt to deal with. I told Mark Arthur from the beginning that our asking price was £2m – but should I have been speaking to manager Billy Davies or even David Pleat, who has a say in their transfers? Apparently the Midlands club has a transfer panel, all of whom has to approve a potential transfer. If you want a hold-up, call a committee meeting.

Forest continued to come back, both to me and our chief executive, Dave Morris. But when they put their offer in writing, they fell a full £500,000 short, with no add-ons and with the money in installments over three years. In contrast, Reading made their move just days before the season kicked off, but came up with a concrete offer which matched our valuation before agreeing personal terms with Matty. I still believe the lad has the ability to become England's centre-half in years to come, but a £2m return on a £300,000 investment wasn't too bad.

In return, we brought in four players during the same week including the experience of John Oster, the former Everton and Sunderland star, Quinton Fortune, once of

Manchester United and South Africa, alongside the obvious promise of Byron Webster, who had been plying his trade in the Czech league, and fellow defender Mustapha Dumbuya.

Unlike Forest, we had no reason to overhaul our squad at Doncaster. Look at the regularly successful sides and you will see that radical change is only occasionally the way forward. Our foundations are based on continuity and, looking at the talent among Sean O'Driscoll's squad, I was happy at the beginning of the summer to see the absolute minimum of incomings and outgoings at the Keepmoat once we'd released the five players from last season.

So am I promising Premiership football for the club that was buried and almost dead eleven years ago? I would be foolish to be as categorical as that. But if you ask me whether Premiership football is a strong possibility for Rovers, that's a totally different question. The answer is that if you Dare to Dream anything is possible.

Take a look at recent Championship history to prove a point. Clubs such as our neighbours Hull City, two seasons in the Premiership, and Burnley, promoted after their play-off success over Sheffield United, have shown that where there is vision and ambition there is hope. Burnley even achieved their excellent feat despite being rock-bottom of the table after the first four matches. I also take into account our superb post-Christmas revival that saw Rovers finish in a highly creditable 14th spot in 2008/09. Look at a table for the second half of the campaign and our 40 points – accrued from a remarkable 13 victories and just one draw from our last 23 games – put us in an automatic-promotion slot. The bookmakers and so-called football experts don't currently give twopence for our chances, but they wouldn't be nearly so smug were we to make the play-offs. For our record in sudden-death football bears comparison with anyone's.

True, we kicked off the 2000/10 campaign once again as

one of the more modestly resourced clubs with a playing budget of £5.9m, yet we have plenty going for us. We have a Premier League manager in Sean O'Driscoll, a hugely talented squad of players who add up to a still stronger collective unit, plus a momentum and belief that comes from the huge progress we have made over the last decade.

Put it this way, I have in my office the blueprint of a Premiership future for Donny Rovers in the form of plans of how I see the Keepmoat Stadium developing. Two sections have been added in a style more akin to Hull City's KC Stadium and our capacity increased to 25,000. I can promise you now that this will become reality should we achieve promotion into the top flight. So the dream lives on…

Talking of the Keepmoat, as I write we are currently in our third full season at our new stadium and it's fair to say that I'm pleased with the progress we have made. Yet there have undoubtedly been teething problems.

Turning a new stadium into a home is not just a case of picking up the keys and playing a few football matches, but I do feel now that Rovers fans are beginning to take to the new place. You hear people talking about 'going down the Keepmoat' and nationally the name has quickly become associated with Donny Rovers. To be perfectly honest, it took us a while to feel welcome here ourselves. The Keepmoat is run by a stadium management company and we have a 25-year lease and pay rent as the principal occupiers. But the first stadium manager, Ian Spowart, certainly didn't go out of his way to help. One example was when I was doing a television interview about the Keepmoat and Ian, in his wisdom, refused permission for the cameras to enter the stadium. Thankfully, Ian and another early official have since left the company and we now enjoy much better relations.

The stadium suffered financial losses in its first year and

that had severe consequences for Rovers as our rent was increased from an initial £250,000 a year to nearer £1m. I think that the stadium management company has learned valuable lessons from staging one or two high-profile concerts that ended up making losses, although dear old Sir Elton John's visit was apparently a great success.

We have since taken another step forward to feeling at home by putting up a sign 'the home of Doncaster Rovers' at the Keepmoat. This is something our fans have requested and I share their view that it is part of the process of settling in.

Important work has also taken place to re-lay the playing surface. When we first came to the Keepmoat, the pitch was good enough not to suffer in comparison with Belle Vue which, for all its faults, always boasted fantastic playing conditions. I'm sure that the staging of other events played its part in the subsequent deterioration of the pitch that came more and more to our notice in the second half of last season. As Martin O'Neill and John Robertson immediately pointed out, the poor and bobbly surface did no favours at all to a side committed to playing passing football. Instead, it played into the hands of teams who were happy to hump and thump the ball and avoid making mistakes.

Personally, I think the pitch played a part in Rovers losing four successive home matches and to our disappointingly low goals tally throughout the season at the Keepmoat. Hopefully the £150,000 we spent in the summer will prove an excellent investment for both our players and fans in the months ahead. This certainly looked to be the case when we entertained Wolverhampton Wanderers in Mickey Walker's testimonial and then hosted Preston North End and Coventry City in our opening home Championship fixtures.

I am now confident that the next very important step forward will see Rovers taking full ownership of the complex in the near future. The wheels have been set in motion following the Mayoral election early in 2009 and it is clear now that the council would like to sell. I believe, at the time of writing, that a deal can indeed be done. The advantages of owning our own home are very clear. It would help us to develop both the stadium and the surrounding complex, provide us with an excellent asset and make the Keepmoat the definitive long-term home of Doncaster Rovers and our supporters. In the last few months I have established good links with the new directly-elected Mayor of Doncaster, Peter Davies, another man who extols good common sense. And I am confident that at some stage we can come to an amicable agreement to benefit both the football club and the rest of the community.

One question I simply can't answer is how long I will remain as the chairman of Doncaster Rovers. I have to take into account the fact that I have already had eleven years in the post and that my next birthday in May will be my 60th. The day will indeed come when I take a step back, I just trust that it will not be any day soon and that I will continue to be involved with my football club in some form until I meet the great referee in the sky. Sir Alex Ferguson regretted setting a retirement date a few years ago and I believe it is more logical to just go with the flow and that I will know when the time is right.

I am sadly part of a rare breed. I'm reminded once again of the wise words of former Manchester City chairman John Wardle who told me a few years back that the age of even multi-millionaires running clubs was coming to an end – the future was billionaire. The concept of a fans' chairman is severely in decline. Everton's Bill Kenwright, Dave Whelan, of Wigan, Middlesbrough's Steve Gibson and Forest's Nigel Doughty are among those who have always supported their respective clubs.

The gambles and sheer risks taken at Championship

level even take my breath away. Birmingham City, for example, had a wage bill of around £20m last season and will no doubt consider that money well spent as they gained the second automatic-promotion spot on the last day of the campaign before going on to attract new and even richer owners in the Premiership. But where would they be now if they had missed out, as could so easily have been the case. You simply can't maintain that sort of expenditure in the second tier of English football. Mind you, even that seems like pocket money compared with Newcastle United who are currently tackling the task of instantly winning back their Premiership place with a playing budget of around £42m.

Not so fortunate in the gambling stakes were Reading who had one of their star players on a wage of £35,000-a-week last season as they, too, sought to bounce straight back after relegation from the Premier League. The early stages of this season provided evidence that they may now be financially stretched.

I accept, of course, that Donny Rovers may once again need 'The Three Musketeers' to dip into our pockets to ensure that our figures add up. We provided Sean O'Driscoll with a playing budget of £5.9m in 2009/10 and our initial figures, based on the assumption that Keepmoat gates will rise slightly from their current 12,000 average, were expected to be around £1.5m short come April. But those figures look more favourable after the sales of Wellens and Mills.

I'm totally mindful of the fact that we can't take the commercial side for granted. The first thing on the list of potential savings for a hard-up business is sponsorship and executive boxes etc, and I am aware of our responsibility not to price ordinary folk out of football. For the third successive season we froze our season ticket prices for 2009/10 in a bid to keep our VIPs on board.

The playing field out there is extremely uneven and, as a Championship chairman, I share some of the guilt. It is surely wrong that of the monies distributed by the Football League, 80 pet cent goes to the Championship, with just 12 per cent for League One clubs and eight per cent going into League Two. This picture is more distorted than ever when you bring the subject of the Premier League into the equation.

There is a complacency among the elite clubs but in a way it is well justified. You can view football today as the Premier League feasting at a banquet and the rest of us, the Championship included, waiting in the wings for any scraps to fall from the table. The wages paid at the highest level are obscene and bear no relation to the well-being of the sport in general. But while clubs stay in the Premier League they are protected from any contact with the real world, due largely to the lavish deals they receive from TV companies.

One issue that really makes me furious is the cynical ploy to create a Premiership 2 incorporating so-called major clubs currently outside the top-flight. Worst of all was the idea there should then be no promotion or relegation between the extended Premiership and the Football League. Perhaps it said it all that the proposal came from the chairman of Bolton Wanderers, who may be feeling uneasy about their own future among the elite. The whole thing emphasises the sheer greed among today's top clubs as they attempt to ensure that the big money stays with them and have no regard at all for the many clubs who have very uncertain futures. Also, the closed-door concept is totally contrary to the romance of the game. If clubs were denied the capacity to dream, the game would be infinitely poorer. I can assure you that even if Rovers become a Premiership club in future, I will fight my corner on this one.

The need for financial justice is even more paramount for, even as a successful and ever-optimistic businessman myself,

I can't see things getting better for some time yet. In my view, the current economic downturn will continue until the end of 2010 and then we have to face the fact that this country will be paying back its debts for generations to come.

Obviously I am talking about a problem that is far wider than football. It is a situation in which I can fully appreciate that some folk will look at others such as yours truly who are financially extremely well off with increasing suspicion and hostility. And I do have a lot of sympathy with their views. For example, I understand the growing public anger toward folk who have seemingly made personal fortunes whilst playing a large part in creating the financial meltdown that is now affecting so many ordinary people.

Personally, I am shocked and disgusted by the antics of bankers who have led their organisations to the financial brink and needed bailing out by the Government. But I can't honestly say that I am that surprised. In truth, they have lived down to the very low opinion I have always held of them. I got a big insight into banks when Barclays very nearly caused the downfall of Transform, my successful cosmetic surgery business, back in 1990.

This year I have again been extremely unhappy with the way the banks have dealt with us at Doncaster Rovers. On this occasion I don't want to name names but we decided to change banks after they demanded changes in our overdraft facility and a big increase in their fees. Before we had time to wipe the dust off our feet, the second bank came back to us wanting to change the goal posts fairly significantly. There's a message there for football clubs generally – don't think for a moment that banks see your club as a priority when it comes to giving financial help unless they're already among the super rich in the Premier League, of course.

Banks don't seem to do the job they are supposed to - protecting the interests of their clients - but appear to have a different agenda altogether. They seem to thrive on creating debt and are all too ready to swoop to close the coffin lid on businesses that have always been successful. I blame bankers 100 per cent for the credit crunch and, in particular, their irresponsible dealings in the sub-prime sector. Their motives seem to have been fuelled more by personal greed than public concern. I would never condone violence but I can certainly understand the anger directed against bankers such as Sir Fred Goodwin, the now-retired head of the Royal Bank of Scotland. How individuals can walk away with huge sums of money from organisations they have driven into the wall is totally beyond me.

Obviously there is some truth in the oft-repeated claim by current Prime Minister Gordon Brown that this is merely a symptom of a global recession - economies are indeed being hit in many parts of the world - but this does not explain the full mess that we have got ourselves into. Brown and his predecessor Tony Blair acted totally irresponsibly when they basically got into bed with fat cats who far from pointing the economic way forward were acting on the verge of criminality.

It's crossed my mind over the years to go into politics, although I've always been reticent. To be honest I think that I am much too straightforward and outspoken to make it in the political world. My first problem would be – which party would I represent? I've voted for all three major parties over the years and still find it very difficult to decide whom to support. So I suppose that if I'd ever gone down this particular road, it would have been as an independent.

I make no pretence about the fact that I am a multi-millionaire – and that was always my intention. From a very young age I wanted to cast off the trappings of my modest council house background and steady jobs, and make a lot of money. I got where I did through a lot of hard work and effort, allied to a sprinkling of inspiration and good judgement. Instead of going down the path of the worthy, but not particularly financially rewarding world of forensic science, I got involved with the cosmetic surgery Transform – and the rest, as they say, is history. Throughout the years the business went from strength to strength, providing me with very good dividends. And eventually in 2002 I had my windfall moment when I sold the business for £25m, ten per cent of which had to be paid in tax. Since then I've gone back into the cosmetic surgery business by forming another company MYA (Make Yourself Amazing), which is also proving to be very successful.

I have several business interests, including Bowden Properties which owns 14 properties for let in the Doncaster area, and also in the production of model trains. Plus I have invested in property for myself and my family, such as my prime base in Knutsford and our homes in Majorca and Cape Town. Both came about as they were regular holiday destinations and I wanted to spend time there. I regard Cape Town very fondly as one of the best places on the planet for its climate, its food and its people. My wife Lynne and I look upon the house there as our palace in the sun. And, for the record, I also believe it is a safer place in which to live than Manchester. Furthermore, I have two apartments in Dubai – one of which is being built as we go to press – but these are for letting rather than as homes.

But I didn't – and don't – believe in wealth purely for wealth's sake. My ambition was to be the person who could lead my football club out of the wilderness and I wanted financial security for both myself and my loved ones. As you can gather from reading this book, I do go out of my way to help people when I feel that I can – but to go into too many details would be defeating the object. If you do good things entirely for the publicity it brings, it loses its meaning.

Hopefully, the credit crunch will provide some benefits for football by sobering up the demands of agents and players. This would be very timely as the knights in shining armour who have frequently swooped in to save football clubs in recent seasons are now fewer and farther between. Businesses are, of course, being particularly badly hit by the recession and potential investors are getting the message that supporting a football club financially is not the most sensible of investments.

Naturally, over my lifetime I do have regrets. The fact that my university days came to an end? Not taking on Manchester City? Pouring millions into Donny Rovers? Discovering Melinda Messenger? Actually, none of those. If I have a regret it is signing Justin Jackson and Bruce Dyer and, yes, if I got my chance all over again I'd always ensure Paul Green was on a lifelong contract! Not too long a debit list for a man of my years. I guess Frank Sinatra could list them under 'too few to mention'.

In all seriousness, I've loved almost every minute of my time at Rovers so far and, with my businesses still doing well and my personal life better than ever, I have so much to be thankful for. Even at my semi-advanced age I view the start of a new season with exactly the same enthusiasm as I anticipated my first match at Belle Vue all those years ago.

It saddens me more than a little that the dear old place is still derelict with very little news of what, if anything, will happen to the land where I first fell in love with the beautiful game. The vision that the council had of the magnificent racecourse stand on one side of the road offering views to an auspicious development on the other has yet to be fulfilled and all we see today is an eyesore. Every time I drive past on my way to our training ground at Cantley, I recall that fateful day when all hope appeared to be lost and I received that tap on the shoulder. The body and shell of Doncaster

Rovers may still be funereal, but the heart and soul of the club is more vibrantly alive than ever before. And, for that, I thank once again each and every Rovers player, official and, most importantly of all, every supporter for being part of this wonderful story.

As Kevin Keegan said in his kind introduction, this is a story that is still being written with every game that Rovers play. I hope you have enjoyed re-living recent history and hopefully in these difficult times it will encourage you to look again at your own personal dreams and believe. There is no magic formula – but if you have a vision and are willing to pursue it unceasingly, whatever the circumstances, anything, literally anything, is possible. Even if you ultimately fail, providing you have been true to yourself and given 100 per cent effort, you will be able to look yourself in the mirror and stand tall.

Allow me to leave you with one last thought – one that shows that, despite the uneven playing field, the spirit of Robin Hood is well and truly alive in football and that the last can indeed still be first.

Last season we were delighted to be provided with an independent judgement on our rise to grace from an organisation called The New Football Pools. They came to the Keepmoat in October 2008 to acclaim Rovers as officially the most over-achieving club in England since the Premiership years began in 1992. In doing so, they provided an answer to a question often posed by fans in the pub and in their friendly banter with each other.

They assessed clubs according to their status and resources back in 1991 and followed them all the way to the end of the 2007/8 season. They took into account each club's 'starting position' in 1992, stadium capacity and average attendances, changes in club ownership and associated investments, financial difficulties, including administration, transfers in and out since 1992 and League and Cup performances each season. Starting with a score of 100, they charted how each and every team has progressed over the past 15 seasons. Of course, the merits of their findings can be argued about forever as, although the organisation described its research as scientific, that will no doubt be disputed by some of the nation's bigger clubs who didn't find themselves near the top of the table. But, to argue over the finer details is to miss the point. Unlike many football books, I've spared you endless league tables and statistics. But just feast yourselves on this, Rovers fans. And perhaps supporters of other clubs will get a better idea of just how well or badly their club has actually fared.

1 Doncaster Rovers
2 Portsmouth
3 Reading
4 Hull City
5 Wigan Athletic
6 Cheltenham Town
7 Aldershot
8 Carlisle United
9 Scunthorpe United
10 Accrington Stanley
11 Morecambe
12 Bolton W
13 Yeovil Town
14 Colchester United
15 Sunderland
16 Hereford United
17 Swansea City
18 West Bromwich Albion
19 Northampton Town
20 Stoke City
21 Dagenham & Redbridge
22 Plymouth Argyle
23 Preston North End
24 Walsall
25 Rochdale
26 Macclesfield Town
27 Arsenal
28 Watford
29 Manchester United
30 Southend United
31 Blackburn
32 West Ham United
33 Chelsea
34 Wycombe Wanderers
35 Burnley
36 Barnet
37 Chesterfield
38 Everton
39 Blackpool
40 Rotherham United
41 Newcastle United
42 Crewe Alexandra
43 Gillingham
44 Bristol City
45 Liverpool
46 Barnsley
47 Leyton Orient
48 Hartlepool United
49 Port Vale
50 Lincoln City
51 Stockport County
52 Aston Villa
53 Birmingham City
54 Charlton Athletic
55 Peterborough United
56 Bury
57 Huddersfield Town
58 Fulham
59 Ipswich Town
60 Brighton & Hove Albion
61 Middlesbrough
62 Tottenham Hotspur
63 Derby County
64 Swindon Town
65 Crystal Palace
66 Darlington
67 Queens Park Rangers
68 Bristol Rovers
69 Chester City
70 Bradford City
71 Millwall
72 Tranmere Rovers
73 Oldham Athletic
74 Bournemouth
75 Grimsby Town
76 Sheffield United
77 Southampton
78 Norwich City
79 Leeds Utd
80 Exeter City
81 Cardiff City
82 MK Dons
83 Shrewsbury Town
84 Brentford
85 Leicester City
86 Luton Town
87 Notts County
88 Manchester City
89 Coventry City
90 Nottingham Forest
91 Wolverhampton W
92 Sheffield Wednesday

*

INJURY-TIME

HARRY BACON, fellow Rovers fan: "There is only one John Ryan! The man should be knighted and have the stadium named after him. I started watching Rovers about the same time as John did, when we were in the old Second Division in the 1950s. Today, I sit six seats away from him in the East Stand at the fantastic Keepmoat Stadium. There can't be many chairmen like him. I've watched him banging a drum behind the goal standing with the fans – his fellow fans – and I see him stand up every few minutes and shout with a passion and enthusiasm that is an inspiration to us all. I had a chance to meet John as part of the Founders Club after our Johnstone's Paint Trophy final triumph and on other occasions. He immediately struck me as 100 per cent genuine.

"My life was nearly ended at about the same time as Rovers looked like going to the wall under Ken Richardson. I had three heart attacks on the same day and my memory of those bleak times is hazy. But the medics came to the rescue and my football dream has also lived on – thanks to John Ryan. When he first made his comments about taking us back into the Football League, Wembley and getting us into the Championship, I thought it was a publicity

stunt. Yet everything he promised then has happened and I don't think it's over. Belle Vue was my second home and now the Keepmoat is too. It is a great place to be and houses a friendly, family club. When I first started watching Rovers, my father put me in the kids' pen because he knew I'd be safe there. I still feel safe coming to watch my football to this day.

"I was thrilled in October 2008 when invited to give my views on Rovers, as we were named the most over-achieving club in the Premiership and Football League by The New Football Pools. That was proof that thanks to John in particular, Doncaster Rovers are worth every penny. Thanks John, and here's to the next 50 years!"

PETER DAVIES, directly-elected Mayor of Doncaster: "There is a link between the fortunes of our town and Doncaster Rovers, so I should thank John Ryan for making my job easier! He has transformed the club's fortunes, taking it from the Conference to the Championship and providing us with a watershed moment when we beat Leeds United at Wembley. And I do understand the parallels John draws between our two jobs. There is evidence to suggest that the success of a football club has a direct effect on the local economy and the feelgood factor should never be underestimated. John remains ultra-committed to driving Rovers forward, while my aim is to make Doncaster into one of the most successful large towns in the north of England.

"After the Donnygate scandal and the children's services debacle, the town is starting to make the most of its huge potential. Like Rovers in the past, we have under-achieved but can emerge as a top-class town. I thank my predecessor Martin Winter for helping to provide Doncaster with a stadium of the quality of the Keepmoat. It is no secret that I am exploring the idea of the football club taking over its ownership. Quite apart from on-field success, Rovers is very well-run and recently won two major awards from the Chamber of Commerce. I wish John Ryan and Doncaster Rovers well. Here's hoping that we can all move forward together."

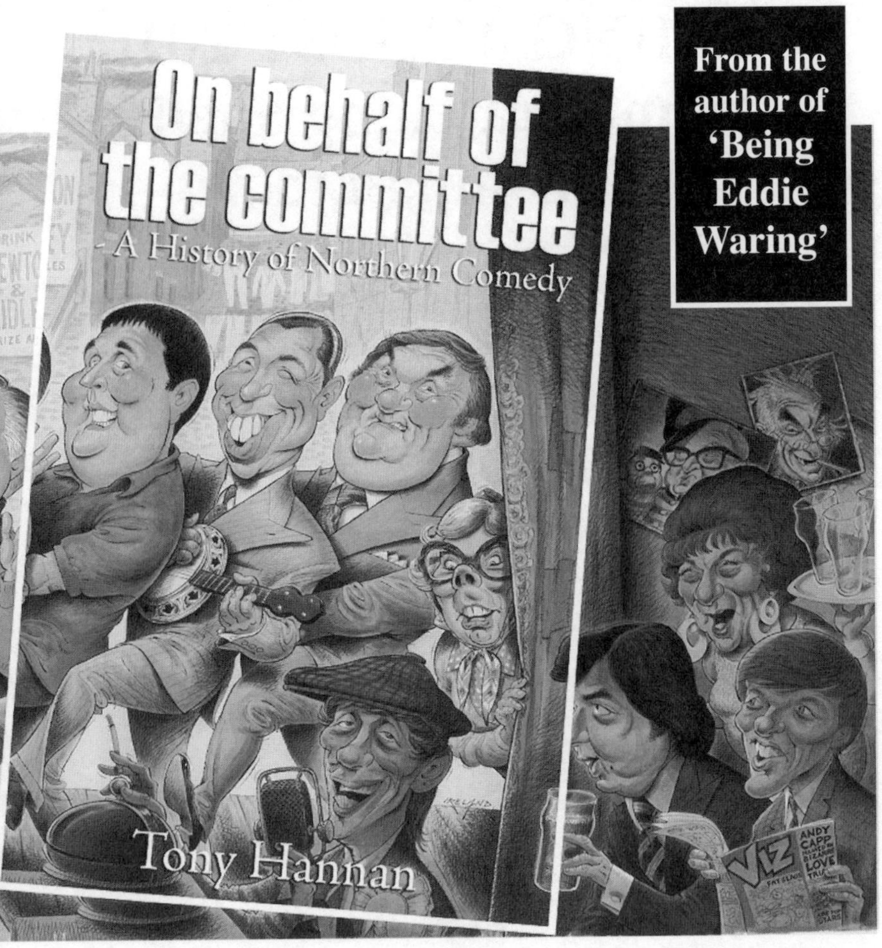

From the Industrial Revolution to our own comfortable 21st century digital age - via music hall, Variety, working mens clubs, radio, cinema & television - Northern-born comedians have consistently been at the heart of popular British comedy culture, tickling the funny bone of the entire nation.

This witty and informative book questions why that should be so, all the while charting an entertaining course through the careers of George Formby, Tommy Handley, Gracie Fields, Frank Randle, Al Read, Jimmy James, Hylda Baker, Jimmy Clitheroe, Les Dawson, Morecambe & Wise, Bernard Manning, Alan Bennett, Monty Python, Victoria Wood, Ken Dodd, Chubby Brown, The Young Ones, Vic and Bob, Steve Coogan, Caroline Aherne, the League of Gentlemen, Johnny Vegas, Peter Kay and many many others. Along the way, it also wonders why such a huge contribution to the British entertainment industry should be so often under-appreciated.

Mostly, however, it is a rich celebration of British comedy history & confirmation that you really do have to laugh - or else you'd cry...